CO-AVA-045

THE SOCIAL STRUCTURE OF CHRISTIAN FAMILIES

THE SOCIAL STRUCTURE OF
CHRISTIAN FAMILIES

A HISTORICAL
PERSPECTIVE

Brian W. Grant

Chalice Press®
St. Louis, Missouri

BT
707.7
.G73
2000

© Copyright 2000 by Brian W. Grant.

All rights reserved. No part of this book may be reproduced without written permission from Chalice Press, P.O. Box 179, St. Louis, MO 63166-0179.

Biblical quotations, unless otherwise noted, are from the *New Revised Standard Version Bible*, copyright 1989, Division of Christian Education of the National Council of Churches of Christ in the USA. Used by permission. All rights reserved.

Cover art and design: Elizabeth Wright
Art direction: Elizabeth Wright
Interior design: Wynn Younker

This book is printed on acid-free, recycled paper.

Visit Chalice Press on the World Wide Web at
www.chalicepress.com

10 9 8 7 6 5 4 3 2 1   00 01 02 03

Library of Congress Cataloging-in-Publication Data

Grant, Brian W.
  The Social structure of Christian families : a historical perspective / Brian W. Grant.
        p.   cm.
  Includes bibliographical references and index.
  ISBN 0-8272-3446-5
  1. Family—Religious aspects—Christianity—History of doctrines I.Title.
  BT707.7 .G73   2000   261.8'3585'09—dc21
  00-08624

Printed in the United States of America

Contents

Acknowledgments

Like any book, this one owes much to many people. Particular thanks are due to Christian Theological Seminary, whose liberal research-leave policies created the time to do most of the research behind this book. A faculty development grant from the Lilly Endowment made research assistance available, and the scholarly help of the Reverend Mrs. Joyce Keilman Smith, thus enabled, gave great impetus to the early stages of the research. At a later point the Reverend Claudia Ewing Grant made major contributions with research assistance, manuscript review, and general encouragement. Colleagues at Christian Theological Seminary, especially Clark Williamson, Newell Williams, Marti Steussy, and Felicity Kelcourse read and commented helpfully on several chapters. Many others provided the incentive of at least appearing to be interested in the progress of the work. David Bundy and his staff at the Christian Theological Seminary library were repeatedly the source of materials otherwise unavailable.

There is also a community of people who taught me to love and be curious about families. Some appear as sources for this manuscript: John Chrysostom, Augustine, Martin Bucer, Philip Greven, Margaret Sanger. Others are or were known privately but helped me understand that families are worth learning about: Lurah Phillips, John Ewing, Esther Apisdorf, Roberta Stratton, and my daughters—Donna, Mary, and Helen. I am indebted to all of them and hope through this volume to give back a small part of what I owe.

CHAPTER 1

Introduction

Families in the United States—secular families, Christian families, families of other faiths—have been careening through a wild set of passages for four decades. A series of voices have clamored for change, for stability, for experimentation, and for adherence to tradition. Church bodies, political parties, and mass movements have labeled the family everything from a prison for women and children to the last hope for an orderly society. Huge changes in economic structure, contraception, longevity, and ideology have made it impossible for the family to be the same as it was fifty years ago and have made it impossible to predict what it will be in the next decade. In the midst of this tumult the church has struggled to understand its ministry to families and its existence as family and often has found itself behind the curve in grasping and responding to the changes sweeping through the society.

In the last ten years the debate has focused more intensely, and the countervailing positions have been drawn more sharply. Two particularly important books have described the current debate, the social realities on which it is founded, and the response of church bodies and other institutions to the changes. Stephanie Coontz's third book, *The Way We Really Are*, a beautifully researched and strongly argued volume on the history and structure of American families,[1] has presented a secular feminist analysis, strongly influenced by economic theory and a keen awareness of class

---

[1]Stephanie Coontz, *The Way We Really Are* (New York: Basic Books, 1997).

structure. She argues that our creation of a "winner-take-all" economy, coupled with the government's abandonment of responsibility for the poor, has created a situation in which single parenthood, child poverty, father absence, high divorce rates, and communities shorn of an institutional infrastructure are almost inevitable. Yet she is optimistic about our apparently increasing ability to respond to the divorce crisis, the now gradual decline in divorce rates, and the hope for further involvement of fathers in family life. She does not take a theological position but expresses concern that the most visible family-oriented religious movements would try to stabilize families at the expense of the recent gains for women, attempting an equilibrium that recent structural economic changes have made impossible anyway.

A more churchly treatment of the same issues is offered by the monumental series *The Family, Religion, and Culture*, edited by Don Browning and Ian Evison. In its capstone volume, *From Culture Wars to Common Ground*, the five-member team marshals an argument for the "intact, equal-regard, public-private family."[2] It is a deeply theological argument and even more deeply an ethical one, strongly informed by biblical scholarship and the philosophical tradition. It looks closely at several contemporary pro-family movements (the same ones Coontz finds troubling in most cases) and finds much to admire while identifying them as failing to adequately ensure the intersubjective dialogue they find central to Christian faith.

The Browning volume is the penultimate in an eight-volume series. The set provides the first serious scholarly attention that the mainline or liberal church has offered in decades to questions of the biblical witness and record concerning families, denominational traditions and family, marriage law in the church, family and economic life, feminism and the family, and the interaction between genetic technology and the lives of families. But there are significant omissions in the coverage of this effort. It does not address the actual sociological fabric of the family as it developed from the end of the New Testament era to the Baby Boom generation. And it touches only lightly on the interaction between the structural forms of family in different epochs, the historical forces bearing on and shaping those forms, and the contemporary theological reflections about family.

This book contends that God has always been leading human communities to form themselves in healing, saving ways, when those communities are confronted by circumstances that change too rapidly for whole societies

---

[2]Don S. Browning, Bonnie J. Miller-McLemore, Pamela D. Couture, K. Brynolf Lyon, and Robert M. Franklin, *From Culture Wars to Common Ground* (Louisville: Westminster John Knox Press, 1997).

to arrive at a settled, holy condition. It contends that the church's theology of family in any epoch is decisively shaped by the family structures of that time and is part of the political/philosophical debate of its era. That theology cannot claim independent, divinely ordered status even in its own epoch and is even more limited and limiting a witness when it is made normative for other eras. Yet it has often had profound impact on the family forms of later periods, often for good and sometimes for ill, particularly when it has claimed divine endorsement for forms that evolved in one set of conditions but have been imposed on those of another. Such clashes have weakened the witness of the church by making demands that many of the faithful see as absurd and that are immediately dismissed by those with no Christian loyalty. This volume recounts the history of the church's rhetoric about families in dialogue with the actual families it was addressing, hoping to focus the question "What is/was God doing with families in this era?"

This book makes these contentions on the basis of a process theological understanding of God's work in the world. It holds that God's nature is to perpetually offer possibilities for every actual entity, including families and societies, possibilities that lure those entities toward the maximum intensity of harmony and contrast, building on the givens that the past makes available for each present moment. It does not see God as all-powerful, but as an indestructible (not unopposeable), persuasive force for good, who contends with other forces to provide the goals toward which every existing being strives. Hence, the family is not wholly shaped by God, but is always invited and affected by God, as is every other actual entity.

The stimulus for this book was provided several summers ago by a course I was teaching on the social structure of families. The course was offered in a theological seminary, and a unit was needed on theological thought on family life. In seeking to find a text for that study, I made a surprising and distressing discovery: There wasn't one. There were contemporary theological writings on the family from Protestant positions more conservative than I wanted to encourage,[3] and there were the current writings of Pope John Paul II and other Roman Catholic authorities.[4] All of these were interesting and serious efforts, but far from my own position. Most of the writings from ecumenical Protestantism were less than serious theologically and not historically grounded in any sense. Some of them were awful.

---

[3]Stanley Hauerwas, *A Community of Character* (Notre Dame: University of Notre Dame Press, 1981). See also Anderson and Guernsey, *On Being Family* (Grand Rapids: Eerdmans, 1985).

[4]John Paul II, *On the Family* (Washington, D.C.: United States Catholic Conference, 1981).

As I considered creating a constructive theology of the family, I encountered another problem. A great deal of what has passed for the church's stance on marriage, sexuality, and child-rearing had grown out of theological pronouncements responding to specific historical circumstances that no longer exist. Basically, the biblical statements about marriage and family were made about a social institution so different from what exists today as to be prescriptively irrelevant, though they may be indispensable principles on which to base our family codes. The institution of the family was so different by the fifth century in western Europe, and again by the ninth century, the thirteenth century, the seventeenth century, as to be unrecognizable. Again, when the story moves from Europe to North America, some, but not all, aspects of the Continental family made the Atlantic crossing but were radically different in seventeenth-century New England than in eighteenth-century Georgia; they had changed drastically again by 1880 throughout the country and underwent a further revolution in the last half of the twentieth century. The attempt to understand and utilize the theology derived from any of these epochs as normative for the families of today is impossible without tracing the changes in the institution as it shifted and following the theological changes that accompanied those relational and societal moves.

This volume is an attempt to provide a grounding in history and historical theology so that a contemporary theology of the family—which might address such questions as "What is God doing with the family now?"—could draw on historical resources without unknowingly importing the societal structures that informed them. It provides the background for asking questions about God's current purposes for marriage and sexuality by looking at the thought of earlier generations of the church about those purposes, and at what marriage and sexuality, child-rearing and economics actually were in the centuries in which those theologies were written. In the context of that history, it will be possible to argue that God is doing a new thing with the contemporary family, something that represents hope as much as chaos. But that argument would be implausible without an awareness of the historical changes documented here.

Any current book on family requires some specificity about the phenomena it will include and needs to be careful about the distinction between normative and descriptive choices. I do not claim with certainty that God includes or excludes particular groupings from the title "family." I accept the variety of structures that people in their own time have defined by the term. In the discussion of contemporary families, I hope to be as inclusive as possible, including persons joined by choice, sex, blood, and/or church.

A great deal of this book is about marriage, and I understand a committed, sexualized, legal relationship between persons of different sexes as central to the idea (though not necessarily to all the historical incarnations) of family. That centrality, however, is temporal (such a relationship is in the history of almost every one of us, if not in our present) and conceptual (even if such a relationship is not at the core of a present household, one can usefully generalize from such a relationship to whatever is at the core of the current reality). I recognize that there are large numbers of single-parent households/families, families headed by homosexual couples, and persons living alone. This book intends to exclude none of them from consideration as families or parts of families, though I recognize that there are particular problems for each of those forms (as for households headed by married couples) that have implications for persons living in such structures. Though I believe that for most people, for most of their adult lives, marriage is the optimal framework, I recognize that there are persons for whom it is either inappropriate, unavailable, or unwise but whose lives are fully as holy and familial as those who are married. I am hopeful that the history presented here will have something to offer them and that they will sense their stories as having impacted this effort.

Because this book is written primarily for North American Protestant readers and those who wish to know what has formed their traditions, its criteria for inclusion bear those marks. It is a white, male, feminist, heterosexual, middle class, American Protestant book. I do not contend that that is the only important community or the superior community, but it is the community that I know best. It has taken the better part of a decade to develop such mastery of its literature as is represented here, and I have little confidence that even more years would produce real competence in the literature of communities to which I would always remain an outsider. I hope and trust that there are persons working on similar questions from the perspectives of homosexual, working class, ethnic minority, non-Western, and non-Protestant communities. I will read them with interest and hope for the same respect from their authors. I suspect, for better and worse, that the family developments chronicled and critiqued in this overtly dominant part of the modern world have a great deal of power vis-à-vis the other communities and that an understanding of them will be useful even for people who define themselves over against the structures represented here.

The book proceeds sequentially. It begins with a brief account of the way families were structured in Old Testament Israel, from its nomadic, polygynous, patriarchal roots to its more settled and monogamous, exogamous, postexilic structures. It examines the family structures of the New Testament Christian community, as it changed from almost unanimously married in the time of Christ to the more sexually and relationally ambivalent atmosphere of the Pauline and post-Pauline church.

The narrative then explores the immediate post–New Testament church's struggles over the role of sexuality, starting with the struggle over whether widows and widowers should remarry, entering the politically and spiritually charged struggle over the importance of virginity, climaxing in the never fully resolved Catholic disputes over clerical celibacy. All of this is cast against the background of the Roman world's deep distrust of sex, its excitement over the sexual austerity of the desert fathers and mothers, and religious/ philosophical traditions ranging from Manicheism to neo-Platonism. It culminates in the powerful and lasting synthesis forged by Ambrose and Augustine that formed the basis of Catholic marital and sexual theology for a thousand years.

As that synthesis was being forged, the Mediterranean world was collapsing in the face of Germanic and other invasions. The survival of the church, let alone theology, was far from certain for a handful of centuries as whole communities of people swept across Europe and North Africa displacing their often Christianized predecessors, only to be gradually evangelized and domesticated themselves by heroic monks and missionaries. During these years the battle between the Germanic tribes' view of marriage as a way of amassing and transferring property and the church's attempt to spiritualize and individualize it (not without the church's own interest in weakening the dynastic power of the tribes) was largely waged over issues of marriage law by bishops and church lawyers rather than by theologians. Only as populations began to restabilize in the early and high Middle Ages, nation states began to form, and theologians like Bernard of Clairvaux, Bonaventure, and finally Thomas Aquinas reworked the Augustinian synthesis, did the church firmly establish custody over marriage among the faithful.

Even as this stabilization of church-structured marriage was taking hold, the seeds for its dissolution were being sown. The plagues of the fourteenth century opened up the society, technological and philosophical changes in Italy advanced individualism, and the papal schism humiliated the church. Reformation emerged in Germany, Switzerland, Bohemia, and England and brought with it a frontal challenge to the Roman Church's views on marriage and sexuality. Luther led the charge for the legitimacy of marriage and its equality with celibacy, and the Calvinist writers, particularly Bucer and Milton, argued eloquently for dignifying the companionate and even sexual aspects of married life.

This accompanied, perhaps generated, a rapid increase in the percentage of the population that married and increasingly gave marriage a visible role in the spiritual development of spouses. It especially identified the spiritual headship of men, as increasing privacy also meant less community protection for those with limited ability to protect themselves; and it produced the first clear statements that parents, especially fathers, were critical, and potentially culpable, agents in the spiritual health of children. Childhood began to be identified clearly as a separate stage of life, and the responsibility of parents to break the will of children before they were far into it was emphasized.

These were the issues dominating family life and theological reflection about it when the first colonists came to North America. Circumstances of migration, however, so changed the European patterns that a new trajectory developed—and our narrative moves to this side of the Atlantic. There had not been a migration of peoples like the one to and then across North America since the Germanic invasions of Europe, and this one produced a massive reordering of society. Social and family patterns were different in each colony, but in every one land was plentiful, conditions were healthier than in the European cities (except in the first vulnerable months), and labor was scarce. Family size burgeoned, and paternal economic power expanded. Then as the areas of earliest colonization became crowded, families began to scatter, first into new households and then new settlements, and the pressure for westward expansion intensified. Early in this process, through most of the eighteenth century, the Great Awakening generated a theological struggle between the more settled, worldly, theocratic Old Light Calvinists and the ascendant New Light conservatives, and much of the struggle focused on the family. Jonathan Edwards and John Wesley and their followers besought parents to distance themselves from grandparents and to discipline desire out of their children, so that they might be more attentive to the will of God. They were much more restrictive than the Puritans and increasingly controlled church life and theological thought until the political stirrings that brought on the Revolution took center stage.

For the next century or longer, it was impossible to speak about families or theologies with any sense of nationwide similarity. Developments in the Northeast and Mid-Atlantic states had a similar character, but with each hundred miles or so to the west the cultural conditions changed— cities became scarcer, smaller, and rougher; women became rarer; churches became less frequent and less under the control of Eastern authority; men became more and more independent and monarchical in their organization of life. Drinking intensified as people went further west, violence became harsher and more frequent, and families became less able to count on one another for support.

The United States in 1800, except for Maryland, was an almost entirely Protestant country and proud of it. But as land opened up in the West and Eastern cities began to industrialize, political and economic circumstances in Europe made emigration desirable. An increasing segment of nineteenth-century immigration was Catholic. Cultural differences, political fears, and the increasing wish of the wealthier Protestant elites for distance from those who were both poorer and domestically different intensified the development of class distinctions that had only been rudimentary before.

The almost exclusively Protestant middle and upper classes developed a model of femininity that transposed the seventeenth-century male responsibility for the spiritual health of children into a womanly duty. As men became more and more embroiled in the competitiveness of laissez-faire capitalism, women increasingly were seen as the moral guardians of households and the enforcers of class boundaries (often seen as the same thing). Romantic preachers and theologians Horace Bushnell (in the 1840s) and Henry Ward Beecher (in the 1880s) brought attention to the emotional life of spouses and children, and the social movements that developed out of the Second Great Awakening involved middle-class women in leadership in abolitionist, temperance, suffragist, and moral purity crusades. Roman Catholic women were more often allied with their husbands in a strong working-class consciousness that supported a more public, emotionally expressive style of life.

Throughout the nineteenth century birth rates were falling, divorce rates were rising, and women were increasingly assuming prominence in the leadership of social and, increasingly, political movements that challenged the unrestrained aggressiveness of the largely male economic and social worlds. Theology followed suit, with the Social Gospel movement of the late nineteenth and early twentieth centuries both demanding better treatment for the poor and beginning to think theologically about the connection of sexuality, companionship, and child-rearing. That began to flower in the work of Walter Rauschenbusch but was cut short by his untimely death.

The century that we have just completed started with the work of Margaret Sanger, whose work made the facts and materials of contraception available to the masses, intensifying the gradual decline in the birth rate that, except for the 1950s and 1960s, has continued since the Revolution. The divorce rate, also rising throughout the same period, continued its gradual increase until the 1940s, jumped after World War II, faltered, leaped up again as the Baby Boomers' parents met the frustrations of large families, and has leveled off and slightly shrunk since 1980. And of course, women went (back) to work. Though women have made major contributions to human economies in every age, as the class-consciousness of the Protestant majority asserted itself in American cities in the nineteenth century, it became their religious and moral duty to exert their efforts primarily in home and family. That had begun to slip during the early years of the twentieth century and changed mightily if temporarily during World War II. But from the late 1940s through the mid-1960s women worked less outside the home, married earlier, and had more children faster than any age cohort in American history.

Many factors combined to change that: Women's boredom and poor health grew out of isolation from the adult population and from economically productive work; changes in the economy promoted a higher rate of acquisitiveness at a time when men by themselves could not earn enough to meet it; and women became increasingly aware that the divorce epidemic made them very vulnerable if they couldn't produce an income. By the last decade of the twentieth century, more than half of the married mothers of preschool children in this country were working outside the home, whether their economic circumstances required it or not.

Another huge change in this century, making perhaps as much difference to family style and theology as any, has been the rapid expansion of life expectancy. Most couples who stay married now live together longer after their last child has left home than they lived with children, which has brought attention to the erotic and relational components of post-childbearing married life. Sexual pleasure for its own sake is attractive to this population, and theology is only beginning to consider whether it may be attractive to God as well.

As one follows this unfolding story, tantalizing questions emerge. Were the human beings in second-century Rome in fact unable to combine intimate companionship and reproductive marriage, as their philosophers maintained? Was that only a belief compelled by ancient sexism or political necessity, or have human beings actually changed through species-wide learning, or perhaps cultural advance, in the ensuing centuries? Did the gradual ecclesiastical preference and then dominance of virginity over marriage that emerged in both Eastern and Western churches in the fourth and fifth centuries depend primarily on political necessity, or was there something about the way those early Christians went about being sexual that was incompatible with spirituality? If there was then, is there now? If not, how did it change? Did the medieval insistence that persons within seven degrees of relationship (seventh cousins, basically, even through the status of in-laws or even godparents) were not eligible to marry one another actually create a field of persons with whom lust did not enter relationship, as they claimed? And if so, was that a good thing, or did it merely create a wonderful opportunity for bribery and politically expedient exceptions? And did the public objections of many American denominations, including the Disciples of

Christ, to contraception well into the 1930s represent a faithful reading of the will of God or merely a commitment to keeping women in the roles that nineteenth-century Protestantism had designed for them?

The answers to these questions are, of course, beyond the competence of a theological history, but knowing the history and the theology are indispensable to a responsible approach to the questions. My hope in this volume is to trace the emergence of the social realities and theological rationale for what Browning, and others, call the "intact, equal-regard, public-private family." I would add to those adjectives "sexually invested" and "emotionally responsive" to correct for the arms-length feel of the Lilly team's model. It appears that God may be bringing a new thing into being in the educated classes of the industrialized West (and, increasingly, else-where)—not necessarily the best thing and certainly not the final thing—but a new and potentially redemptive thing, and a required part of our stewardship of the history we have been given is to seek to understand it.

CHAPTER 2

Biblical Judaism and the Apostolic Church

Both Jewish and Christian communities have wrestled with questions about what God is doing with families since biblical times, with noticeable bursts of attention at major transitional points: the conquest of Canaan, the establishment of the monarchy, the return from exile, the second Christian century, and so on. Different segments of these communities have emphasized different issues: Jews, the honoring of father and mother; Catholics, marital sexuality vis-à-vis virginity; evangelical Protestants, the family as authority structure; and ecumenical Protestants, values of relationship and re-creation.

Most twentieth-century ideas and images of family life would have seemed foreign to biblical writers in either testament. Those writers, and the families about and to which they wrote, were facing a radically different environment. Its social structures were all but unrecognizably dissimilar to our own, and the motives that propelled both institutions and individuals were not the same as today's. Yet this century's family serves many of the same purposes as those very different structures, and the tensions that shape the modern family were not unknown 3,500 years ago.

The Hebrew Testament words referring to family refer to more inclusive groupings than does contemporary usage. There are two crucial terms, one more inclusive in its reference but without a clear boundary separating it from the other. The broader, *mishpaha,* usually translated "family," means family only in the widest sense in which we use the word, the broadest strain of extended family over time. In the authoritative work of Johannes Pedersen, "Therefore family, *mishpaha,* is the designation of those who are of the same kind, have the same essential features, and it is the essential

11

factor of the community…All that forms a whole, a homogenous community with its own characteristics, is a *mishpaha.*" [1]

More recent scholarship achieves a bit more precision, though the same ambiguity remains. Carol Meyers, writing in the *Family, Religion, and Culture* series, notes that neither family nor clan is a very good translation. The *mishpaha* was a group of at least partly related family units that settled a given area, the nucleus of an agricultural village. Not all members would have been related by blood, though many would have been, but all would have been committed to the same territory and to shared economic and military effort.[2] It was the intermediate structure between tribe, on the one hand, and household (*bayith*) on the other.[3]

The more intimate grouping is designated by *bayith*, household, or *beth abh*, the father's house. This designates all who live within or around the dwelling and "represents kinship in its most intimate sense."[4] An adult man was always understood as having a house, if married (and an adult man would, in almost all cases, be married), though he might also still be understood to be a member of his father's house and of his grandfather's if the latter was still living.

The definitions of these terms and of the boundaries between them are not exact in biblical usage and probably changed through the biblical centuries. House and family are often used interchangeably, and a person could be said to belong to more than one of either. However, when differentiations were made, *mishpaha* was always the more inclusive term. More important is that neither represents anything as limited or exclusive as our contemporary nuclear family, having more in common with the patriarchal clan, including uncles, cousins, and adoptees, extending over time.

There are some widely applicable generalizations that can be made about these groupings. They centered around men. It was a man who had a house and a family. They served to accomplish many things, including defense, production, inheritance, and companionship; but most importantly, they served to provide a man a house, a lineage, so that he did not suffer "the great terror of the Israelite: to perish from the family and be blotted out."[5]

Women were obviously crucial to that effort, but their widely understood duty was to assist in achieving that male objective. He had far more freedom than she in regard to sexual choices (polygamy was lawful, polyandry not; intercourse between a married man and an unmarried woman was not

---

[1]Johannes Pedersen, *Israel, Its Life and Culture,* Vol. 1 (London: Oxford University Press, 1973), 48.

[2]Carol Meyers, "The Family in Early Israel," in *Families in Ancient Israel,* ed. Leo Perdue, Joseph Blenkinsopp, John J. Collins, and Carol Meyers (Louisville: Westminster/John Knox, 1997), 13.

[3]Joseph Blenkinsopp, "The Family in First Temple Israel," in Perdue, et. al., 51.

[4]Pedersen, 51.

[5]Ibid., 81

defined as adultery), economic matters, and divorce (he could, she could not), but it was not a relationship of complete abasement and subjection. Wives came to marriage with a gift from their families, which for families of means gave a woman independent property and therefore influence in her new family. And there was the presumption of an intimacy, or at least the awareness of the possibility and desirability of such. Pedersen deals with that in his discussion of man as *ba'al,* possessor or master of the house and its occupants. *Ba'al* "always presupposes a psychic community, a whole, and *ba'al* designates the ruling will within this. The word does not mean one-sided sovereignty."[6] There is another word for that, which is appropriate with a conquered nation or a slave.

> The word *ba'al* therefore not only characterizes the man as master of the house, but also tells us something of the character of his rule. He is not an isolated despot, but the center from which strength and will emanate through the whole of the sphere which belongs to him and to which he belongs.[7]

But this should not lead the reader to believe that this husband-wife *ba'al*-centeredness was at the essence of the unit. It primarily served the parent-child bond and existed for its sake. Pedersen points out that in the Samson stories, for instance, when Delilah complains that he didn't tell her the riddle he had told the Philistines, his answer was that he hasn't even told his parents. The implication is clear that they would have had first claim on the information. "The relation between parents and children is the innermost kernel of this community of kindred."[8]

The earliest consistent biblical affirmations about family were twofold and establish a tension that remains today: It is not good for man—and they apparently did mean "adult male"—to live alone; and that the parent-child relationship (usually father-son) was the decisive one—"Honor thy father and mother, that thy days be long upon the land which the LORD thy God gives thee." This tension, between companionship and parenting, stretches between these two poles of family purpose throughout the centuries, with the relationship between the poles governing the shape of family life in each epoch. As the meaning of each term has changed over time, its relation to the other changes and the shape of the resulting family has also shifted. A major thesis of this essay is that each of these shifts further reveals God's possibilities for human bondedness and with them new data about the nature of the human experiment itself.

---

[6]Ibid., 63.
[7]Ibid.
[8]Ibid., 72.

The early Hebrew family, like the Hebrew nation during its early history, was a very inclusive unit. Both expanded by including the sojourner in the desert, hiring servants, marrying (often multiple) wives, and forming alliances. Abraham circumcised his slaves as well as his son, and family identity and obligations were readily taken on—and not so readily shed. The land was sparsely populated and unforgiving to the isolated, and it greatly favored those whose band increased. Families were large, many children were the rule, and sons especially were a major economic asset.

The cohesiveness of these family groups was critical to survival, producing (at least in part) a reverent attention to the nature of familial authority. There is a lengthy Jewish tradition of commentary on the commandment to "Honor thy father and mother," the center of Jewish family ethics. Gerald Blidstein has distilled this tradition into four major affirmations: (1) Parents are co-creators with God; (2) Gratitude for that creation is a moral requirement and in turn humanizes the grateful; (3) Parental authority is a necessary structurizing force in human community; and (4) Reverence toward parents is a natural response to the above.[9]

Those emphases can be harmonized as follows: God, by means of the faithfulness of the ancestors, has articulated a community that can enjoy the fruits of covenant with Godself if its members attend to the requirements of that covenant; to do so is a great gift and joy, for which gratitude and response in turn will bring harmony with God and result in divine protection.

Blidstein notes that the position of the fifth commandment makes it a transition between those precepts regulating human relation to God and those regulating relations with other persons. Hence, parents stand in a nearly divine and interminable relation to the Jew, because this relationship is the determinative one over how long his/her days will be in the land. The causal link between filial reverence and long life is not a mechanical or retributive one. Rather, the awe and gratitude owed to a father and mother are a prototype for an attitude toward God that reminds the now grown child of total dependence on the creative acts of both God and parents.[10] Philo wrote in the first century, "Parents…are to their children what God is to the world, since just as He achieved existence for the non-existent, so they in imitation of His power…immortalize the race."[11]

There is disagreement between first-century and medieval Judaism over the most important stimulus to this gratitude, with the early rabbis more

---

[9]Gerald Blidstein, *Honor Thy Father and Thy Mother* (New York: Ktav Publishing, 1975).
[10]Ibid., 6.
[11]Philo, *The Special Laws,* in *Philo,* II, 225, trans F. H. Colson (Cambridge, Mass.: Harvard University Press, 1968), 447.

impressed with the gift of life itself, and the later ones arguing that care and nurture are what properly calls forth the loving response. This reverence extends equally to both parents, though at times the balance appears to favor the mother, while it remains true that the demand lies more overtly, though not more substantively, on the son than on the daughter.

Blidstein continues, holding that the good effect of filial piety cannot be cleanly separated into God's explicit reward and natural human wisdom, since the divine reward is often mediated through natural processes. He cites Maimonides' claim that obeying the fifth commandment builds up a stable society, thus benefiting all. Further, as medieval scholars pointed out, if parents are revered, the tradition is preserved, which is even more important to Jewish thought than the stability of the secular state.

The command for both honorable behavior and reverent attitudes are required regardless of the behavior of the parent. Again, quoting Blidstein, "Nothing is to be done that might diminish the dignity, and hence the feeling of worth, of one's parent—either father or mother. Reverence is expressed by this unegalitarian reserve, which demonstrates behaviorally the qualitative gulf in status separating parent and child. Indeed, parental dignity is here virtually identical with inviolability and superiority."[12] In one rabbinic story a mentally ill mother is beating her adult son with a shoe, drops the shoe, and the son picks it up and returns it, saying only, "Enough, mother." The rabbi writes, "However trying the provocation, the honor of the parents remains an absolute in relation to the difficulties of the son. The…suffering of the son is never to be relieved at the expense of the parent, even when the parent is their cause."[13]

The core of the Jewish commandment is the honoring of parents in personal service, in noncontradiction, in protection of the esteem and the place of the parent. In no case should the faithful Jew of any century act in such a way as to expose the parent to the ridicule of others, or even to evoke doubt in others that the parent has a less than completely respectful child. Any right the child might claim to equal consideration in stating opinions or determining the outcome of decisions is to be abandoned as a matter of religious obligation.

The overall cultural heritage of the Middle East is helpful in understanding the functions of this structure. The head of the clan had quasi-monarchic prerogatives throughout the nomadic tribes in the area, then as now. Sons stayed in their father's household along with their wives, children, slaves, and so on, and all moved in a body. The father fulfilled the function of the civil ruler of a small, mobile, political unit. Wives, in almost

---

[12]Ibid., 39.
[13]Ibid., 44.

all cases, were either already part of the clan (marriage among first cousins being the preferred choice in patriarchal Hebrew society, and remaining so until the Islamic period throughout the Middle East) or left their father's house to become part of a nomadic band. Again, in almost all cases, those marriages were arranged by the fathers with the most minimal participation by daughters and often not much more than that by sons.[14]

This created a tension between the very wide-ranging honor a parent is due and the love a spouse is due. The tradition separates those explicitly,[15] requiring behavioral service to a parent as the sign and substance of honor. There is little treatment in Talmud or Midrash of situations where those requirements come into conflict, but the impression from what is stated is that behavioral obedience and deference is due the parent, regardless of the emotional priority that may be granted the spouse. Again, recalling the nomadic basis and clan-sized household on which this society was developed, the notion of such a conflict would not often have occurred to the early Hebrew. Citizenship in the father's house was the primary identity. Marriage was a means of fulfilling several responsibilities of that identity, but it was not understood as conferring a new or competing identity on the husband. His first obligation was to his father's house. As his wife joined that household as well, her obligation was to support her husband in fulfilling that commitment. Though the boundaries around the nuclear family apparently became more defined as the nomadic period ended and settled agricultural and urban life began, they never reached anything approaching the central loyalty to the marriage found in much Western society today.[16] And in the contemporary Middle East, they still don't.

Every adult male Jew was to be married, since marriage throughout the tradition is the fulfillment of a divine command. There was no place in society for the single woman, and widowhood was so unpleasant that remarriage was always sought when possible.[17] The Code of Qaro in later Judaism stated that "every man is bound to marry a wife in order to beget children, and he who fails of this duty is as one who sheds blood." Celibacy was considered impiety, not part of even the most ascetic Jewish practices.

In filling out the meaning of "It is not good for man to be alone," Jesuit scholar Joseph Kerns argues that the promises of God in Exodus 23 and Deuteronomy 7 that no one in the land, man or woman, would be

---

[14]This discussion is drawn largely from Raphael Patai's *Sex and Family in the Bible and the Ancient Middle East* (Garden City: Doubleday, 1959).

[15]Ibid., 56.

[16]John J. Collins, "Marriage, Divorce and Family in Second Temple Judaism," in Perdue, et. al., 104–8.

[17]David R. Mace, *Hebrew Marriage* (London: Epworth, 1953).

childless, establishes the universality of marriage.[18] Many have argued that this is a heritage of the early Israelites' Bedouin tradition. Since offspring (essentially sons) were the only enduring creation of a nomadic Hebrew, not to have them would leave the world as if one had never been. Further, it would diminish the power of one's father's house and fail to realize the advantage that should rightfully accrue to one's father for one's own conception. Marriage performed a more utilitarian than relational or romantic function. It is only when a more individualized view of marriage develops in the modern West that some may not find a match and/or choose to remain single. That was not the expectation in biblical Israel.

As Patai points out at length, barrenness was the greatest evil that could befall a woman.[19] It was typically seen as the consequence of sin, often sexual sin, the punishment of God, and rendered the woman vulnerable to displacement and scorn. Magical remedies were sought, an elaborate folk medicine developed, and recourse was often made to offering a servant-girl or second wife to the husband so that offspring could be ensured. A woman who made such provision for her husband's progeny could not be divorced, whereas barrenness was otherwise grounds for divorce.

Kerns notes that the initiative in the Yahwist account is with God, who presents Eve to Adam; hence the specific partner is seen as God's gift. But one should not conclude that it is a gift aimed primarily at producing romantic or relational happiness. Raising heirs to the covenant and to one's father's name remained central, and childlessness was a great curse. Apparently the alone in "not alone" meant not only without companion but also without offspring to link one to the ongoing life of the covenant community, so that marriage was primarily a means to produce children.

There is substantial writing in the Wisdom tradition (especially Proverbs 31) about the advantages of a good marriage, both from the sexual and companionate standpoint, but nothing that prioritizes those boons over the creation of offspring. It points mainly to the domestic effectiveness of a good wife, an effectiveness not rooted in beauty, Proverbs points out, but in knowledge of the word of God. The evidence of that goodness was primarily in domestic productivity, making life easier for man by relieving him of inconvenient and crucial tasks. The effect was to increase his esteem, primarily in the company of other men, and to ease his commerce with them. This woman could own no property, could take no public role in ordinary times, and was subject to the death penalty for adultery (a man's sexual adventures outside marriage were only understood as adulterous if the partner

---

[18]Joseph Kerns, *The Theology of Marriage* (New York: Sheed and Ward, 1964).
[19]Patai, 73–80.

were also married or betrothed). The relative status of men and women is further suggested by the fact that the period of purification after the birth of a daughter was twice as long as it was following the birth of a son.

There were some provisions for the welfare of a married woman and some moderating of her disadvantages over time. Though the bride price was paid by the father of the groom to the bride's father, it was typically returned as part of the dowry. However, it was to be preserved intact so that it could be returned to the wife's family in the event of a divorce (note that it would typically be a durable commodity, such as land, livestock, or house, hence easily preservable or replaceable), so there were some guarantees for her welfare in that unfortunate circumstance.[20] Visible influence on public life was rare for married women, or for unmarried women, but their rights to seek influence on issues or to pursue justice on personal matters considerably exceeded those of their counterparts in other Middle Eastern societies.

As the Talmudic and medieval periods unfolded, Jewish marriage changed significantly. The nomadic economy had largely disappeared during the biblical period and with it the immense households—small armies really—that typified preagricultural Israel. Settled agriculture meant smaller and more dispersed households, though high birth rates, wives, and children still remained economic assets. With the diaspora, ghetto existence produced a sharper division between life in the family and life outside the family, and woman's role as the custodian and architect of life in family was elevated. The custom developed of the husband's weekly singing at the Sabbath of the ode to the virtuous wife from Proverbs 31, and monogamy became obligatory rather than merely customary. Postemancipation changes further altered Jewish marriage, diminishing the birth rate and producing the necessity for many Jewish women to work in the community. It is only in the last two centuries that marriage choice has become a matter for individual spouses, and more recently yet that average marital ages have become as high as or higher than those of the Gentile population.[21]

A further intriguing sidelight to this tension between marital and parental relationships is that there is no marital commandment comparable to "Honor thy father and thy mother." One is not commanded to a specific level of attitudinal commitment to one's spouse, the prohibition of adultery being more behavioral than emotional and as much a protection of property as relational rights.

---

[20]Collins, in Perdue, et. al.108ff.

[21]Stanley R. Brav, "Marriage with a History," in *Marriage and the Jewish Tradition* (New York: Philosophical Press, 1951), 83–102.

When we examine the New Testament church community, we find the same linguistic ambiguity as in the biblical Hebrew—specific words for *extended family* through the generations and for *household* that designated the smaller unit, which still included slaves, servants, apprentices, and other borrowed members. This New Testament family is far different from the family that Western industrial society invented, which neither testament could have anticipated, though each structure has been an attempt to respond to similar needs.

As is well known, the discussion about family shifted ground within the developing church. The leadership of the earliest church was, for the most part, married. Peter's wife accompanied him on missionary journeys, and Paul makes it clear that that prerogative was available to all, though he did not utilize it. The apostle Philip's children were known to the church. Throughout the pastoral epistles and Paul's letters there are instructions for how various aspects of marriage should be conducted. The Bible is replete with marital imagery, symbolizing the relationship of Christ and the church, the soul and Christ, and so forth. But the purpose of the institution seems to have changed. Companionship, the gratification of sexual need, and the production of children were more equally at the center. Children remained the means to increase the numbers of the faithful, add covenant partners for Yahweh, and provide soldiers for the armies and laborers for the harvest; but in the new church marriage was mainly a vehicle for the domestication of sexuality. History was going to end soon, and long-term societal and population concerns were not pressing. But sex was a problem, and marriage was seen as a solution, at least for some. But it was a solution that fit a very different Greco-Roman world than the Jewish world from which the church had sprung. Though Roman antiquity had harbored as intense a patriarchal extended-family tradition as the Jewish one, it had been substantially altered by the expanding Greek influence. According to many historians, the Greeks had a considerably less demanding view of sexuality than had the Jews or the early Romans, and the struggle among these three patterns for organizing family life was crucial to the formation of early church practice and thought.

CHAPTER 3

Family Theology in the Greek and Roman Churches

Within a couple of centuries, the delay of the parousia had produced a further change in the discussion. New questions about the legitimacy of marriage and about the created status of sexual feelings competed for attention. Issues of the status of marriage, celibacy and virginity, the remarriage of widows, the role of sex in marriage, all confounded by Roman understandings of will versus passion, competed for attention. While the Hebrew tradition and the early biblical church are largely intelligible on the basis of a Palestinian worldview, the further we move into the Christian centuries the less help we get from a Jewish understanding of sex, family, and society. The Roman Empire lived from a very different philosophical base and by a very different set of sexual and familial codes, which themselves varied considerably from the Greek East to the Latin West, and they evolved significantly from the time of Paul to that of Augustine.

Despite trenchant criticism by the biblical church, Rome and its territories were not a sexually chaotic and dissolute society. Especially in its upper classes, which the church penetrated with remarkable speed, there were firmly established expectations about sexual and familial practices.

Rome and its satellite cities were organized with a highly public, highly political view of human behavior. The city was the bulwark against the biological chaos of the unconquered continents, the provider of order and structure. It was the creation of a group of interconnected families who both assumed and demanded from others the responsibility to continue begetting politicians, officers, and soldiers. Each male citizen's obligation was to produce three children, and no son could inherit from his father

21

until he had done so. The inheritance laws underscored the reality that fertility was an obligation that one owed one's family and one's city. Those structures were the primary decision makers on issues of human reproduction.

Though Roman law required that neither man nor woman could be married involuntarily, in practice fathers of families dictated and arranged marriages to further political and social alliances. Girls were almost always married before the age of fourteen, typically to men twice their age or more, and often to men they had not met.[1] It was not uncommon for a girl to be pregnant before she had her first period and for her to have done her reproductive duty (three children) to city and family well before her twentieth birthday. A woman could keep her property (her dowry from her family) if her marriage ended after she had had children. But inheritance and marriage remained linked, so her capacity to inherit in later life would depend on her marital status at that time.[2] Since early death was common, so was widowhood. The fact that Roman widows with children had their own property (unlike Greek widows, who returned to the households of their fathers) had huge importance to the developing church.

Both divorce and concubinage were widespread. Since marriage was considered primarily a public and political/familial responsibility, rather than a private and affectional one, when it had served its civic function (childbearing) it was easily dissolved. Both men and women could initiate divorce, though it was easier for men, simply by establishing residence with another partner. The new relationship canceled the old. Typically these new relational choices were self-made, rather than arranged by family, and more represented the sexual and companionate interests of the parties. Most often these partners would not marry, however, because marriage would make the offspring of the new union eligible to inherit, thus making them rivals for the legitimate children of the partners' earlier unions. Since grandparents had a proprietary interest in already legitimated grandchildren, there was often significant family pressure for new unions to avoid disrupting the inheritance pattern through marriage.

There were, however, clear standards for behavior in such concubinage as in marriage. Again, because of the concern for inheritance, sexual behavior, especially for the upper classes, was tightly regulated. Adultery was punishable by death in some cases. A father had the right to kill his daughter and her lover if her virginity had been compromised, and a man whose wife

---

[1] Aline Rousselle, *Porneia. On Desire and the Body in Antiquity,* trans. Felicia Pheasant (Oxford: Blackwell, 1988), 46. See also Peter Brown, *The Body and Society: Men, Women, and Sexual Renunciation in Early Christianity* (New York: Columbia University Press, 1988), 6.

[2] Rousselle, 93–107.

had been found guilty of adultery had to repudiate her or be legally culpable himself.[3] Adultery was defined differently under Roman law than in our contemporary society and differently for men than for women. A man could have intercourse with actresses, prostitutes, or slaves and be guilty of no crime, though a woman who did so would be an adulteress. There was a further category of punishable sex, *stuprum,* that applied to sex with persons not permitted by the law but not representing a clear violation of the marital contract. Like adultery, it was punishable in some cases with death by the sword.

The development of medical gynecology, on the one hand, and professional consultation on selecting a legal sexual partner, on the other, make clear the public importance that Roman society placed on sex and inheritance. Greek physicians Galen and Soranus moved to Rome in the second century and wrote widely on how Roman husbands could tell if a prospective preadolescent bride was likely to be fertile and bear sons.[4] A significant market developed in self-help books for fathers on choosing wives for one's sons, as well as for books on how to ensure conception (and therefore inheritance).

This was complicated for the Romans by a set of philosophical beliefs that preceded Christianity and combined with it to create a volatile and decisive mix. Roman men believed that to have sex too often would feminize them, cause them to lose their precious "dryness," blur their boundaries, and damage their health. Moderate sexual intercourse was preferred by some of the physicians, abstinence by others. The philosopher Epicurus believed that intercourse in itself was harmful to men, and some physicians, Soranus especially, agreed.[5] The loss of semen was thought to weaken men.

This produced a situation in which men thought intercourse to be dangerous for reasons of health, not morality, but necessary because of the inheritance laws. Their doctors and philosophers told them to allow it to occur as infrequently as was consistent with producing heirs quickly. At other times they regarded the company of women as dangerous (since they were seductive), less interesting than that of men (partly because their wives were likely to be much younger and much less educated), and likely to undercut the toughness on which Roman male identity rested. For young women of high rank, courtship in the modern sense did not exist. Her husband was chosen for the Roman woman and might well be a stranger. Her first sexual experience was to be with him, but it would be repeated infrequently. She joined his household, but only rarely his intimate circle,

---

[3]Ibid., 78–85.
[4]Ibid., 25–40.
[5]Ibid., 12.

since that was largely composed of men. If she had children quickly, her period of commitment to him, and his to her, was likely to expire while she was still in her teens. He could take a concubine, without violating the adultery laws, at any time; she could not and was most disadvantaged during those early years of legal marriage.

Children born to this union were typically raised and breast-fed by nurses, who would often have to leave their own children to take care of those children of the senatorial class. Though our knowledge of Roman child-rearing is limited, we do know that fathers had the right to accept or reject any child at birth, and that those who were rejected were exposed, either picked up to be raised as slaves, or eaten by beasts. Malformed children and girls were the most often rejected, but a father in the pre-Constantinian empire had to give no reason for refusing a child.[6] A child was not legally one of his family if the father did not pick it up when it was laid at his feet after its birth.

Children were swaddled in early infancy, kept in a confinement involving almost total sensory deprivation for the first two months.[7] Once children were old enough to understand blows, the advice manuals on child-rearing suggested blows and threats to facilitate desired behavior from weaning on. In response to this harsh and limiting childhood, Galen observed that Roman women were believed throughout the Mediterranean to care little for their children.[8]

Such was the relationship of sex, morality, child-rearing, and society when Paul began preaching Christianity in the Mediterranean basin. Though these arrangements well served the production of sons and soldiers, they were indifferent or destructive to relationships between husbands and wives, and parents and children. No wonder continence looked so good when the church began challenging the sexual assumptions of the empire.

The concern about sexual self-control among the Roman elite gave Christianity an obvious entrée to the empire. Justin, one of the earliest Christian theologians, in addressing the Stoic emperor Antoninus Pius, wrote circa 150, "Many, both men and women of the age of sixty or seventy years, who have been disciples of Christ from their youth continue in immaculate purity…It is our boast to be able to display such persons before the human race."[9] Justin's arguments reveal that sexual abstinence among

---

[6]Ibid., 50–51.

[7]Ibid., 60.

[8]Ibid., 48.

[9]Justin Martyr, *The First Apology*, vol. 56, *Ancient Christian Writers*, ed. Walter J. Burghardt, John J. Dillon, and Dennis D. McManus; trans. Leslie William Barnard (New York: Paulist Press, 1997), 15, 32.

a significant minority of Christians was part of the life of the church by the second century.

Brown and others point out, however, that the meaning of continence was very different for the apostolic and subsequent first-century church than for the Roman world around it. It came out of Jewish apocalyptic thought and the eschatalogical hope for the triumphant parousia, a background different from the mind-body and/or conscious-unconscious dualism of the Greeks, and even more so, of the Romans. There had been no permanent celibacy in the Jewish community. Even the Nazirite vows and the sexual abstinence of priests during their rotation at the altar were temporary. The Essenes were the first monastic community known to Judaism, and their vows were also time-limited and connected to the life of this body in this world.[10] Hence the unitive, temporary, political celibacy of the Essenes, and the early missionary church was transformed in meaning by its encounter with and need to make itself acceptable in the world of the dualistic, philosophical, and self-manipulative celibacy of the Romans.

Within the first hundred years following the death of Paul, there was active controversy from one end of the church to the other over the value and necessity of sexual abstinence. Most of the apostles, who became the early missionaries, had been married. Most of their converts were adults, which, in the Roman world, meant that they also were married. But given the alienated state of sexuality in that world, and the emphasis on single-mindedly seeking the kingdom of God (again, a largely Jewish concept), a pattern developed of many married converts renouncing sex at the time of their conversion.

In the second century, postmarital continence, or continence within the marriage of two Christians, became widespread.[11] A principle was quickly established in more ascetic communities that Christians who were widowed (as many were, since women so often died in childbirth) or divorced would remain single and continent; but the majority of clergy were still married and actively sexual with their wives. During the bishopric of Ignatius in Antioch (110–117), pastors who attempted to make celibacy mandatory for their baptisands were forbidden to do so, and those who boasted of their celibate marriages were instructed to practice their celibacy in secret.[12] A hundred years later, as vigorous an exponent of virginity as Origen

---

[10]Henry C. Lea, *History of Sacerdotal Celibacy in the Christian Church*, 3d ed., rev. (London: Williams and Norgate, 1907), vol. 1., 9–10. See also Brown, 38ff.

[11]Lea, 19.

[12]Brown, 58.

(185–254) condemned those who abandoned their spouses to live in celibacy,[13] which tells us that a significant minority were doing it.

Hermas, a Jewish Roman Christian who wrote in the early second century, obviously assumed a married readership and was himself married, though striving for continence with his wife. His understanding of virginity was not as a sacred symbol of purity, but as a time of danger before the family could see that the young girl got married.[14] He was a member of the popular prophetic movement, focusing on singleness of heart, who felt that lust and all other private longings interfered with his transparency of spirit. Yet he advised those who had lusted for other women to think of the charms of their own wives. This was not the recommendation of a man who found all sexual feelings inappropriate, though they were distracting to a prophet and interfered with the freedom to show forth the Spirit.

Almost a hundred years later, across the Mediterranean in Carthage, we find the Montanist prophetic movement represented in the rhetoric of Tertullian, who linked soul, body, and celibacy. He was a Stoic and believed that control of the body directly benefited the soul. "For continence will be a means whereby you will traffic in a mighty substance of sanctity: by parsimony of the flesh you will gain the Spirit."[15] His writings reflect another tension prominent throughout the early church. The church at Carthage was strong and as such attracted the attention of Roman persecution. However, Tertullian's readers were educated and well-off, providing a certain immunity from the persecution and martyrdom that many Christians faced. Though Tertullian agreed with the Montanists that martyrdom is the perfect union with God, his semi-immune followers required another way to intensify their intimacy with the divine. Continence was the chosen method. Brown writes, "With Tertullian, we have the first consequential statement, written for educated Christians and destined to enjoy a long future in the Latin world, of the belief that abstinence from sex was the most effective technique with which to achieve clarity of soul."[16]

Tertullian made powerful contributions in two other areas. He was among the first to argue that no *digamus,* or man in a second marriage, could be ordained to the priesthood (clearly indicating that once-married men constituted the bulk of the ordained). The controversy over the ordination of *digami* lasted another century before Tertullian's position triumphed, and it is clear that second marriages for laity were only beginning

---

[13]Lea, 19.

[14]Brown, 71.

[15]Tertullian, *On Exhortation to Chastity,* chap. 10 in *The Writings of Tertullian,* vol. 3 of *Ante-Nicene Christian Library,* ed. Alexander Roberts and James Donaldson, (Edinburgh: T. and T. Clark, 1869), 15.

[16]Brown, 78.

to become controversial in this early third-century church.[17] The other intense conviction Tertullian advanced is the belief that sexual desire can never be removed, the body being real and inescapable, and that women are basically seductive and therefore must be veiled and kept at a distance, baptism notwithstanding. The gravitational pull of human, and especially female, nature would never allow relaxation of the will or the precautions.[18] With those views Tertullian was one of the first to encourage Christians to be suspicious of all contact between the sexes.

Contemporary with Tertullian, but at the other end of the Mediterranean, two important developments were shaping the very different development of the Eastern church. East of Antioch in the mountains of Syria, in close contact with Judaism, a tradition was developing of total continence for all baptized Christians, in communities called Encratites, which means Abstainer. These groups formed villages in which Christian men and women lived and from which they traveled together, observing continence and teaching faith in a manner not unlike that of the Jewish and Montanist prophets. They developed a theology that was radically unlike the Roman and has strong echoes in the Eastern Church today. They saw the human soul as existing to be married to the Spirit. They believed in an almost ecstatic mysticism, "a benign state of permanent possession gained by the Christian at the moment of baptism."[19] Images of spiritual marriage, with its bonding and nurture by a distinctly feminine Spirit, abounded. Such a powerful love could accept no rival, so human sexuality was outcompeted. They, like the desert fathers who followed, developed a regime of fasting as one of the methods of cutting down physical desire. There was a clear split with nature among the Encratites and a belief that baptism and fasting would enable one to control, and ultimately eliminate, sexual desire. Hence, the Roman preoccupation with separation of men and women was unnecessary, since in their spiritual freedom they would have no sexual need for each other.

Only a couple of hundred miles south, in Egypt, Clement of Alexandria, who like Tertullian was a Stoic, was preaching a very different gospel than that of either the Encratites or the great Carthaginian. He was deeply offended by the Encratites, scoffing that "they set their hopes on their private parts." Death, not sex, was the great enemy for him,[20] and sex should be ordered like the other passions. Ultimately, that meant it should be undertaken in the service of God, consciously planned, not to be enjoyed to excess, and not beyond the times necessary for the conception of a child.

---

[17]Lea, 25.
[18]Brown, 80–82.
[19]Ibid., 91.
[20]Ibid., 132.

(The first prominent appearance of this theme.) But the objection to excess here was neither moral nor mystic, but aesthetic, in the standard Stoic sense. Clement expected the purification of the Christian to be a gradual thing and, with it, for sexuality to wither away. But a Christian home should have children conceived as a Stoic tribute to God.

Probably Clement's most remembered contribution to the church's struggle to understand sexuality and family is his involvement in the early education of his successor and student, Origen. Origen became the center of a philosophical circle in Alexandria by 202, when Clement left the city, and he continued as the great sage of the Eastern Church until his death in 253. A spurt of persecution, rare for Egypt, martyred his father while he was still in his teens and made him the head of a philosophical community. As a Platonist, he was much less convinced of the immutability of the body than was his Stoic teacher, Clement; instead he advocated a fluid view of physicality that was infinitely malleable under the pressure of the soul.[21]

Origen was the first strident advocate in the church of lifelong virginity. Prior to his time, continence was almost exclusively a postmarital phenomenon, with marriage being a preparation for continence. But he saw virginity as preserving a preexisting identity, "already formed in a former, more splendid existence and destined for yet further glory."[22] He sought an immaculate spirit, preserved in the original state of the joining of body and soul, "a fragile oasis of human freedom." He saw virginity as a social and even a political choice, a rejection of the claims of society, "the assertion of a basic freedom so intense, a sense of identity so deeply rooted, as to cause to evaporate the normal social and physical constraints that tied the Christian to his or her gender."[23]

Here we see the beginnings of the Catholic understanding of celibacy, for Origen argued that not to belong to society, nor to a spouse, was to free one's self to belong more intensely to others, especially to the great communion of angelic beings he saw as closely surrounding the virginal person. It was his great hope to free Christians from the attachments and distracting pleasures of this world in order to enjoy the even greater pleasures of the spiritual senses in another, more intensely joyful world. What was at stake was not a legalistic or works-righteous continence, but "the fragile growth of a spiritual sense of preternatural sharpness."[24] Physical pleasures nourished a counter-sensibility, dulling the spirit's true capacity for joy, he held. "The spirit was destined for a moment of startling, unimaginably

---

[21]Ibid., 167.
[22]Ibid., 169, 171.
[23]Ibid., 197.
[24]Ibid., 173.

precise knowledge of Christ, of which the subtle knowledge of a partner gained through physical love was but a blurred and—so Origen was convinced—a distracting and inapposite echo."[25] Ultimately the virgin's purity of spirit would lead to a falling away of the physical, a body made holy as the resplendent vehicle of the soul. He objected vigorously to Paul's writing that young widows should marry and bear children, since marriage furnished bodies in which to imprison souls.

By the time of Origen's death, two other movements that would powerfully impact the ethos of Western Christianity were gaining momentum in the East. In Egypt, Christians were fleeing the Diocletian persecution that killed Origen, taking up solitary life in the desert. And in Syria, an Encratite wanderer named Mani was putting the finishing touches on a philosophy that would profoundly affect the Roman world and shape the Christianity first imbibed by the young Augustine.[26]

When Anthony moved to the desert in 270,[27] a generation of ascetics had preceded him. Word came back to the Roman West that Egyptian ascetics had found a way to achieve continence in the desert, and by the beginning of the fourth century pilgrims from the West were daily visitors to the monks' cells, and collections of the writings of the desert fathers were circulating in several Western languages.[28] In their attempt to find God and solitude, these anchorites also discovered the power and ineradicability of sexual fantasies, longings, and processes, and the lure of those realities carried them toward human society and relationship.[29] Fornication, looking on a woman, homosexuality, and even sleep were found to be powerful links to settled society and interferences with the monks' attempt to focus completely on God. They found that abstinence from sleep and severe limitation of food, coupled with repetitive work, would diminish sexual feelings and fantasies. Many monks regularly restricted their intake to about a thousand calories per day, well below the level necessary for sexual functioning.[30] Nocturnal emissions were carefully noted. When a monk could restrict these to one or two a year, it was understood that an advanced state of holiness had been achieved.

Despite the intense attention to sexual renunciation among the anchorites, they did not believe that sex was either evil or basic in itself. It was assumed that there would be occasional lapses, some physical and intentional, especially among younger monks, but neither shaming nor ostracism were

---

[25]Ibid.
[26]Rousselle, 137.
[27]Ibid., 139.
[28]Ibid., 142ff.
[29]Ibid., 176.
[30]Ibid., p. 157.

typical. It was only held that sexual activity was harmful to the goals of ascetic union with God and to freedom from the structures of human society.[31] Ultimately, Brown concludes, "The most bitter struggle of the desert ascetic…was not so much with his sexuality as with his belly."[32] Starvation and insanity in his isolation and the immensity of the desert were even greater risks, in the face of which sexual thoughts were an anchor binding the monk to settled society. The goal was to find oneself and God without the security of society or relationships. To stand alone in the face of God and the demons was seen as the only route to the ultimate purification.[33]

Ultimately it was the longing for corporate help with the temptations toward sex and the settled life that produced the grouping together of the anchorites into desert monasteries, which were thriving institutions by the early fifth century. In 400, there were five thousand monks at Nitria, near Alexandria,[34] which was one of a score of monastic centers in the Egyptian desert.

In a parallel development in Christian Syria, around the time when Origen was forty years old, a twelve-year-old boy received the first of a series of visions that led him to found the "only independent universal religion to emerge directly from the Christian tradition."[35] Mani had grown up as a follower of a Jewish Christian leader named Elchasai in a settlement on the banks of the Tigris, and moved from that community's focus on ritual washings to a total repudiation of marital sexuality. He combined basic Christian teachings with a Zoroastrian vision,[36] believing that the kingdom of light had been invaded and traumatized by the kingdom of darkness. But light had regained its balance and created a means for the pure spirit to find its way through the physical world to reunite with God.[37]

Manichaean religious communities organized themselves in two tiers, a structure that was also developing in the orthodox Christian community. There were the elect, who vowed lifelong continence and strict attention to a vegetarian diet, and were seen as "the Sun and Moon come down to earth" to forward the liberation of the world.[38] And there were the auditors, of whom the young Augustine became one, who were not bound by rigorous vows but attended the elect, fed them, learned from them, but were themselves married and only fasted at specified times of the year.

---

[31]Brown, 218.
[32]Ibid., 220–21.
[33]Ibid., 215.
[34]Ibid., 197.
[35]Lea, 34.
[36]Brown, 199.
[37]Ibid.
[38]Lea, 33.

Though Mani himself was flayed alive by the Persian king in 276 and his communities in Persia exterminated,[39] the optimism that sexuality could be overcome and humans could be perfected, even if slowly, gave his followers great popularity in the West. Sex symbolized the horrendous opposite of true creation, the greedy drive that enabled the kingdom of darkness to spread and obstruct the kingdom of light. Sex clearly served evil for the Manichaeans, but it could be totally transcended. Sexual desire could be entirely excluded from the inmost self, whose soul could be fully suffused with light and utterly at peace.[40]

The early fourth century was utterly revolutionary for the church. Antony and the other desert fathers were attracting thousands of pilgrims to their cells in Egypt. The Council of Elvira, a local gathering of Spanish clergy, ruled in 305 that married priests must totally abstain from sex with their wives to keep their positions—a stance that was not mandated in the broader church for at least another century.[41] Constantine was converted in 312, effectively ending the persecutions except for a brief surge under Julian half a century later. The great Council at Nicaea (325) grappled with the Arian controversy and prohibited a form like priestly concubinage.[42] Arguments began to appear that the growing wealth of the church, now that it was the official religion of the empire, made property and inheritance dangerous temptations and inappropriate concerns for its priesthood.

Shortly after the mid-fourth century the intellectual leadership of the Eastern Church had passed to the Cappadocian fathers, many of whom were married. Their region, eastern Asia Minor, had long been Christian, and priesthood and bishoprics were passed down from father to son.[43] One such son was Gregory of Nyssa, whose *On Virginity* introduced a new strain of thought, linking the fall, death, sex, and virginity. Without the fall there would have been no death, he argued, so God activated the previously latent sexual differences of men and women to produce new persons to replace those who had died. So sex was a gift for even the reluctantly married Gregory, but a double-edged gift that bound humans to society and thereby to death. Death had created a new sense of time, bound by the fear of death, thus creating a deep sadness over the world.[44] Virginity, on the other

---

[39]Brown, 200-1.

[40]Lea, 43.

[41]Lea, 45–48.

[42]Brown, 285.

[43]Ibid., 293–99.

[44]Gregory of Nyssa, *On Virginity*, in *St. Gregory of Nyssa, Ascetical Works*, vol. 58 in *The Fathers of the Church*, ed. Joseph Deferrari (Washington: Catholic University of America Press, 1966), 48.

hand, was a restoration of our original condition (à la Origen) and removed one from anxiety about the perpetuation of families and cities. It shifted the concern to the eternal kingdom in which death is not a decisive event.

> Therefore, such a life, because it is stronger than the power of death, ought to be preferred by the intelligent. For the bodily procreation of children...is more an embarking upon death than upon life for man. Corruption has its beginning in birth and those who refrain from procreation through virginity themselves bring about a cancellation of death by preventing it from advancing further because of them, and by setting themselves up as a kind of boundary stone between life and death, they keep death from going forward. If, then, death is not able to outwit virginity, this is clear proof that virginity is stronger than death.[45]

Three Westerners and a great preacher from Antioch dominated the final years of antiquity and established the final outlines of Roman Catholic and Greek Orthodox theologies of sex and family, at the same time that the popes and councils were hammering out the ecclesiastical syntheses that have governed, or attempted to govern, the lives of clergy, monks, and consecrated virgins for the entire history of the Catholic church.

Ambrose of Milan, born sixteen years after Gregory of Nyssa (in 339), Jerome (born 342), and John Chrysostom (born 347) furthered the reverence for virginity, the institutions of monastic and convent life, and the demand for an exclusively celibate clergy, at least in Western Europe. All three were important parts of the intellectual and ecclesiastical history of Augustine of Hippo, whose writings crowned the intellectual production of the early church and established the theories that govern Catholic thought on sexuality to the present day.

Ambrose had been imperial governor in Liguria (northern Italy) before becoming bishop of Milan, by then the center of the western Empire, in 374.[46] His sister, like many educated and wealthy women throughout the empire, was a consecrated virgin and as such a major challenge to a Roman society still deeply committed to the continuity of noble families. Ambrose was unceasingly embroiled in the struggle against the Arians and well aware of the military vulnerability of the region, and the whole empire, since the collapse of the Danubian frontier. He lived in unsettled and anxious times.

---

[45]Brown, 341.
[46]Ibid., 347–50.

He was a thinker with a strong preference for clear distinctions, absolute dichotomies, and the centrality of the Catholic Church in the life of the empire. Virginity was utterly central in his thought, aided by the dualism he imbibed from his readings (in the original Greek, a capacity then lost to many churchmen) of Philo, Origen, and Plotinus. He emphasized the primacy of the will, actively maneuvering to challenge both emperors and pagans with his thought on the one ugly scar on every human body—sexuality.[47] Many who contemplated baptism at his hands, including Augustine, firmly believed Ambrose would not baptize a married person.

It is difficult to separate the theological and the ecclesiological concerns that impelled Ambrose. The wealthy consecrated virgin was a major source of church funds, and thereby of church safety in an unstable time. Ambrose's intense preoccupation with the perpetual virginity of Mary, which he elevated to a point of established doctrine, was strongly connected to the question of whether consecrated virgins could be ordered out of the convent by their families, to marry and place their wealth in the hands of the chosen husband and his family, rather than those of the church.

For him, baptism was closely connected to virginity. It initiated the ascent into tranquility that flowed from the spotless flesh of Christ, spotless because it was conceived without lust and itself knew no lust.[48] The data for Jesus having known no lust is not as convincing to the modern reader. His "sexless birth and unstirred body acted as a bridge between the present, fallen state of the human body and its future, glorious transformation at the resurrection."[49] Only a body whose virgin birth was exempt from sexual desire could redeem human beings scarred by that desire. This established for Ambrose the absolute boundaries between the church and the world and reinforced his disgust for all forms of "admixture." The church, like Mary, had integrity, "the precious ability to keep what was one's own untarnished by alien intrusion,"[50] like the penis and sperm of a man. Because Mary had avoided all admixture, she was chosen by Christ as the source of his own flesh. She was an *aula pudoris*, a royal hall of undamaged chastity, an image that conveyed to the Milanese the inviolable central court of the imperial palace. Mary's womb was closed and stood for all that was unbroken and sacred in the world.

During the episcopate of Ambrose, Pope Siricius intensified the campaign for total clerical celibacy, an objective never totally achieved even

---

[47]Ibid., 348–49.
[48]Ibid., 351.
[49]Ibid., 354.
[50]Lea, 64.

today, though it has been official doctrine for sixteen hundred years. In 385 he wrote Himerius, a bishop in Spain, expressing his horror that the Spanish clergy "had so little regard for the sanctity of their calling as to maintain relations with their wives."[51] He maintained the binding nature of celibacy for bishops, priests, and deacons and demanded expulsion of all who resisted. Apparently even his firmness had different levels for different regions, for a letter the next year to the church in North Africa takes a softer position, imploring clerics to preserve purity, and makes no threats or even allusions to the custom or law of the church.[52] Bitter polemics broke out over Siricius' attempts to mandate celibacy. Jerome was enlisted to argue the pope's point; and ultimately the prime opponent, Jovinian, was beaten and exiled by imperial decree.[53]

Jerome was often invoked to strengthen the church's growing anti-sexualism. He had come to Rome in 382 from scholarly and ascetic pursuits in Constantinople, but by 385 the Roman clergy had been so angered by his arrogance and insults to their style of life that they banished him from the city. He went to Bethlehem, joining virginal friends Paula and Melania. For a time he wrote, following his mentor Origen, that men and women were spiritually and intellectually identical and should enjoy one another's spiritual company. But Roman protests against this dangerous doctrine and the increasing suspicion of Origen as possibly heretical turned his exegetical writings more and more to the dangers for virgins of either sex in contact with their opposites, writing in floridly sexualized language about the dangerous pleasures that awaited.[54] Brown concludes that "he contributed more heavily than did any other contemporary Latin writer to the definitive sexualization of Paul's notion of the flesh."[55]

His importance is evenly divided between political and intellectual realms. He zealously attacked and hounded those who argued against virginity's superiority to married life and was merciless in his rage at married priests. Jovinian, Evagrius, and their followers were exiled largely due to Jerome's intense polemic efforts.[56] He ultimately argued, quite unlike Origen, that in heaven men and women would have precisely the same flesh, though without physical desire. And he was a vigorous opponent of Pelagius, basing his arguments against possible human perfection on the

---

[51]Ibid., 65.
[52]Ibid., 70.
[53]Brown, 366.
[54]Lea, 69–72.
[55]Brown, 376.
[56]Ibid., 384–86.

enduring nature of sexual desire.[57] "What others will hereafter be in heaven, …virgins begin to be on earth."[58] The intensity of his preference for virginity is seen in his very atypical (for a Roman) demotion of Peter to the least of the disciples, because he was married.[59] After Jerome it was never again possible for a Roman Christian to doubt that virginity was preferred by the church, if not by God, or to lack for reams of intensely argued justifications for that view.

Chrysostom, like Jerome, is more important for his political, polemical, and homiletical activity on behalf of virginity than for the originality of his thought. From the time he was ordained a priest in 386 until the beginning of his ill-fated and brief tenure as patriarch of Constantinople in 397, he preached the contrast between the Christian's gift of his or her own body to God and the city's demand that the body be available for civic purposes. Antioch was the empire's third largest city during Chrysostom's tenure as bishop there and was famed for its public eroticism—bawdy games in the Arena, naked young women (nereids) cavorting in the pools flanking the games, and marriages as an open celebration of ribald sexuality. But the city was surrounded by the Syrian mountains, which had been the home of the Encratite movement and continued as a center of ascetic Christianity.

As a young man, John Chrysostom had spent two years as a hermit in the mountains, but his health failed, and he returned to Antioch and the settled church. But he retained his loyalty to the virginal life, preaching that "your bodies belong to yourselves, not to the city."[60] He also pled for the sanctity of Christian marriage. Chrysostom combined the themes of sexuality and poverty as a modern social critic might, arguing that the poor—and Antioch's civic structure was based, like that of many cities, on the necessity of poverty—were more vulnerable to sexual exploitation, whereas the rich could protect the bodies of their women. "For the body was the most vocal spokesman of all, in its manifest vulnerability, of the common descent of all human beings from Adam. John preached a brotherhood of bodies at risk."[61] And he ultimately, like his contemporary Jerome and his successor Augustine, moved to separate the men and women in his church and diminish the opportunities for the exploitation of the one by the other.

His fame as a preacher won Chrysostom elevation to the head of the church in Constantinople, but his radicalism on sexual matters brought

---

[57]Jerome, *Against Jovinian* I, 36. 374 in *The Nicene and Post-Nicene Fathers,* Second Series, vol. 6, ed. Philip Schaff and Henry Wace, trans. W. H. Freemantle (Grand Rapids: Eerdmans, 1892).
[58]Lea, 38.
[59]Brown, 307.
[60]Ibid., 316.
[61]Lea, 86.

him down. He was exiled in 404, driven to death in 407, by a city unwilling to tolerate his challenge to both its sexual and economic habits.

Augustine was seven years younger than John Chrysostom, spent his entire career between North Africa and Italy, and forged the final synthesis of the ancient world's thinking on sexuality.[62] His thought pulled together the various strands that we have considered to this point and continues as the dominant Roman Catholic position.

As an auditor among the Manichaeard since the age of nineteen (373), Augustine had drunk deeply from the Encratite and subsequent neo-Platonic traditions. He longed for and struggled with the hope for a pure union with God, but he also lived monogamously and passionately with a lawful concubine for thirteen years, pursuing his career as a minor governmental official in the North African provinces. In 384 a promotion took him to Milan, the seat of imperial power, and afforded an escape from a looming marriage arranged by his mother. He felt both the marriage and the loss of his concubine as giving up his freedom in order to gain earthly power and experienced a disturbingly powerful need for sex in the transitional periods between established relationships.[63] He began attending the sermons of Ambrose, was touched by the power of the purity Ambrose demanded, and was baptized by him in 386. Five years later he was a priest, leader of a small North African monastery, and shortly bishop at Hippo. He moved into an all-male world without the cultured women of Rome or Milan and spent the rest of his life exploring his own consciousness and its meaning for the private and societal lives of Christians.

Unlike Jerome, and to a lesser extent Ambrose and Chrysostom, Augustine was not against marriage. No virgin himself, his praise of virginity, though real, was measured. He placed a high value on friendship as the basis for marriage and on the superiority of reason and will over passion. He was especially concerned that sex between a man and a woman could destroy their friendship, the latter being better sustained by rational will. He observed that passion often did not obey the will, rising when the will would not have it, refusing to appear when the will would choose it. Hence, it was an undependable ally of the true friendship between men and women, more often disrupting that friendship and leading to the subjugation of one by the other for the sake of passion or profit.

For Augustine, therefore, if marriage was to preserve the maximum portion of that friendship, marriage must banish passion to the fullest extent

---

[62]Brown, 392–93.
[63]Augustine, *City of God*, in *The Fathers of the Church*, ed. Roy Joseph (Washington, D.C.: Catholic University of America Press, 1966), 399. Reference is to *City of God* XIV, 23.

possible and be governed by rational will. For rational will the only good use of sexual intercourse was the production of children, and to admit sex at any other time invited passion to govern the relationship at the cost of the friendship. Much of his position stemmed from his exegesis of Genesis, which he read as indicating that there was only non-lustful, rational choice for intercourse and children before the fall, with sex being corrupted as fully (but no more so) by the fall as all other human capacities. Then lust entered,[64] and sex could never again be wholly subject to rationality. His views are spelled out particularly in *On Marriage and Concupiscence* and *The Good of Marriage*.

> The union then, of male and female for the purpose of procreation is the natural good of marriage. But he makes a bad use of this good who uses it bestially, so that his intention is on the gratification of lust, instead of the desire for offspring.[65]

> Of this bond the substance undoubtedly is this, that the man and woman who are joined together in matrimony should remain inseparable as long as they live; and that it should be unlawful for one consort to be parted from the other, except for the cause of fornication.[66]

> But those who resort to [contraceptive measures], although called by the name of spouses, are really not such; they retain no vestige of pure matrimony, but pretend the honorable designation as a cloak for criminal conduct.[67]

> Wherefore the devil holds infants guilty who are born, not of the good by which marriage is good, but of the evil of concupiscence, which, indeed, marriage uses aright, but at which even marriage has occasion to feel shame.[68]

> The very embrace which is lawful and honorable cannot be effected without the ardour of lust, so as to be able to accomplish that which appertains to the use of reason and not of lust. Now

---

[64]Augustine, *The Good of Marriage*, in *The Fathers of the Church*, ed. Roy Joseph Deferrari, vol. 27 (New York: The Fathers of the Church, 1955).

[65]Augustine, *On Marriage and Concupiscence*, I, 5. 265 in *The Nicene and Post-Nicene Fathers*, First Series, volume ed. Philip Schaff, trans. Peter Holmes (Grand Rapids: Eerdmans, 1956).

[66]Ibid., 268.

[67]Ibid., 271.

[68]Ibid., 274.

this ardour, whether following or preceding this will, does some-how, by a power of its own, move the members which cannot be moved simply by the will, and in this manner it shows itself not to be the servant of a will which commands it, but rather to be the punishment of a will which disobeys it.[69]

Augustine ultimately holds that to marry is good, but not to marry is bet-ter, for it preserves the freedom to be a friend. He distances himself consid-erably from Ambrose and Jerome, arguing that marriage is not out of date, but that the "concord of husband and a wife pointed forward to the final unity of the city of God."[70] He ultimately does not even condemn sexual pleasure, but indicates that it is lawful if it is completely coincident with the will. In a marvelous passage, Brown notes that "the sweet attractive power of physical beauty and the delicious onset and sharp climax of sexual delight, traditionally associated with the act of conception, may not have been absent in Paradise; but, in Paradise, such delight would have coin-cided entirely with the will."[71]

There were two realities facing Augustine that are quite different from those we face. To begin with, he inherited the Greek and Roman cultural-philosophic traditions that had vastly more confidence in conscious will than any other human capacity. That was the strength that won the empire, and it had not been faced by either psychoanalytic or Christian skepticism about a rationality unswerved by emotion and self-interest. For Rome it was self-evident that reason was pure and could be separated from passion. Contemporary readers find that difficult to assume.

And Augustine lived in a time beset with and preoccupied by heresy. The doctrines of the church were in active, intense evolution. Arian, Donatist, and Pelagian heresies rivaled the beliefs of the bishops for en-dorsement as orthodox. Heresy and schism were considered the greatest sins. To hold such a position one must believe that conscious will can dic-tate what one believes, that belief, like literally everything else, is subject to reason, and that reason is subject to nothing but God. Hence, it is natural to believe that the same combination of reason and will, which ensure one's safety against the sin of heresy and resultant damnation, must govern all of life. To let anything challenge it, like sexual passion, would undercut the philosophic basis of the defense against the far more serious stain of heresy. So a rational and conscious control of passion was established as the bul-wark of Christian sexual orthodoxy.

---

[69]Ibid., I, 27. 275.
[70]Brown, 403.
[71]Ibid., 407.

CHAPTER 4

Church and Family in the Middle Ages and Reformation

The End of Antiquity

Throughout the theological flowering of late antiquity, Rome's political and social structures were slowly collapsing. Migrations of Goths, Vandals, Huns, Franks, and Lombards were bringing increasing pressure on gradually retreating legions. The empire's birth rate was too low to replace her officers and soldiers. The guiding vision of civility and rationality had lost its persuasiveness. Property increasingly found its way into the hands of the church. Alliances with the subject peoples led to barbarians' holding key roles in the military and civil administrations. Rivalry between Constantinople and Rome, later Milan or Ravenna, made it easier for increasingly powerful leaders of the challenging nations to divide and weaken, if not conquer. Use of barbarian mercenaries, then of barbarian allies, made it harder to draw a clear distinction between friend and enemy; and, in the end, many of the empire's strongest champions were Gauls, Vandals, and Goths.

During those last two centuries of the empire, administrative and philosophic interest that had once ordered imperial Rome was increasingly concentrated in the fledgling church. As political and military structures weakened, the church often was the most dependable and well-organized segment of society. From the time of Constantine on, the empire was so dependent on the stability of the church that heresy and schism were considered intolerable threats to military security, and force of arms was regularly used to enforce or alter doctrine. Many persons of primarily political motivation saw the church as the way to preserve the structures of society. Hence, men like Ambrose of Milan could be an unbaptized provincial governor one day and bishop of the capital city of the West the next, and as bishop, crucial in the empire's struggles against Arian heretics—many of whom were those same threatening Goths and Vandals.

The So-called Dark Ages

At different times in different parts of Europe and North Africa, the constant ebb and flow of warfare altered the communities and institutions that had stabilized and humanized society for centuries. By the late fifth century, the dependable structures were largely gone in the West. Rome had been sacked by Goths, Vandals, and Lombards. Africa had been lost to the Vandals, cutting off the corn supplies. Famine, plague, and massacre visited every city. Years of warfare reduced whole populations to poverty. Cities were stripped of art and wealth, and rural and tribal nations increasingly became the military powers. Political centrality shifted from Rome to the capital of the duke or king with the strongest army at the time, and popes were made and unmade depending on political alliances and military victories.

Despite all of this, the church had the best communication network and leadership structures of any of society's institutions for several centuries. Even so, hierarchical discipline collapsed. The church community, and especially the monastery, became the most dependable source of order and safety in Europe. Though whole nations suffered drastically decreased standards of living, and bishops were often generals who had to lead armies to survive, the structures of the church persisted, while those of empire did not.

But they persisted in a radically different society, or set of societies, than the ones that had gone before. Values were totally inverted, social and governmental structures were less formal and rigid, warfare was endemic, cities were diminished, and families served quite different purposes in very different ways. Priestly marriage became common again, and monasteries were often invaded and defiled. Since survival was much more of a struggle, and so much energy went into blending the old culture with the several new ones, leisure for theology was subordinated to the practical difficulties of working out new ways to live and trying desperately to stay alive.[1]

---

[1]Much of the previous discussion was drawn from Justine Davis Randers-Pehrson, *Barbarians and Romans: The Birth Struggle of Europe, A.D. 400–700* (Norman: University of Oklahoma Press, 1983).

As the relentless pressure of migrating tribes from the East continued, northern and central Europe were ravaged for six hundred years by almost uninterrupted warfare, as tribe fought tribe for space. Boundaries were fluid, tenure was uncertain, and the primary occupation of almost all men of means was combat. Furthermore, incessant warfare made the development of other resources exceedingly difficult. Human population in these areas had been sparse, and tribe after tribe would settle an area and begin to develop the rudiments of civilized life, only to be displaced by the next wave of wanderers, raiders, and pirates. One century's wild, fur-clad barbarians were the next century's victims before yet another onslaught.

Among the most enduring of the invaders were the Franks, originally (or at least most recently) from the North Sea littoral of Belgium, Holland, and farther east.[2] They were first known to the Romans as raiders, then as suppliers of mercenaries, then as allies, and finally as a pressure of population that could not be pushed back. They gradually occupied the north of what are now France and Germany, struggling with the Alemanni and the Burgundians to the southeast and with the Gallo-Romans and the Goths to the southwest. They filled in much of the space north of the Loire River between more scattered settlements of Gauls and Saxons, though they were often beaten back from the coast by the depredations of the Scandinavian pirates and raiders.

For the first several hundred years of their presence, they were a loosely organized movement, more a mass of separate, distantly related families than an organized state. By the late fifth and early sixth centuries, under the leadership of Clovis, they successfully overcame the challenges of both Alemanni and Goths and became the dominant people in the land. Clovis accepted Christianity around 503, and the long struggle between Frankish customs and Christian doctrine was joined.

Roman cities had been based on the expectation of established, permanent populations, with representative governments delegated by familiar constituencies. Frankish society was fluid, based on large extended families, in early times polygamous, inbred, and so mobile that one's neighborhood and neighbors often differed from year to year. There was no shared space, except within the extended family's crude wooden barnlike house, hence no fixed relationships between fellow citizens. Since location was not fixed, there were almost no real property, no public realm, and few established institutions. There were human sacrifice, a fierce traditional code of vengeance, law that protected movable property, and such a keen sense of

---

[2]See J. M. Wallace-Hadrill, *The Barbarian West, 400–1000* (New York: Hutchinson's University Library, 1952). See esp. 66ff.

the privacy and inviolability of family boundaries that even the state and its offices were considered private property well into the ninth century.[3]

In the traditional Frankish religion, vengeance was a religious duty. The talionic principle was the law of the tribe, down to very small details—literally a right eye for a right eye, a finger for a finger. A man or family who did not avenge kinsmen were shamed, subject to being wiped out without fear of retaliation. Violence and death were so common and masculine aggressiveness so prized that when law began to substitute civil penalties for vengeance, murder was punished by a lesser fine than arson and many degrees of theft.

The Frankish family was very different from the Roman, hence very different from the family about which the early church had theologized. It was almost always extended, several generations (including occasionally multiple wives) and collateral lines living under one roof with cows, pigs, and chickens. Like the Roman family it was male-headed, but unlike the Roman it favored (always parentally arranged) intermarriage between cousins and other members of collateral lines, as had the early Hebrews. The limited amount of accumulated family property was thus kept together.

There were elaborate marriage customs, which honored male decision-making, preserved property, and protected children. Though women had considerably less freedom than men, they could inherit most property and maintain their inheritance after divorce or a husband's death. The position of women in this mobile society was mixed. To begin with, for the poor, women were a luxury. Population research on northern France in the sixth through the ninth centuries makes it unmistakably clear that female infanticide was widely practiced, especially among poorer families. Sex ratios in the population were as high as 262 men per 100 women in some poorer villages, with ratios dropping to 115:100 among the better situated.[4] Though both church and state opposed infanticide, the church's concession to its economic necessity is reflected by the reduction of penance for the act from fourteen years to seven if the mother was poor. The survival chances of women were further reduced by the high death rate in childbirth, so that women who survived infancy still died several years earlier, on average, than men. Despite the constant warfare and endemic political violence of this society, the risks for women remained significantly greater than for men.

Several consequences ensued. It was a very young society, with more than half its members being under twenty. As many as half of the men

---

[3]Michel Rouche, "The Early Middle Ages in the West" in Paul Veyne, ed., *A History of Private Life*, vol. 1, *From Pagan Rome to Byzantium* (Cambridge: Belknap, 1987), 485–510.

[4]Emily Coleman, "Infanticide in the Early Middle Ages" in Susan Stuard, *Women in Medieval Society* (Philadelphia: University of Pennsylvania Press, 1976), 48ff.

never married, adult women being in such short supply. But such women as there were had significant influence. Many were landowners (after the populations stabilized sufficiently enough for land to be held), with significant political and economic power in the fledgling towns and estates. Because men were absent frequently fighting in the almost constant warfare and often did not return, surviving women accumulated large amounts of property and local political clout. But women also remained vulnerable, because families were patrilineal, and a woman's economic power had to be wielded on behalf of a family. Hence, her decisions had to respect the male-headed family's sense of its own long-term political interests. Divorce was easy for men to initiate, and wife-murder was frequent and almost always unpunished, until well after the time of Charlemagne.[5]

The church's influence over marriage, family, and sexuality was very limited from the fifth well into the ninth centuries, and it was not firmly established until the eleventh or twelfth. During the Germanic migrations of the third through seventh centuries, and the constant warfare among the newly settled tribes through at least the tenth, the relatively easy transportation that had kept the Roman Empire somewhat connected had disappeared. Road systems and bridges collapsed, law and order vanished. Hence, ecclesiastical discipline had little power in outlying regions, at precisely the same time that successful evangelism among the Germanic peoples was increasing the regions over which Rome had at least formal ecclesiastical authority. The church grew, but adherence to Roman rule shrank. Local bishops were as often military leaders as committed churchmen, and the fine points of church doctrine were often and easily dismissed. Married priests again became the majority, often inheriting pastorates from their fathers, and even the few early monasteries were often inhabited by married couples or monks with their mistresses.[6]

This situation was compounded by the political situation in Italy, where for several centuries the papacy was either the captive of local Roman political rulers or barbarian captors, or itself became the political power. Many of the popes themselves were openly contemptuous of celibacy and had no interest in enforcing it in the provinces, even if they had been able to exert authority in territory that was often under the control of rival political factions. Since the bishops in those territories were usually appointed by the local political leadership, ecclesiastical matters were often decided according to the political needs of the local king or duke. He typically needed

---

[5]Jo Ann McNamara and Suzanne F. Wemple, "Marriage and Divorce in the Frankish Kingdom," in Stuard, 95–113.
[6]Lea, 130–82.

a loyal local church, which meant a church that was not being asked to abide by and enforce unpopular regulations.[7]

The Return of Church Authority

Two movements gradually strengthened during these centuries, returning the church to sufficient power and freedom that it could turn its attention to theology: the spread of monastic orders and the alliance of a small number of crucial episcopal sees with political leaders who saw potential power in identification with orthodox Catholicism.

Wandering forest hermits of the Egyptian style had been in the West for hundreds of years, but organized monasticism and a formal rule began only after 494, when the youthful Benedict of Nursia renounced the world and went to the mountains south of Rome.[8] After wandering for a time, he founded the monastery at Monte Cassino, eventually the model for hundreds of houses throughout Europe. Lea contends that these monasteries "exercised a more potent influence in extending Christianity over the Heathen than all other agencies combined."[9] While the Benedictines worked in southern Europe and gradually northward, Irish monks from Iona were establishing mission points and ultimately monasteries along the Atlantic and channel coasts and working their way up the river valleys.

All these efforts were vulnerable to constant disruption. Looting and murder by local nobles, Danish or Hungarian invaders, and roving bands of robbers would stamp out a group of monks in a region, only to have the nearest bishop or monastery send out yet another outpost. Hence, Corbie on the Somme, Corvey in Saxony, and Cluny in Burgundy became centers of reform and extension of the monastic movement from the mid-ninth and early tenth centuries onward. From these newly established houses stricter adherence to the Benedictine Rule penetrated Europe. These centers also became cultural havens, homes for historians of the Germanic tribes, and ultimately for theologians. Through their restoration of monastic celibacy, spirituality, and scholarship they renewed a model of clerical life that exercised increasing, if often uneven, influence over bishops and local clergy.

Many of the latter group were struggling to increase the church's influence over marriage and family life, trying to counter traditional Germanic customs with more egalitarian and gender-neutral habits, and ultimately to return the priesthood to a more celibate and disciplined order. Though little theological writing on these subjects survives from the early Middle

---

[7]See especially Eleanor Duckett, *Death and Life in the Middle Ages* (Ann Arbor: University of Michigan Press, 1967), 34ff, 84–93, 111–26, 183–201.

[8]Lea, 124.

[9]Ibid., 125.

Ages, it is clear that many church leaders were convinced that the combined Germanic emphases on the purity of bloodlines, the danger of emotionally intense connections between husband and wife, and the demand for male authority in the family all combined to encourage the violence and chaos that kept life impoverished, ignorant, and brief.[10]

A number of changes worked to counter the old ethos. Parish priests, under the influence of the Ionian monks, began the practice of the private confessional, which in turn created the need for standards for the level of penance required to absolve particular sins. By the ninth century penitential books were widely used by priests to guide them in assigning penance, and these books were the vehicles for substantial change. Though they were organized much like the old Salic Law, with very specific crimes carrying very specific penalties, the priorities were reversed. Murder and rape carried very heavy penance, with wife-murder carrying the heaviest of all. The penalties for adultery were increased and applied equally to both sexes, and increasingly both polygamy and divorce were penalized. As Rouche tells it,

> They opposed any union that did not mirror the union of Christ with the Church, that is, monogamous and indissoluble. They sought a natural order, at once divine and human, both in society and in psychology. It followed from this that women needed some measure of protection from men, that blood vengeance had to be quelled, and that desire had to be channeled toward useful ends.[11]

Though the theology of penitential practice was primitive, emphasizing both purchase of absolution and justification by works, the content of the life that was desired was gradually shifting toward compatibility with settled and economically productive civilization.

A key figure in this shift was Hincmar, powerful archbishop of the dominant see of Rheims from 842 to 882. He functioned as judge over marital cases in his diocese and wrote extensively about the reasons for his judgments. In 860 he wrote,

> A marriage is lawful only when the wife's hand was requested from those who appear to have power over her and who are acting as her guardians and when she had been betrothed by her parents or relatives and when she was given a sacerdotal benediction with prayers and oblations from a priest and at the appropriate time established by custom was solemnly received by her husband, guarded and attended by bridal attendants requested from her nearest kin and provided with a dowry. For two or three days, they should then

[10]Rouche, in Veyne, 525–40.
[11]Ibid., 533.

take time out for prayers, guarding their chastity, so that they may beget good offspring and please the Lord. Then their children will not be spurious but legitimate and eligible to be their heirs.[12]

By the end of his career, he had established in that locale that marriage was indissoluble for any reason (a unique achievement in Europe to date), that incest and adultery were punishable by the state, that wives could not be repudiated for barrenness, and that church law was primary in matters of marriage. This signal accomplishment in the most prestigious see in the Frankish kingdoms set a standard that was only intermittently kept for several centuries but increasingly established the content of canon law and the objectives of the church regarding marital life.

The principle that secular arms could be used to enforce church law is illustrated by the decision of Louis le Debonair in 817 that any who seduces a nun is, along with the nun, subject to the death penalty along with the forfeiture of all property.[13] However, the frequent repetition of this and other laws concerning celibacy makes it clear that the church's control, even among its own, was geographically spotty and temporally inconsistent. In 742 it was still necessary for a synod to decree that bishops be celibate. In 762 all intercourse was forbidden for priests, with the lash and prison as penalty.[14] But it was necessary in 811 to repeat that married priests be subject to penance.[15] Norman invasions in the early ninth century again freed hundreds of monks and nuns from convents, and restored royal power imprisoned many. But still, in 893, after Hincmar's death, a public wedding of a priest is reported in Vasnau.[16]

In the midst of open tenth-century licentiousness even among popes, in addition to the murder and kidnapping of more than one, another council in 967 in Ravenna demanded that married priests give up either wives or ministry. Some argued that they needed their wives to support them, but dissenters were ultimately thrown into prison.[17] In eleventh-century Italy the situation deteriorated further, with open episcopal marriage and papal concubinage. Leo IX attempted to restore some order, leading a council at Mainz in 1049, condemning simony and priestly marriage. In 1051 he utilized the secular power to make the wives of priests in Italy slaves of the church and drove them out of the cities.[18] Hence, we come to the close of the early Middle Ages with the church struggling to reassert the discipline

---

[12]McNamara and Wemple, in Stuard, 106–12.
[13]Lea, 154.
[14]Ibid., 152.
[15]Ibid., 153.
[16]Ibid., 162.
[17]Ibid., 173.
[18]Ibid., 222.

of celibacy, having established the content if not the jurisdiction of the Roman view of marriage and having consistently relied on the power of pious kings and emperors to work its will on dissidents.

Between the gradual dissolution of Carolingian power in the late ninth century and the accession of the French Capetians and the German Ottonians a century later, European feudalism began to emerge as the dominant social organization. It was largely a rural society, with no European cities outside of Muslim Spain surpassing fifty thousand people; and it was a politically fragmented society, with duchies and counties carrying more military power and patriotic loyalty than anything we would recognize as a national state.

Though early feudal lords enhanced their power by seizing many church lands, the lack of centralized political authority created a vacuum that favored the more unified approaches of canon law, monastic learning, and sacramental piety. It was a mixed period for the church's control over sexuality and the family, with canon law being much more fully elaborated, but the power of the hierarchy to impose its increasingly well-articulated will temporarily diminished.

Although the sexual discipline of clergy again diminished, and concubinage for laity and clergy alike increased, the rediscovery of Roman law by the canonists and the study of Aristotelian thought in the monasteries were paving the way for increased papal and canonical control, as the High Middle Ages increased in intensity.[19]

Feudal Europe

The late tenth and eleventh centuries witnessed a decisive change in European society, further altering the place of marriage and family, and preparing for the economic, intellectual, and theological flowering of the thirteenth century. As the Carolingian Empire deteriorated, the power to keep order was increasingly localized. Aristocratic families' lives were increasingly geared again to incessant local warfare, which led to the enclosure and fortification of noble residences throughout western and southern Europe.[20] Although a married couple (it being the duty of nobility to marry) were at the core of the castle, which was itself the symbolic and administrative center of the fiefdom, the couple functioned as the creation

---

[19]James A. Brundage, *Law, Sex, and Christian Society in Medieval Europe* (Chicago: University of Chicago Press, 1987), 176–225.

[20]Dominique Barthelemy, "Civilizing the Fortress: Eleventh to Thirteenth Century," in Georges Duby, ed., *A History of Private Life,* vol. 2, *Revelations of the Medieval World* (Cambridge: Belknap Press, 1988), 397ff. See also Georges Duby, "The Aristocratic Households of Feudal France," in Duby, *A History of Private Life,* vol. 2, 35ff.

and representative of the lineage. This absence of independent standing for the couple is evident in a number of ways.

There is no word for the *married pair* in any of the relevant medieval languages. The words referring to what we think of as *family* all designate the lineage, primarily though not exclusively the paternal extended family, or the collection of kinspersons, servants, vassals, and bastards that made up the household. Married women only became half-members of their husband's lineage and upon a husband's death were returned to full membership in their father's house. Property, especially the family lands and castles, did not become theirs to control at a husband's death, though under some circumstances they could continue to live there and enjoy the income. They could not sell the property and could be forced to remarry a spouse of the lineage's choosing. Further, since life expectancy was brief, the typical span of a noble marriage was brief, and society's choices favored the more enduring network of lineal ties.

If the couple's independence was limited, that of the groom's younger, hence unmarried, brothers was even more so. Because of the dedication to passing on the patrimony undivided, and with it the family's stature and viability, marriage was typically not allowed for younger sons until the mid-thirteenth century. Many went into the church, but the bulk remained as knights, spending their time in the Crusades, debauchery, and political intrigue. Their sexuality was less disciplined than that of their older brothers, and no one took offense if they took concubines, or fathered bastards from the serving girls or the bastard daughters of other lords. But much offense was taken, by both church and lay moralities, if they used the crowded conditions of the great houses, and the circuit of tournaments and festivals, as opportunity for adultery with the wives of their lords or for abduction of their legitimate daughters. As these were the only potentially legitimizable outlets for their sexuality, and often their only routes to the wealth and power available by birth to their older brothers, abductions were very common up through the eleventh century; and adultery, romanticized in the literature of courtly love, was viewed by younger sons as both popular and heroic. The church struggled with the questions of whether rape or other prior intercourse disqualified a couple from later marriage and, after many reversals on the subject, ultimately decided that if the woman consented, the indissolubility of marriage was a more important value than was avoidance of the stain of prior intercourse.[21]

---

[21]This discussion is drawn from John F. Benton, "Clio and Venus: An Historical View of Medieval Love," in F. X. Newman, *The Meaning of Courtly Love* (Albany: State University of New York Press, 1968), 19–37; Georges Duby, *Medieval Marriage* (Baltimore: Johns Hopkins, 1978), 5–15; and Georges Duby, *The Knight, The Lady, and the Priest* (New York: Pantheon, 1983), 37–45.

This was a society in which the web of relationships, essentially an extended family web, was stronger than the links between any two people. Marriage and child-raising served that web, with marriageable women being valuable prizes to exchange for services, loyalty, and property. Honor was the central value, accruing primarily to families. It represented the difference that their combination of wealth, power, and stability established between them and the often squalid and desperate lives of the increasingly enslaved serfs, who directly tilled the land. However, honor was vulnerable and could be compromised by a wife's adultery or a daughter's improper marriage. Honor was thought to be transmitted genetically, so that the current scion of the house in a sense replicated the virtue of father or grandfather, and thus the seigneur controlled the breeding of sons and grandsons. Daughters were kept close to home, usually within the castle, and were closely watched by mothers and servants. They had too great a value in the purchase of alliances to be allowed to squander their virginity in casual dalliance, or to be abducted by some landless younger son. Even bastard daughters could be a family asset if they came from the proper lineage.

The High Middle Ages—a Turning Point for Marriage

This pattern, and the great families and fiefdoms that were its building blocks, was largely established by the end of the eleventh century and set the framework within which the great advances of the next two centuries occurred. The security established by feudal organization undergirded a wave of population growth and technical advance in the twelfth and thirteenth centuries and with it an increasing tension between ecclesiastical and aristocratic views of marriage.

The most indisputable change was an immense growth of population. Although the data is spotty and inconsistent geographically, it is consistent in direction. The population of England tripled between 1086 and 1340. Towns grew rapidly, yet the cultivated land also increased; thus rural population remained at least constant. Major civil engineering projects controlled the flooding on the Po River, and the Flemish tidal lands were drained. Churches grew, cathedrals were built, and settled towns replaced seasonal fairs.[22]

Throughout this period, society was organized in a series of communities that were suspicious or intolerant of privacy for individuals or couples. The monastery, in many ways the paradigmatic institution of the High

---

[22]Leopold Genicot, "On the Evidence of Growth of Population in the West from the Eleventh to the Thirteenth Century," in Sylvia Thrupp, *Change in Medieval Society* (New York: Appleton-Century-Crofts, 1964), 14ff.

Middle Ages, was organized so that the monk was never alone. He slept in an open area with other monks and the abbot or his subordinates, with a candle that burned all night. Books were rare, so such reading as was done was done aloud to groups of the faithful.[23] A solitary man might be thinking heretical thoughts, and heresy was the most feared offense of this highly collectivized age.

Aristocratic houses were similarly organized, with little provision for privacy. One indicator of this is that the marital ceremony (strictly a family and secular ceremony until at least the beginning of the twelfth century) usually included a procession to the couple's home, placing them in the bed, and blessing both the bed and their issue. Marriage was for the sake of the family in a way that the sexuality of younger sons was not, and the family as a whole celebrated this advance into the next generation. Further, the bed was not considered a totally private area, as noble couples often received guests in their bedroom, and servants often slept in the same room as their wealthy masters and mistresses. A further indication of the absence of private space is that keys only began to appear in the thirteenth century.

As Georges Duby has argued and documented exhaustively, the eleventh and twelfth centuries were a time for the collision and ultimately the blending of the aristocratic and churchly views of marriage among the very highest classes. The lay aristocratic vision has already been presented. It focused on the duty of the seigneur to extend his family's values and property into the next generation. The ecclesiastical view coming out of the Carolingian period, as we have seen, could be reduced to three principles: monogamy, exogamy, and the repression of pleasure.[24] Monogamy was crucial because of the church's insistence on the protection of women and centered in these centuries on the struggle against the time-honored Germanic male prerogative of wife-repudiation. The latter was central to the aristocratic morality because of the lord's responsibility to produce an heir, which in an era of warfare, jousting, and low life-expectancy required multiple and robust male offspring. The families understood this, and customs existed for compensating women (and their families) after such a repudiation. But for the church it constituted a breach in a relationship that was supposed to be a sign of the perpetual union of Christ and the church. It may not be irrelevant that repudiation and remarriage also enabled the aristocracy to strengthen its political power, at a time when the church was an active political competitor.

---

[23]Georges Duby, "Solitude: Eleventh to Thirteenth Centuries," in Duby, *The History of Private Life,* vol. 2, 509–17; see also Duby, "The Aristocratic Households of Feudal France," in Duby, *History of Private Life,* vol. 2, 35–47.

[24]Duby, *The Knight, The Lady, and the Priest,* 31.

The repression of sexual pleasure seems to be rooted in the monastic ideal, the need for an ideology to advance the papacy's never fully accepted insistence on clerical celibacy and the persisting belief that desire and intercourse compromise ritual purity. The attempt to find historical reasons for the prohibition of marriage to cousins to the seventh degree, including those related by marriage or prior intercourse (and even godparental ties) has never found satisfactory answers.[25] No biblical or patristic code demands it, and it may be another way the church sought to prevent the continued concentration of aristocratic power. These prohibitions spawned careful genealogical memory and record-keeping and an incredible confusion of cases in which public knowledge of closer relations was ignored until it became convenient for a family to repudiate a no-longer-advantageous match. Then the lord would penitently notify the church of the "unnoticed" blood link, and the church would demand the divorce that would not have been possible by any other means.

The period's crucial shifts in marital practice center around a small number of controversial cases. In the first, in 1092 Philip I of France repudiated Bertha, his wife of twenty years, who had given him only one son, who was still very young and weak. In her place he took Gertrude (who was at the time married to the Count of Anjou) with all the typical ceremony: procession, dowry, and celebration.[26] Controversy followed for decades, far beyond the lifetime of any of the participants, because the interpretation of the outcome was critical for marriage law and practice. Pope Urban II, prodded into action by Bishop Ivo of Chartres and Hugh of Die, challenged the king's right to repudiate and remarry. There were three excommunications for Philip, several councils, and finally a solemn penitence and mutual vows by the couple to cease all conversation and intercourse; after which they moved back into the royal palace, the excommunication was lifted (1104), and they lived together as husband and wife until their deaths. They had ceded to the church the right to call their behavior into public question, but not to govern it.

The early protests against this transaction focused on the adultery, with both the pope and the bereft husband terming it so—yet the bishop of Senlis still blessed the marriage, which was crucial to the king in his need to present its issue as legitimate claimants to the throne. The bishops also complained of bigamy, protesting that his repudiation of Bertha was not a legal divorce. The Pope vacillated on the matter, and ultimately Ivo, the key advocate for the excommunications, settled on the incest (on the basis of

[25]Ibid., 35–36.
[26]Duby, *Medieval Marriage*, 29–45.

their premarital intercourse) and abduction as the most dependable bases for banning the marriage.

Ivo became the church's central authority on marriage during those decades, and Duby outlines for us his gradual change of belief.[27] Increasingly, consent became the crucial determinant of the validity of marriage, prohibiting unconsenting capture and parental coercion. The claims for marital indissolubility strengthened vis-à-vis the previous demand that adultery required divorce. Bigamy diminished as a clerical complaint. The church's influence over marriage solidified.

A further critical transition followed the divorce of Louis VII of France from Eleanor of Aquitaine, who then became wife of Henry II (Plantagenet) of England. Henry was also Duke of Normandy. Louis and Eleanor had been cousins in the fourth and fifth degree, which was widely known at the time of the marriage in 1137. The two had gone on crusade together, during which time rumors of her adultery with an uncle reached Pope Eugenius III. He feared a separation, and when the royal couple passed through Italy on their return, he specifically blessed the union and their bedchamber—obviously diminishing the appearance of papal outrage over incest. Having produced no sons, Eleanor was dismissed, papal blessing notwithstanding, in 1152. Louis remarried two years later. A literature of comment on the divorce developed, since it was a key act in the history of both countries. It agreed on only two things: The divorce was wrong, and wrong because it violated indissolubility, not because of incest.[28]

Bernard of Clairvaux was a key actor in this and other crucial marriage cases, volleying letters all over France, preaching the importance of indissolubility, and accusing those who appealed to incest of seeking mere political advantage. Bernard was also responsive to political concerns, of course, being intensely anti-Capetian and exercising his rhetorical gifts exclusively in behalf of opponents of the royal house.[29] Partly through Bernard's good offices, incest rarely appeared as an ecclesiastical objection to marriage after the middle of the twelfth century. Obedience to the church and willingness to pay for its agreement had replaced it as a governing principle.

Church reform, and with it a major tightening of clerical discipline (read celibacy), was also intensifying through these years. The papacy of Innocent III (1190–1216) was its high point. His struggle with Philip Augustus of France over the latter's divorce was critical, in that the king agreed to separate from his wife until the church made a decision. He and the rejected wife fled the council before a decision was rendered, but papal

---

[27]Ibid., 41ff.

[28]Ibid., 59–62.

[29]Ibid., 67–72; see also *The Letters of Bernard of Clairvaux,* trans. Bruno Scott James (London: Burns Oates, 1953), 71–75, 76, 257–61.

power did prevent the legitimation of a remarriage. The case made obvious the abuses of the incest laws, which led to the Fourth Lateran Council's 1215 decision to remove the bar to marriage beyond the fourth degree of relationship.

A final shift in family practice began to appear around 1150, in consequence of increasing wealth and population. Smaller fortified houses began to appear around the seats of the great fiefdoms, occupied by married younger sons. A combination of new developments in feudal contracts enabling sons to hold land in fief to their fathers or elder brothers and the need for an occupation for these sons appears to have increased the percentage of the noble population that could marry. Increasingly, that meant to marry permanently, unless lineages were threatened; to marry monogamously; and to marry with less attention to the complexities of affinity and incest. But still, it meant to marry on behalf of family and under the authority of the seigneur.

Obviously we know far more about the familial practices of the nobility, since their family histories were recorded and their property transactions (essentially the only ones that occurred) were often contested in civil and ecclesiastical courts, from which registers survive. Almost nothing is known of the extent to which their practices were duplicated among the peasantry, free or enserfed, other than that land records show that couples typically stayed together and bound to the land. Since marriage was not a rite of the church until late in this period, only assumed sacramental status with Gratian's *Decretum* in 1140,[30] and little or no property requiring legal protection was involved, it is not clear whether we can speak of marriage at all in the peasant or craftsman communities. It is clear that in many fiefdoms the seigneur made mating decisions for some or all of the poor and that it was to his advantage to keep the peasant on the land and contented. But the role of love in the joinings of the poor is unknown. It is clear that there was little protection for the sexual freedom or concern for the sexual modesty of poor women and little official control on the sexual predations of poor men, unless they ventured out of their social class. Class being a crucial component of medieval honor, such wanderings were harshly suppressed.

Formal theology was rare in the Middle Ages before the development of universities in the thirteenth century; so the canonists, confessors, bishops, and popes of the earlier years were largely applying Augustine's doctrines on sexuality and marriage to medieval conditions. Modifications and new applications developed in response to historical situations, but little new conceptual ground was broken.

---

[30]Brundage, 236–54.

There were, however, subtle but important shifts in the feelings that church thinkers expressed toward sexual pleasure. Heloise's letters to Abelard in the early twelfth century and Hugh of St. Victor's almost precisely contemporary theology reopened consideration of Augustine's conclusion that marital sex ruins the friendship between a man and a woman. Each author highlighted the importance that sexual desire has in intensifying this closeness, while arguing that its spiritual richness is greater if that desire is not consummated. That is not because of an intrinsic evil in sexual fulfillment for either thinker, but of the danger in its leading either to egoism or violence for Hugh, and to the loss of freedom for Heloise.[31] For Hugh the ideal would be a celibate, but erotically charged, marriage; for Heloise, the less clearly bounded erotic longings of courtly love.

A similar feeling-tone, though with different verbal content, flows through the writings of Bernard of Clairvaux. As a Cistercian reformer, Bernard sets a high value on virginity,[32] and though he does contend that carnal lust always involves sin,[33] there is none of the contempt for marriage that marks earlier writers. In his *Steps of Humility* he carefully points out the lack of enmity between soul and body,[34] and in his lyrical sermons on the Song of Songs he takes a fully sensuous text and uses its sensuousness as a guide for the spiritual life. He praises love warmly,[35] uses the marriage bed of the Song of Songs as an image for the religious houses,[36] and takes the citation "he abides between my breasts" as referring to congratulation and compassion.[37] My point is not that Bernard endorses the heartily and directly erotic celebration of physical love of some twentieth-century theology, but that he neither found sexual imagery offensive nor affective intensity in relationship to it an obstruction to prayer or faithfulness.

A century later Aquinas' contemporary Bonaventure arrives at very Augustinian conclusions in a more scholastic and precise manner.[38] In very familiar terms he argues that there is no conception without lust (since the fall), that the integrity of matrimony depends on its being a cure for lust, and that matrimony was a sacrament even before the fall, though it had a different purpose.[39] There is an interesting concession to the growing

---

[31]Eric Fuchs, *Sexual Desire and Love: Origins and History of the Christian Ethic of Sexuality and Marriage* (New York: Seabury, 1983), 120–26.

[32]Bernard of Clairvaux, *Letters*, 174–75.

[33]Ibid., 292.

[34]Bernard of Clairvaux, *The Steps of Humility* (Cambridge: Harvard University Press, 1940), 4.

[35]Ibid., 127–29.

[36]Bernard of Clairvaux, *On the Song of Songs* (London: Mowbray, 1952), 140.

[37]Ibid., 131.

[38]Brundage, 424–26.

[39]Bonaventure, *Introduction to the Works of Bonaventure,* vol. 2 (Paterson, N.J.: St. Anthony Guild Press, 1963), 98, 124–33, 269–70.

interiority of the culture in his argument that Adam and Eve attended to the perishable external reality in the garden, hence "failed to read the internal book."[40] This is another sign of the gradually growing respect for the private mind and uncertainty about the superiority of the observable.

The great theological production of the medieval church comes, of course, from Thomas Aquinas, who extends Augustine's ideas of marriage and family perceptibly, though without offering substantial challenge to their central points. Like all medieval theologians (with the possible exceptions of Bernard and Hugh) before him, Aquinas is concerned about the dangers of pleasure in general. In his treatise on kingship he warns the king of Cyprus, "If a country is too beautiful, it will draw men to indulge in pleasures, and this is most harmful to a city."[41] He goes on to argue that men's giving themselves up to pleasure dulls the senses and corrupts judgments, since "nothing conduces more easily to immoderate increase which upsets the mean of virtue, than pleasure. Pleasure is, by its very nature, greedy." Like the progression from one drug to another, shameful pleasures enter easily if lawful pleasures are overenjoyed, leading to weak-mindedness, laziness, and the avoidance of duty. A little is all right, but it needs to be rationed carefully.[42] The pleasures of sex appear central in his thinking.

Thomas specifically treats marriage in the third part of the "Supplement" of the *Summa Theologica*, where he argues that marriage is natural,[43] that marital sex is not in itself sinful and may be meritorious if it is done either to pay the marital debt (to meet the clear canonical requirement for both husbands and wives that they make themselves available for intercourse whenever the partner requests it) or to produce children for the worship of God.[44] Such uses are a means of grace, providing a cure for concupiscence.[45]

Aquinas differs from some canonists of his day by arguing that intercourse is not necessary to marriage,[46] and that marriage is holier without it. Note the link to Hugh of St. Victor. It is not sex, but consent, for Aquinas and much high medieval thought, that is indispensable to marriage; and the consent must be both verbal and sincere—again moving the discussion to the interior of persons.[47]

---

[40]Ibid., 115–16.

[41]Thomas Aquinas, *On Kingship, To the King of Cyprus* (Toronto: Pontifical Institute of Medieval Studies, 1949), 78.

[42]Ibid., 79–80.

[43]Thomas Aquinas, *Summa Theologica* (London: Burns, Oates, and Washbourne, 1920), 3d Part (Supplement), XX, XXXIV–LXVII, 77–78.

[44]Ibid., 84–85.

[45]Ibid., 93.

[46]Ibid., 94.

[47]Ibid., 118–20.

The crux of the discussion of marriage for Aquinas is in his presentation, again following Augustine as transmitted through the canonists, of the marriage goods: children, faithfulness, and the sacrament.[48]

> If a man participates in sex strictly for these goods, there is no sin. But if it is not as a wife but as a woman that a man treats his spouse, and that he is ready to use her in the same way if she were not his wife, it is a mortal sin; wherefore such a man is said to be too ardent a lover of his wife, because his ardour carries him away from the goods of marriage. If however, he seek pleasure within the bounds of marriage, so that it would not be sought in another than his wife, it is a venial sin.[49]

If a man acts in this way, it makes him unfit for spiritual things, Aquinas argues, but does not make him the enemy of God. It is not the fact of pleasure that makes the act sinful, but the seeking of it and the failure to have rationally established a limit before the act, restricting the pleasure to that necessary to accomplish the goods of marriage. This follows Augustine's insistence that both desire and pleasure be subject to reason, while sharpening the distinctions within the experience.

Two other contributions of Aquinas should be cited. In his discussion of impediments he advances the clarity of the rationale for the broad incest prohibitions.[50] What God seeks, he argues, is "the extension of friendship."[51] That is, there should be a broad set of intimate friendships, extended family, and close friends (and their families) of the sort one would ask to be godparents to one's children, in which lust should be completely out of the question. His belief is that that should be the church's goal, so that the impossibility of marriage should prevent one from considering the sexual possibilities presented within that field of relationships. It sought the same effect as a modern rule that persons within a workplace won't date each other and thereby will be more free to focus on the other aspects of their relationship. The historical data, limited though it is, does not suggest that these prohibitions prevented lust in these relationships, only marriage.

The other advance Aquinas offers us is the beginning of attention to the way the sexual relationship, by intensifying the link between parents, makes it more likely that they will fulfill their responsibilities to their children. He suggests at one point that intercourse can enhance the friendship between husband and wife, which in turn benefits "nourishment and

---

[48]Ibid., 145–50.
[49]Ibid., 157–58.
[50]Ibid., 194–245.
[51]Ibid., 207.

instruction, until the offspring comes to perfect age."[52] This is argued as a reason that the parents must stay together, for the "rearing and instruction of the child," and is one of the first links in Christian theology between the quality, or at least the existence, of the marital relationship and the welfare of children. The previous arguments for indissolubility had centered almost exclusively on grounds of morality or ritual purity.

By the end of the thirteenth century, the marital structure in noble families paralleled in many respects that in late imperial Rome: It centered in the extended family, dominated by parents, crowded in by servants. But there were also significant differences: Spouses were usually closer in age; primitive (or at least ethnic German) passions were less tightly controlled by reason; the society was agrarian rather than urban; divorce was very difficult; couples who lived long lives tended to stay together; and the culture was in an expansive and optimistic mood about its future. The culture of the peasantry was even more different from that of Rome, with more stable relationships, rooted more firmly in the land. But all this was functioning on a very similar theological foundation to that of fifth-century Rome, with the exception that the Aristotelian tone of the Schoolmen placed an even tighter cognitive structure on these explosive subjects than did Augustine's Neo-Platonism. So a culture in its roots more expressive and explosive than the Roman, first ordered and structured by a Roman and Catholic leadership and ideology, was now increasingly faced with the attempt to regularize and cognitively structure all things and especially its sexuality.

At this point the church had the temporal power to effect its will, but change was on the horizon. An increasingly individualistic and emotional ethos was gaining ascendancy, the cities were growing and freeing themselves from their feudal lords, and the developing monarchies were gradually consolidating their power, thus becoming less malleable at the hand of the church. The fourteenth century was on the horizon.

The 14th Century—Schism, War, and Plague

Though it must have appeared in 1300 that a great flowering was underway and was bound to expand further, processes were underway that delayed and diverted the movement into modernity. Already in the late thirteenth century, the rivalries of local Italian politics had created a vacancy in the papacy for three years (1268–1271). Further struggles, notably those between the Capetian kings of France and the German Holy Roman Emperors, ultimately displaced the papacy to Avignon from 1308

---

[52]Ibid., 361.

to 1367, and produced the thorough absurdity of the Papal Schism—also largely a creature of European politics—from 1378 to 1450.[53] By the end of that period the popes had lost the power and prestige they had held through the previous two centuries and were no longer the unifying quasi-government of Europe. Furthermore, in the struggle to finance two papal regimes, expenses had risen astronomically, and both parties had settled on the sale of indulgences—in addition to simony, the already rampant sale of offices—as a means to feed the competition. The moral authority of the office was severely compromised, and the resulting conciliar movement elevated the nobles of the church, the bishops and cardinals, to such an extent that they limited the freedom of popes to act—rivaling the limitation that dukes and counts were beginning to place on kings.

As those struggles were gutting the moral and financial resources of the church, large-scale war was depleting the resources of the English and French monarchies, doing major damage to the developing French infrastructure and shutting off the population growth. Though the origins of the Hundred Years' War blur into the ongoing feudal struggles of the great families, the increase in scale of combat is conventionally dated to Edward III's 1339 campaign from the English-allied Flanders into northeastern France.[54] The end is easier to date with a battle at Castillox, near Bordeaux, in the fateful year of 1453—when Gutenberg produced his first Bible, and Constantinople fell to the Turks.[55]

The changes wrought by this war were enormous. When it started, loyalties were to families and fiefdoms; by its end, national states could be said to exist and patriotism to apply to them. Because of the war's huge expenses and the need for regular taxes to pay them, nobles and cities were able to extract concessions from monarchs in exchange for the right to tax. When the war started, decisive and honorable combat was the privilege of the armored nobility. France maintained that strategy for a century and suffered defeat after defeat. England made much better use of its peasant archers, hence English lords ruled large areas of France for generations. When France found a way to use its less-honored archers, its larger population and local resource base enabled it to expel the English.[56] The war produced a leveling of society, demonstrating to the nobility the power of the peasants and to the royalty the power of the nobles.

In the midst of this war raged the plague. First appearing on ships arriving in Italy from the East in the fall of 1347, it swept across Europe for

---

[53]Barbara W. Tuchman, *A Distant Mirror: The Calamitous 14th Century* (New York: Ballantine, 1978), 590–91.

[54]Ibid., 401.

[55]Ibid., 593ff.

[56]Ibid., 71, 86, 146–50, 519, 584.

three years. No region, save Bohemia, was spared. In some cities 90 percent of the population died, and the figure for Europe as a whole was at least a third of the population. The young died in greater numbers than the old, so the blow to population was more severe than the mortality figures themselves would predict. Whole monasteries and ships' crews perished. People died faster than they could be buried. The recently expanded towns stood empty. Agricultural lands went uncultivated, fields unharvested, wild animals returned where they hadn't been seen for decades. Some whole regions were depopulated.[57]

The economic dislocation from this catastrophe was enormous. Agricultural labor became scarce, wages quadrupled, landowners organized to demand that wages go back down, and peasants moved into the homes of lords who had died. There was a sudden opening up of a previously tightly organized society. Wealthy orphans were married to whoever could protect them. People fled plague-ravaged regions for hoped-for safety elsewhere, so populations that had been stable suddenly intermixed. Bizarre cults of death were formed, anti-Semitism intensified, flagellant sects toured the cities, and confidence in the ability of either church or state to protect the masses vanished.

The post-plague fourteenth and fifteenth centuries were a time of suddenly expanded space, physically and psychically. The plague lowered the population density, and the gradual reconquest of Spain expanded Christendom. Warfare shifted sovereignty over and over again, allowing space for new sets of relationships. Universities were growing, despite the population losses, and church control of thought was decreasing.

These global shifts were producing crucial, if subtle, changes in the way people lived. Houses became larger, shifting from one room to two in poorer sections of towns; development of long houses in rural areas separated people from livestock.[58] Interior walls began to be built in poorer homes, creating rooms where privacy was a possibility. In the Italian cities especially locks came into common use.[59] The increased availability of books and writing materials and the increase in literacy made privacy more possible. Italian merchants developed a tradition of private journals, both diaries and business documents that were never to be seen by others.[60] When more could read and there were more books, there was stimulation for private thought. Portraits began to dominate late medieval art, with attention

---

[57]Ibid., 92–125.

[58]Philipe Contamine, "Peasant Hearth to Papal Palace. The Fourteenth and Fifteenth Centuries," in Duby, *A History of Private Life,* vol. 2, 443–63.

[59]Ibid., 455.

[60]Philippe Braunstein, "Toward Intimacy: The Fourteenth and Fifteenth Centuries," in Duby, *A History of Private Life,* vol. 2, 616–21.

to details of facial expression and emotional tone unknown in earlier medieval painting.[61] The idea of individuality was emerging, as leading citizens began to be publicly fascinated with what was unique about themselves and those they were familiar with.[62] This created a situation in which the uniqueness of the spouse was noticed and celebrated in literature, and the way was opening for a less functional and more personal model of marriage.

As this opening of society broadened throughout Europe, it increasingly came into tension with the attempts to domesticate it in the great collectivities of feudal estate, parish, and dogma. Wycliffe's challenge to orthodoxy and clerical control of religious knowledge in England, and Hus's profound if temporary success in Bohemia, showed the readiness of the masses to take the new respect for individuals seriously and to resource it with the broadened access to the Bible and secular knowledge. The consequences for the theology and practice of marriage and family life were at once shattering and seminal.

---

[61]Ibid., 561–66.
[62]Ibid., 567.

CHAPTER 5

Renaissance, Reformation, and Colonial Expansion

Germany and the First Reforms

What is now Germany was a fragmented, largely rural, politically restive region at the dawn of the sixteenth century. Capitalism was subtly emerging, but cities were small, and political power was divided and rarely free to act. Maximilian I, king of Rome, was Holy Roman emperor-elect and trying vainly to match the authority of kings in France, Spain, and England. The absence of a national church as a buffer against the power of the pope kept huge tithes pouring out of the realm to Rome, and developed increasing, seething resentment. German princes continued to follow the principle of partible inheritance, treating their realms as private estates to be divided among their sons at death.[1]

The center of European life was shifting from the external sociabilities of guild, parish, and village to the more private realities of locked chests, secret diaries, printed Bibles, and the primacy of conscience. And in Germany all this was accompanied by intense disaffection with the church of Rome, boiling up in response to the tithes and the methods of collecting them. The church held marriage in low esteem, and marriage rates were low—about 40 percent of women were single, and many youngsters were forced into monastic life because their families couldn't afford to endow them with lands or money.[2] The official view of the church remained that

---

[1]Paula Sutter Fichtner, *Protestantism and Primogeniture in Early Modern Germany* (New Haven: Yale, 1989), 7–10.

[2]Steven Ozment, *When Fathers Ruled: Family Life in Reformation Europe* (Cambridge: Harvard University Press, 1983), 1–3.

virginity was the most sacred of estates, that marriage was spiritually inferior to the life of the cloister.[3]

In the years immediately following the posting of the Ninety-five Theses, Luther did little to address or challenge family practices. His initial statements in this area were impulsive, conservative, monkish, mutually contradictory, and naive.[4] But pastoral experience as leader of a mushrooming religious movement soon deepened his understanding, and events in 1523 forced him to rethink his position. He had been advising monks and nuns to abandon their cloisters on theological grounds—despite its being punishable by death—when word reached him of Cistercian nuns at Nimbschen, Saxony, wishing to leave their cloister.[5] Luther arranged with a local merchant, who had access to the convent, to aid the women in their escape. He took nine of the twelve into his own home, pending their return to relatives or securing a husband. His future wife, Katherina von Bora, was among them.

After receiving them he wrote the tract *That Maidens May Honorably Leave Their Cloisters*, addressing openly the circumstances that led him— and he hoped would lead others—to this direct violation of canon and civil law.[6] His theological arguments for the act included the moral imperative to "save their souls and their consciences," the condemnation of leaving young women to maintain chastity without regular exposure to God's word, and the typical Lutheran insistence that there "can be no enforced and unwilling divine service." He finally declared that celibacy is such a rare gift of God that it should never be made obligatory: "It is impossible that the gift of celibacy is as common as the cloisters are chosen."[7] In closing he said that the normal course of life for women is to marry and "have a family full of children."

Martin and Käthi did marry on June 13, 1525, after an exchange of correspondence among relatives and associates that bears little or no resemblance to a modern courtship, instituting a partnership that was more reproductively and theologically fertile than romantic.[8]

His theology of marriage had been ripening since 1522, increasingly being expressed in terms of marriage as "an estate of faith." He combines this positive view of marriage with the more negative "remedy against sin"

---

[3]Ibid., 9.
[4]See especially William H. Lazareth, *Luther on the Christian Home* (Philadelphia: Muhlenberg Press, 1960), 180–84.
[5]Ibid., 12–15.
[6]Ibid., 14.
[7]Ibid., 16.
[8]Ibid., 22–28.

theology he brought from his Augustinian days. He clearly states that marriage is pleasing to God.[9] He links marriage to "the opportunity for the noblest and most precious work of all," the rearing of children in the knowledge and love of God. Civil and religious authority come together in parenting, and Luther more comfortably exalts this parenting than the more intimately dyadic details of sexual or relational life. He consistently holds that the institution of marriage is preferable to the institution of monasticism, though the individual celibate may be the very closest to God. Faith, however, can be put to work for others in marriage and lacks such an outlet in monastic life.

Though Luther is no more consistent and systematic in relation to marital life than elsewhere in his vast writings, there are several common themes throughout his mature writings on the subject. They are typically conservative, domestic, and patriarchal. He advocates all but perpetual pregnancy for women, obedience to their husbands' (not arbitrary) will, fidelity, and modesty. Men are enjoined to protect, to respect a wife's individual personality, and to enjoy sex, but not to make it more central than the glory of God. He inveighed against the practice of secret (illegal, but binding in canon law) marriage and exhorted parents and children to respect one another's wishes in regard to marital choice.[10] And he spoke sympathetically, if ambiguously, about divorce, wondering "whether...it might not ...be the most loving solution when the alternative is a faithless and loveless union held together publicly by the compulsion of canon law while violated privately in infidelity."[11]

John Calvin further eroded the orthodox position on marriage by declaring that procreation was not its primary purpose. He reinterpreted procreation as a secondary blessing flowing from companionship, which became the central Protestant theological focus. Calvin, along with Martin Bucer, propounded the image of covenant for marriage.

Luther's elevation of marriage gave energy to two often-opposed streams in family life and theology over the next several centuries: free choice and enjoyment of marriage and of spouse, on the one hand, and an emphasis on child-rearing, leading to the ideology of husband as lord of the home, on the other. It could be argued that they only began to come together in the West in the nineteenth century, and that we are still working out the turbulence of their union today.

---

[9]Martin Luther, "The Estate of Marriage," in *Luther's Works,* vol. 45, ed. and trans. Walter I. Brandt, gen. ed. Helmut T. Lehman (Philadelphia: Fortress Press, 1962), 38

[10]Idem., "That Parents Should Neither Compel Nor Hinder the Marriage of Their Children, and that Children Should Not Become Engaged Without Their Parents' Consent," ibid., 385–93.

[11]Lazareth, 192.

Marriage as a Companionship

In Zwinglian Strassburg, and later in England, Martin Bucer was working out the ethical implications of Christian freedom in marital law. As a married priest, in 1525 he urged development of civil legislation (adopted 1529) on marriage and divorce. The marital age without parental consent was set at 24 and 20 for men and women, respectively. Parties being married had to consent. Divorce was possible for a variety of grounds.[12] He writes of "holy marriage," presaging the English usage he later contributed to Thomas Cranmer's *Book of Common Prayer*. He argued that "where there is no love, there is no marriage," hence divorce and remarriage are permissible.[13] However, desertion, adultery, or "deadly hostility or incorrigible harshness" are required as grounds.[14] He later added impotence and incurable disease.

In 1548, Bucer refused to sign Emperor Charles V's Interim Agreement, which he believed too severely compromised Protestant principles, and was forced into hiding. He had a number of offers to go abroad and teach and finally accepted Cranmer's offer to aid in the English Reformation,[15] an offer stemming from earlier Strassburg stays of exiled English reform figures. Bucer had dedicated his 1536 *Commentary on Romans* to Cranmer[16] and had an ongoing correspondence with the English archbishop and other Anglican leaders. After arriving in England he had a major influence on the form of the embryonic *Book of Common Prayer*, being in constant dialogue with its primary authors. The young King Edward VI was personally generous to Bucer,[17] and it was to him that Bucer dedicated and directed his final work, *De Regno Christi*. It laid out a vision of Reformation England's social and ecclesiastical shape[18] and dealt extensively with matters of marriage and divorce.

Bucer, as usual, took an intermediate position between the Anglicans and the growing Puritan party, who wanted all traces of popish ceremony and polity scoured out of the fledgling English Church. But in regard to marriage and divorce, he pleased neither. Following Henry VIII's Act of Supremacy in 1534, assuming sovereignty over the English church, the Roman policy had been continued: no divorce with remarriage. Under Rome

---

[12]William J. Nottingham, "The Social Ethics of Martin Bucer" (Ph.D. diss., Columbia University, 1962), 220–24.

[13]Ibid., 225–27.

[14]Constantin Hopf, *Martin Bucer and the English Reformation* (Oxford: Blackwell, 1946), 108.

[15]Ibid., 1.

[16]Ibid., 6.

[17]Ibid., 10ff.

[18]Ibid., 99–106.

this had been selectively eased by the always present possibility of dispensations and annulments due to the incest rules, but even this loophole was eliminated by the early Anglicans. A celebrated case resulted in the tolerance of remarriage for the innocent party in an adultery-based divorce, but that sole exception remained in Bucer's time and long thereafter.

In the 1549 *Prayer Book*, which Bucer strongly influenced, Cranmer officially added a third justification for marriage to the classical two, remedy for sin and propagation of Christian children. The additional wording was "mutual society, help and comfort, that the one ought to have of the other, both in prosperity and adversity."[19] In *De Regno Christi,* Bucer fleshed this out substantially: "The proper and ultimate end of marriage is not copulation, or children, for then there was not true matrimony between Joseph and Mary the mother of Christ, nor between many holy persons more; but the full and proper and main end of marriage, is the communicating of all duties, both divine and humane, each to other, with utmost benevolence and affection."[20] In that work, Bucer calls marriage "the first and holiest society"[21] and commends that spouses live together "with such an affection as none may be dearer and more ardent among all the relations of mankind, nor of more efficacy to the mutual offices of love, and loyalty."[22] Having laid out such a high goal for marriage, he then said that when such a marriage is not possible, divorce should be allowed and offered a lengthy scriptural and patristic argument supporting that position.[23]

His stance was not accepted by the English church, and *De Regno Christi* failed of wide circulation, due in part to the early deaths of Bucer and King Edward and the subsequent Catholic reaction under Mary. Bucer's books were burned, his body was exhumed and burned, and his writings were only secretly available in England in small numbers. But his position, followed by many reformers, continued to contribute to the growing sense of marriage as a spiritual and psychological union.

Bucer's thought was utilized by the poet John Milton a century later as a major support for his argument for divorce law liberalization, deepening the support for a companionate view of marriage.

---

[19]Lawrence Stone, *The Family, Sex, and Marriage in England, 1500–1800,* abr. ed. (New York: Harper, 1977), 101.

[20]Martin Bucer, *De Regno Christi,* trans. John Milton and in "The Judgement of Martin Bucer Concerning Divorce," in *The Complete Prose Works of John Milton* (New Haven: Yale Press, 1959), 2: 465.

[21]Ibid., 442.

[22]Ibid., 465.

[23]Ibid., 454–77.

The Primacy of the Father

The other major emphases of Reformation-era marriage and family were the centrality of child-rearing and the primacy of the father. The reformers intensified the growing ethos of individual conscience and experience that was emerging in middle- and upper-class Europe, and placed responsibility for producing such individual excellence primarily in families.[24]

Two sources of family structure and authority had been diminishing throughout the sixteenth to eighteenth centuries: the Roman Catholic Church and the lineages of the great and powerful families. Their power was largely being replaced by that of households, and, especially in urban France and England, by the national governments. These two appear as allies throughout modern history. Rural areas were more informally organized, with villages carrying substantial responsibility for regulating family behavior. In Germany, with its lack of political coherence, autocracies were very powerful within most of the states, and Reformed and Lutheran pastors were given quasi-political authority within their parishes. On the other hand, in more politically centralized France and England, the state was increasingly limiting church authority over family relations.

The core Protestant virtue for family life was obedience. As Ozment puts it, "Above all, the husband was supposed to *rule.* He alone was master of his house, the one on whom all domestic discipline and order finally depended."[25] He was to be the local sovereign, though he was not to be arbitrary or brutal. Yet it wasn't excessive use of parental power that was most feared. "The cardinal sin of child rearing in Reformation Europe…was willful indulgence of children."[26] Children were to be subjected to standards pleasing to God, to produce "the internal and external controls necessary to preserve and enlarge their newly won religious freedoms."[27] The Protestant leaders saw that they had left the Roman Church's authoritarian

---

[24]This discussion draws on different sources for different national traditions but emphasizes themes that are common across state boundaries. Conditions in France are chronicled primarily in Philippe Aries, *Centuries of Childhood* (New York: Knopf, 1962); and in Jean-Louis Flandrin, *Families in Former Times: Kinship, Household and Sexuality,* trans. Richard Southern (Cambridge: Cambridge University Press, 1976). England has been thoroughly researched and documented in Stone, already cited. German materials are recounted in Ozment, already cited. Other material, largely French, is available from Roger Chartier, *A History of Private Life,* vol. 3, *Passions of the Renaissance* (Cambridge: Belknap Press of Harvard University Press, 1989). Of these sources, Ozment draws especially on theological and ethical writings, Aries more on study of paintings, school records, and other primary sociological sources, as does Flandrin. Stone utilizes a great variety of sources, particularly diaries and parish records.

[25]Ozment, 50.

[26]Ibid., 133.

[27]Ibid., 135.

rule and were seeking an internalized self-control to replace the former medieval external constraint.

This is the first age in Western history where there is a widely repeated, self-conscious belief that the raising of children is decisive for character formation, for the kind of society that will be possible, and for the eternal salvation of the child. As a consequence, it was crucial to govern childhood behavior down to very small details, so that the resulting adults would thus govern themselves. Swaddling, which completely denied infants freedom to move their limbs, had been normative in Europe for centuries (though it was to disappear by the end of this period), and very precise and detailed restriction was understood to be appropriate and necessary. Erasmus railed against yawning and laughing,[28] Brunfel's writings emphasized table manners and daily schedule as theologically crucial, and all writers emphasized a civilizing of the will to restrain and transcend the effects of original sin.

This powerful parental influence was exercised during a relatively brief part of the child's life. Huge numbers of children were sent to wet-nurses, over half in many urban areas, despite horrendous death rates among wet-nursed children (double that of children nursed by their own mothers). This was an especially dominant practice in France and Germany. Since weaning was late, rarely before age two and often later, and apprenticeship or boarding school often started by age twelve for boys, this intense influence was to be achieved in ten years or less. Though governance was expected to be strict under apprenticeship, which carried a quasi-parental authority and was increasingly strict in schools, there was a large semi-independent adolescent population that was a constant source of concern.

Aries develops the idea that an understanding of childhood as a defined phase of life to be set apart from other eras first appeared in this period. A new vocabulary for denoting children emerged,[29] children began to appear properly proportioned in paintings,[30] and by the seventeenth century, portraits of children were being painted.[31] Attitudes toward juvenile sexuality began to change. Whereas the court records depicting the childhood of Louis XIII (born 1601) make much sport of his infantile erection,[32] in the same years some pedagogues were expressing concern about children being given indecent books.[33] As the seventeenth century continued, children were increasingly kept away from servants (understood to

---

[28]Ibid., 137.
[29]Aries, 28–33.
[30]Ibid., 33–38.
[31]Ibid., 46–48.
[32]Ibid., 100–102.
[33]Ibid. , 109–10.

have inferior morals), were restricted from drinking and gambling, began to play children's games that were distinctly different from adult pastimes, and were dressed in styles of clothing different from that of adults.

Corresponding moves were made in the structure of education. Whereas late-medieval schoolchildren typically lodged privately in the towns that had schools, with almost no supervision, now increasingly boarding schools emerged. They provided greater opportunity to keep the free hours of students under surveillance. These changes were advertised as improving the moral development of students. [34] By the eighteenth century, much greater attention was devoted to segregating students by age. At the beginning of this epoch it was not uncommon to have students with as much as ten years difference in age in the same classes, but by the beginning of the nineteenth century students started school at about the same time and went through in carefully age-stratified classes.[35]

Along with increased control over student ages, the earnestness of the school's moral task was demonstrated in the severity of punishments. Prior to the sixteenth century discipline was enforced by associations of students through a system of fines, but during that century the masters took over disciplinary responsibility. Corporal punishment became the favored method. Aries calls this a humiliating disciplinary system—"whipping at the master's discretion and spying for the master's benefit."[36] Whippings continued to be the dominant mode of punishment through the age of twenty. This severity continued until the mid-eighteenth century, when revulsion against the authoritarian structure and its physical brutality weakened it, at least in France.

Stone reports that physical severity was also dominant in England, with flogging being the standard punishment in schools by the sixteenth century.[37] He contends that in the sixteenth and seventeenth centuries more boys were beaten for a longer period than ever before and that conditions in the English universities were similar to the prisonlike quality of the monastery.[38] The traditional public-school hierarchy of older over younger boys heightened the repressiveness, as older students had great latitude in their control of new students. He sees this severity as a result of the fear of eternal damnation that the Reformation inherited, and the responsibility of education (replacing that of the sacramental system) to prevent it. He interprets the sternness as the consequence of increased caring about children,

---

[34]Ibid., 170ff.
[35]Ibid., 225ff.
[36]Ibid., 261.
[37]Stone, 117–18.
[38]Ibid., 118.

since given original sin, caring required repression of otherwise inevitable and damnable evil. There was widespread writing on child-raising, especially by the Puritans, who found much biblical advice favoring severity and emotional distance. "No hint of tenderness is to be permitted, since this would undermine authority and destroy deference."[39] Breaking of the child's will was understood to be the early Puritan parent's duty.

Along with the increased authority that parents assumed over children in these centuries came increased authority of husbands over wives. In sixteenth- and early seventeenth-century England, women's right to own property was limited to whatever the specific marriage contract detailed, and husbands could sell wives' property at will unless the contract banned it.[40] The decline in importance of lineage left brothers and uncles less able to protect kinswomen from their husbands, and the priest could no longer be called on as a counter-balance to a husband's authority. Husbandly authority was most severe among the well-to-do, where property gave its owners power over others and privacy was possible. Strong affectional or sexual bonds could not be relied on to protect many women, as these marriages were typically neither romantic nor self-chosen.[41] They were also typically brief, given the average late-marriage age (mid-to-late twenties, except for firstborn sons of the propertied class) and a life expectancy in sixteenth- and early seventeenth-century England in the low thirties (though admittedly longer for those who reached marriageable age).

Strictures against extreme marital cruelty existed, however, and they were enforced. All the reformers wrote against wife-beating and in favor of wives having a right to speak on important matters. That was partly to counter the very popular misogynist literature, but also indicates that official attitudes favored increasing sexual equality after the mid-seventeenth century. Yet, a much higher proportion of women remained illiterate throughout this period, with two-thirds of English women unable to read in 1750.

Among the poor, communities had informal rituals for regulating marital behavior. Overly enthusiastic wife-beating would be punished by public humiliation, as would a man's refusal or inability to control his wife. Normative power relations were one-sided. With people living very close together, they knew one another's business intimately. If a husband was dominated or a couple's violence was excessive, the neighbors would come together and forcibly tie the offending man or couple backward on a donkey

---

[39]Ibid., 125.
[40]Ibid., 136ff.
[41]Ibid., 32.

and parade them around the community, subjecting them to abuse and, sometimes, mortal danger.[42] Wife-beating was explicitly legal in France and elsewhere until the sixteenth century, and it is only in the eighteenth century that French marital literature begins to suggest that husbands should be companions rather than rulers of their wives.[43]

The Puritan Liberalization

Marital companionship and emotional bondedness first emerge as popular public ideals among the English Puritans, developing out of the Bucer-Cranmer emphasis on "holy matrimony" and its related vision of the goals of marriage.

This line of thought first becomes highly visible in the seventeenth-century work of John Milton, the Puritan poet and politician. His personal, theological, and political motivations are intermixed in complex, indecipherable ways. He was a Parliamentarian, and the bulk of his writing on divorce was done during the Civil War. Early in that struggle (June 1642) he married Mary, daughter of a royalist family from Oxford. After a month, she left and returned to her family for what was expected to be a temporary visit. She never returned.[44] Since desertion was not an allowable ground for divorce, and her family would not return her, Milton had no remedy but to seek to get the law changed.

He wrote a series of pamphlets lobbying Parliament to use its new authority to establish a different marriage law. The first of these, *The Doctrine and Discipline of Divorce,* was published in 1643. They carried the bulk of Milton's views on marriage and evoked a firestorm of opposition from more conservative churchmen of all political opinions. Shortly after this writing he discovered Bucer's works on divorce and published in 1644 a partial translation of *De Regno Christi* under the title *The Judgement of Martin Bucer Concerning Divorce* in an attempt to quell the criticism. Two 1645 works presented lengthy biblical exegeses and patristic polemics.

The core of his argument is the contention that "In God's intention a meet and happy conversation is the chiefest and the noblest end of marriage."[45] He specifically objected to biblical interpretations that seemed to designate sex and childbearing as the center of the institution: "He who affirms adultery to be the highest breach, affirms the bed to be the highest of marriage, which is in truth a grosse and borish opinion."[46]

---

[42]Collomp, in Roger Chartier, ed., *A History of Private Life,* vol. 3, 536–40.
[43]Flandrin, 127ff.
[44]Ernest Sirluck, "Introduction," in Milton, *Complete Prose Works,* 2: 137.
[45]Milton, 2: 246.
[46]Ibid., 269.

Milton's primary argument was that marriage was crafted by God because "it is not good for man to be alone." Loneliness is the primary enemy, and loneliness is worse in a marriage both unhappy and perpetual than in single life. Such perpetual marriage is an offense to charity, Milton writes, since it values the institution over the creature it was created to comfort and is responsible for rampant adultery and prostitution. Companionship is the goal of the relationship, he contends; hence,

> He therefore who lacking of his due in the most native and humane end of marriage, thinks it better to part than to live sadly and injuriously to that cheerful covenant (for not to be beloved and yet retained is the greatest injury to a gentle spirit) he I say who therefore seeks to part, is one who highly honors the married life, and would not stain it: and the reasons which now move him to divorce, are equal to the best of those that could first warrant him to marry."[47]

His repeated refrain was that marriage should be a remedy against loneliness, and if it does not succeed in that, "it is no marriage, and useless to the true goals of matrimony."[48] He cites at great length the Old Testament laws permitting divorce,[49] arguing that Christ could not be less gracious than Moses in Deuteronomy, nor than Ezra and Nehemiah after the exile. He argues that God hath not truly joined those who cannot offer this companionship to each other, while further contending that the "what God has joined together, let not man put asunder" passage from Genesis comes before the fall, when men and women were perfect, and no remedy for incapacity was needed. He repeatedly cited Christ's saying he takes not jot nor tittle from the law,[50] hence he should not be understood as revoking the Mosaic law on divorce.

Milton's political efforts did not succeed in his lifetime, and had they, the political effects would have been submerged when the Cromwellian reforms were washed away in the Restoration. But this line of theological thought remains a major part of Protestant thinking to the present.

Milton lived during a transition that Stone terms the passing of the *Open Lineage* family system, and the emergence of the *Restricted Patriarchal Nuclear Family*, a transition he saw as finished by the close of the English Civil War. The former family was low-intensity, very permeable to extended family, servants, and retainers, and driven by considerations of inheritance,

---

[47]Ibid., 253.
[48]Ibid., 250.
[49]Ibid., 303.
[50]Ibid., 317.

lineage honor, and early death. Emerging was a family with stronger affective bonds and clearer external boundaries. With it came a decline in the belief that families are responsible for individual crimes, and the state began to replace lineage as the keeper of broader structures.[51] Fathers' power over their children increased in England as elsewhere and was less subject to interference from the lineage.[52]

As the eighteenth century approached, further changes were underway. The 1660 Restoration produced an English reaction against Puritan introspection and asceticism and ushered in a period of open tolerance of the erotic in marriage and society. Boundaries around families became stronger, apprentices as lodgers diminished (increasingly they lived separately and were paid wages), the invention of the corridor allowed privacy within rooms, and the dumbwaiter allowed a separation of families on one floor and servants on another.[53] Personal hygiene began getting more attention, swaddling disappeared in England, and more affectionate child-raising became normative. John Locke's ideas were central to the changes in child-rearing, as he advocated tailoring teaching methods to the age of the child.[54] Contraception, largely *coitus interruptus*, was widely practiced, and England experienced zero population growth for several decades. Protestant theology had effectively separated procreation and pleasure and established a place for the latter.

By the mid-eighteenth century, marriage based on mutual affection was common, building on the established primacy of values of individualism and privacy.[55] There began to be ways for young people to mix freely and test each other out, which had not been possible before 1700. A series of county marriage markets, and a national one, were established.

Migration to the Colonies

During these latter changes colonization of North America began, and our account shifts to the western side of the Atlantic. From the Puritan exiles' early flight to Holland in the late sixteenth century, and throughout the seventeenth century, floods of English emigrants sailed for the colonies. The emigration produced a fascinating and highly specific mix of England's strata to establish the new communities, and with them the norms for family life and theology in the New World.

Almost all generalizations about the seventeenth-century colonies are misleading. The separate colonies were established by very different groups

---

[51]Stone, 100.
[52]Ibid., 113.
[53]Ibid., 245–46.
[54]Ibid., 255ff.
[55]Ibid., 212ff.

within British society, and communities were separate and locally autonomous. Very different modes of life sprang up.

There were a few common elements. Land was plentiful everywhere. The social structures everywhere were freer than in England, and the migration itself established new economic hierarchies, which were in flux for a time. Almost all men were farmers, at least part-time, and for most of them it was a new occupation. The great majority of free men had come from the merchant and artisan classes of England, with the numerous indentured servants coming largely from the young urban, and largely male, poor. Religious faith and doctrine had a very strong influence on the communities that were formed in most colonies. Beyond these elements, the variety was endless.

In Catholic Maryland, landforms and climate favored large holdings. With malarial mosquitoes, it was a dangerous place to live. Life expectancy was short. Consequently, many planters left their wives in England, and most of the women in the early colony were or had been indentured servants. Women free to marry were at a premium, so the marriage age was high; women thus had significant power both to choose relationships and to influence their direction. Because of the shortage of women, control over morality was less stringent, premarital sex more frequent than in England or New England (as noted by the number of births within nine months of marriage), and support for bastards was mandated.[56] Population grew slowly, because the death rate was high and marriage was late. However, change occurred quickly. For the second-generation settlers, no longer bound by service contracts, women married very early (since demand was still high), and as their numbers increased their power diminished, though not to the point it did in contemporary England.

In Protestant Virginia, things were quite similar. Here the Anglican church was established by law, but the same severe health problems shortened life spans, kept upper-class women in England, and ravaged newcomers. Death rates among the early indentured servants are estimated as high as 80 percent in the first year. After the 1650s Peruvian *Cinchona* (quinine) bark became available as a treatment for the tropical diseases, and population increase became more constant. A further obstacle to population growth was constant warfare with the Indians, who severely limited the speed of expansion of the colony and interfered with food production, leading to periodic famine.

---

[56]Louis Green Carr and Lorena S. Walsh, "The Planter's Wife. The Experience of White Women in Seventeenth-Century Maryland," in Michael Gordon, *The American Family in Social-Historical Perspective,* 3d ed. (New York: St. Martin's Press, 1983), 321–46.

Tobacco was king in Virginia, and the combination of tobacco cultivation and the availability of rivers as direct shipping routes from plantation to Europe produced a semi-feudal pattern of land occupation. Huge land holdings prevailed, from several hundred to tens of thousands of acres by the end of the seventeenth century. Almost no towns developed. Their growth was hindered by the almost total lack of decent roads and the availability of river-to-ocean commerce. So most of the population lived on large estates, with the landowner bringing in both indentured and free artisans, laborers, stewards, and personal servants. The gradual freeing of those indentured and the continued migration of middle-class English who could pay their own passage filled the lands between the rivers throughout the century but supported only slow development of town life.

The bulk of the planters and other immigrants in Virginia, as elsewhere in the colonies, were merchants and artisans. Yet the plantation system produced a new breed of aristocrat. Many younger sons of noble families had come to Virginia, but almost all died of the rampant diseases, and those who established the great Virginia houses were of entrepreneurial origins; not a few of the middle-class planters were freed indentured servants who came from the poorer ranks of English society. Once health and peace were established in the colony, prosperity increased rapidly; however, the introduction of African slaves in 1619 drove down the price of free labor, setting in motion the impoverishment of the yeoman class and a substantial migration to the south and west.[57]

The situation in Massachusetts was very different. Most immigrants came in family groups, so the sex ratio was much more even. They came with a covenant theology, concerning both community and marital life. In Plymouth, the oldest colony, the core group had left England and then Holland for a combination of religious freedom and economic opportunity and saw themselves as bound together in semi-sacred ties. Yet there were other immigrants on the Mayflower, whose motives were strikingly less religious and whose economic ties to the original contract were less binding.

After the first horrendous winter, when nearly half the Pilgrims died,[58] conditions were much healthier than in England or Virginia. Life spans were longer, birth rates higher, food more plentiful, and agriculture less

---

[57]Thomas J. Wertenbaker, "Plebeian and Patrician in Virginia," in *The Shaping of Colonial Virginia* (New York: Russell and Russell, 1958), see esp. i–vii, 1–23, 13–159; also Wertenbaker, *The Planters of Colonial Virginia* (Princeton: Princeton University Press, 1922), 38–59; and also Wertenbaker, *Virginia Under the Stuarts* (Princeton: Princeton University Press, 1914), 1–28.

[58]John Demos, *A Little Commonwealth: Family Life in Plymouth Colony* (New York: Oxford University Press, 1970), see esp. 2–21.

dangerous. Cooperation with the Indians was dependable for the first two decades. Because of the greater balance between the sexes, traditional English family life was more readily established than in Maryland or Virginia. For the Protestant and Separatist, marriage was clearly a contract, not a sacrament.[59] Hence, divorce was possible here, and women were the most frequent petitioners. But it was still a highly ordered, patriarchal community, with plentiful land, religious seriousness, ecclesiastical power, and quickly growing territorial mobility. Population grew rapidly, and new towns sprang up, largely on the open-field model of English villages.

New York, then New Netherland, was also settled very early, with French and Dutch traders on Manhattan possibly before the Mayflower. But due to a combination of poor management in the colony and Dutch domestic prosperity and religious freedom, numbers of immigrants were very small, and the colony grew slowly. New Amsterdam remained a very small town till late in the seventeenth century, despite its geographical advantages for trade; and only a few of the large estates on both sides of the Hudson, stretching as far north as Albany, were successful. Because of struggles among the colonists, between the rural estates and New Amsterdam, between both of these and the French, and between all of the above and the Indians, opportunities to develop a vigorous and permanent Dutch settlement were lost. Gradually the English, who had never recognized the Dutch right to settle in North America, overgrew and outcompeted the Dutch, and in 1644 an English force from Connecticut and Massachusetts forced the surrender of the Dutch claims without a shot being fired. Because the Dutch numbers were small, and English settlers were already nearly as numerous in New York, as they renamed it, as were Dutch, this settlement doesn't appear to have made a major unique contribution to the emerging American family style or theology.[60]

The other colonies were slower to develop, forming their own identities a generation or more behind Massachusetts and Virginia, and beginning to influence the growing synthesis of pre-Republican family structure and ideology in the eighteenth century or later. Pennsylvania is particularly interesting in this respect, forming its amalgamation of Quakers, German Lutheran and Reformed, and Swiss Anabaptists in the last decades of the seventeenth century.[61]

---

[59]Carl N. Degler, "The Emergence of the Modern American Family," in Michael Gordon, *The American Family in Socio-Historical Perspective,* 3d ed. (New York: St. Martin's Press, 1983), 61ff.

[60]See especially John Fiske, *The Dutch and Quaker Colonies in America* (Boston and New York: Houghton Mifflin, 1899).

[61]See especially Oscar Kuhns, *The German and Swiss Settlements of Colonial Pennsylvania* (New York: Eaton and Main, 1900), 1–50; see also Barry Levy, *Quakers and the American Family: British Settlement in the Delaware Valley* (New York: Oxford, 1988), 123ff.

Massachusetts, first settled at Plymouth in 1620 and then at Massachusetts Bay in 1630, became the primary nucleus for English life in North America. Its early successful agriculture, its more balanced sex ratios, its reception of intact families from England, and its economic focus on domestic production and consumption gave it an earlier stability and identity than the other colonies. Its steady population growth, both through natural increase and continued immigration for fifty years, built on that early stability and gave Massachusetts a dominant influence on the shape of the developing continental society.

In both of the Massachusetts colonies, Plymouth Plantations and Massachusetts Bay, life was communal, densely structured, bound by elaborate covenants, highly family-centered, religiously rigorous, and within a decade more prosperous than the immigrants had known in England or Holland.[62] Everyone lived in the towns, fields were worked from these central locations, much land was held in common. Social structures were patriarchal, with town and parish counsels consisting of the oldest males of the families. They then had responsibility for enforcing community decisions. Almost everyone lived in families, with those living singly being fined weekly in Massachusetts Bay and Connecticut, and single men only being allowed to live alone in Plymouth if they successfully petitioned the General Court. Family heads provided the first line of police power, and everyone was subject to such a family head. In many ways this social structure reverted to the earlier period described by Stone.

Though the structures in both colonies were hierarchical, both within and between families, the extent of inequality was carefully regulated in the early years. Land portions were doled out according to prior social standing, but huge inequities were not established. Men had authority over women in marriage, but less than in England at that time, and the courts often took the initiative to correct a man's abuse (physical, economic, spiritual) of his wife, and vice versa.[63] He was often (though not always) seen as her superior, but in his lordship of her he was an inferior to the town and colony governments and could be called to task. Parents did have great power over children, but that power was mitigated by the intense economic need for them, especially for sons.

A crucial economic factor that influenced family shape and theology was the shortage of labor. Most of the first wave of immigrants came in intact families, each with land to clear, plant, and work, all by hand. Wage labor was rare, so natural increase and the work of children were critical.

---

[62]See especially Demos, and Edmund S. Morgan, *The Puritan Family* (New York: Harper and Row, 1944).

[63]Morgan, 29ff.

Birth rates, then, were understandably high, and, since nutrition was good, survival rates were also high after the first couple of years. Sons were crucial to the ability to clear and cultivate the large land holdings, so families delayed sons' emancipation far into, even beyond, their twenties. Marriage was impossible without land, and land could only be had from fathers, who needed the labor of sons. So marriage was late for most, and though a father might settle a married son on part of his own holdings, it was rare for the son to have clear title before the father's death. This was unambiguously the pattern in Andover, as researched by Philip Greven. Demos found less evidence of parental use of inheritance to control adult sons in Plymouth, though Greven challenges Demos' method.[64] Apparently the son couldn't sell, couldn't leave, and saw his economic fortunes inextricably bound with his father's during the latter's lifetime.[65] The difference between reported findings for Plymouth and for Andover may reflect a difference between the earliest settlers' goals and those of the second generation settlements (of which Andover was one), though it is more likely a variant in the methods of effecting control. In both settlements, family bonds were close, the economic interests of the generations bound them together, and fathers and sons functioned as lasting economic units.

With parents' and children's economic fates bound together so inseparably, parents' voices regarding their children's marriages were loud indeed. In a manner paralleling that of England's propertied class at the same period, children were not free to marry without consent, and parental negotiations were indispensable for them to marry at all. Since a livelihood required land, an agreement between the fathers of bride and groom to provide land was necessary, with the groom's family typically putting in about twice as much. Negotiations for settling the new couple required that the families be at similar economic levels, and fathers could refuse to negotiate with a family they found inappropriate for any reason. Once the contract was agreed to, the couple was considered espoused, a somewhat more binding state than a modern engagement. It was a period for testing the possibility that love could develop and for planning the details of setting up housekeeping.[66]

Though the couple was not expected to marry for love, it was expected that love would result. Reason was expected to manage passion in these (and all other) matters, though passion was understood to have a legitimate role, more after than prior to selection of a partner. It was expected that young people would rationally decide that the time was right for marriage

---

[64]Demos, 169.

[65]See especially Philip Greven, *Four Generations: Population, Land, and Family in Colonial Andover, Massachusetts* (Ithaca: Cornell University Press, 1970), 33–40.

[66]Morgan, 33; Greven, 74ff.

and initiate inquiries, largely through family, about prospective partners. The choice was to be based on family interests, similarity in faith, and shared social status.[67] But it was to be the couple's choice, since covenant, the central Puritan theological idea, was always based on free choice.

Love, though not the basis for marital choice, was the chief duty of marriage. It was to be warm, considerate, unambiguously sexual, though balanced with the certainty that the love of God was to remain primary. The documentary letters and diaries of the day make it abundantly evident that these ideals were achievable. The correspondence of many Puritan leaders from both seventeenth and eighteenth centuries are as full of longing and fond memory of the beloved as any modern long-distance romance. John and Abigail Adams, John and Margaret Winthrop among others seem to echo Milton's contemporary view of marriage as a crucial bulwark against loneliness.[68]

Furthermore, sex was important, publicly valued, and openly discussed within Puritan circles. In some ways that is obvious, in that the number of average births per marriage in the seventeenth-century Massachusetts towns was over eight, and the average span of childbearing covered at least twenty years of a woman's life.[69] But the Puritan theologians were very affirming about sexuality and very critical of any attempt by the married to avoid it. John Cotton, in a famous marriage sermon from 1694, upbraided those who sought celibate marriages.[70] Sexual union was the couple's first obligation to each other,[71] and there are cases on record of Puritans' being expelled from their congregations for refusing to have sex with their wives.[72] Sex was never outlawed to Puritans on days when other pleasures were allowed, and almost every recorded Puritan preacher of the seventeenth century spoke of the naturalness and necessity of sex and, in its place, of its goodness. There was also much public discussion of sexual violations, which were frequent. The church court records are replete with detailed accounts of rapes, seductions, broken promises, and paternity suits, making it clear that this was a society that was realistic about sex as attractive, widespread, and powerful for good or ill.

The Dominant Puritan Theology

To this point, I have written as though the largest body of seventeenth century Puritans, those whom Philip Greven calls the moderates,[73] were all

---

[67]Morgan, 59.
[68]See ibid., 51–58.
[69]Greven, 30.
[70]Morgan, 62.
[71]Ibid., 34.
[72]Edmund S. Morgan, "The Puritans and Sex," in Gordon, 312.
[73]Philip Greven, *The Protestant Temperament* (New York: Alfred A. Knopf, 1977).

the colonists there were. Yet though their dominance was secure at the beginning of the colonial epoch, there were conservatives present in the first churches who had different attitudes toward sexuality, community, and human nature. Their numbers gradually increased during the seventeenth century, and they took center stage in the eighteenth-century Great Awakening. It is important to remember their presence, even as we describe the moderates, who dominated the first colonial century. And it should be remembered that thinkers who were moderate on one set of issues were often conservative on others.

The dominant cultural and theological theme throughout seventeenth-century Massachusetts was the covenant, the freely entered bond between individual and community, community and God, and between the several members. It was anchored in a view of God as predictably relational and loving and of humanity as able to respond faithfully from a selfhood that, though fallen, was not utterly depraved. The self was capable of good, and if sufficiently good, of being rewarded with eternal life. There was a detectable Arminian tinge to the dominant Calvinist theology. Family, child-rearing, and marital patterns were erected on and consistent with this foundation.

The theology and social structure of this society were remarkably consistent, each evincing a firm belief in the natural yet freely chosen connectedness of families, localities, and the God who authors them. Because the first colonists tended to stay in one place, with fathers and sons working cooperatively on the land, grandparents were available for most children as a source of continuity and affection.[74] In the absence of formal schools (none were introduced in either colony before about 1650), they did much of the teaching and child care.[75] Grandparents played a particularly strong role in the family of John and Abigail Adams during the colonial period, with John writing on the death of his mother-in-law, "I am sure that my children are the better for the forming hand of their grandmother,"[76] and recalling the equally powerful effect of his own grandmother in his upbringing. This stands in sharp contrast to the conservatives' warnings against grandparental involvement.

What was at issue was the amount of affection and latitude to be allowed to children. Whereas the conservative argued vehemently for breaking the child's will and wrote at length about how to do it, the moderates found the concept abhorrent and devoted much less attention to the details of management. Believing in a less radical fall, they accepted the innocence

---

[74]Ibid., 153.
[75]Ibid., 154.
[76]Ibid.

of children.[77] Samuel Sewall, writing in 1685 after the death of his child, wrote that the infant surely would be in heaven. Wait Winthrop, grandson of the famous governor of Massachusetts, wrote the same sentiments in 1714 after the loss of a grandson.[78] Since the child's nature was not utterly depraved, it required not rooting out, but shaping. As Samuel Willard, one of the first full-fledged theologians in the colonies, wrote in 1703, the government of parents over children "is not Despotical or Arbitrary. The Authority of Parents over their children is Limited. It is so by the Command of God who hath not left them a boundless Authority; but hath told them how they shall, and how they shall not exercise their power over them."[79]

Willard writes, as do many of the moderates, of the centrality of duty, which, in turn, is founded in a relationship.[80] Honoring parents is understood as fulfilling our duty toward them, is required as long as both parties live,[81] and is gender-neutral. But fulfilling our duty is not identical with obedience. In terms of the duties of parents and children, males and females are equally bound and gifted. Willard urges an intense and influential love of parents for children, like God's love for humanity, love which requires caring for the child's physical needs, training and establishing the child for adult life (particularly choosing a calling and equipping the child for it),[82] and providing him/her a suitable portion of their estates. Parents are urged to avoid the extremes of rigor and indulgence, and children are to be made to know both parents' affection and their rule. "Instruction is to be oftener applied than correction," Willard writes.[83] Recreation is to be allowed but balanced carefully with learning the tasks that make the child useful.

Obedience to parents is required of children, but parental authority is limited, and children are to use their consciences to evaluate the rightness of their parents' commands.[84] Obedience must be voluntary, not coerced. Children are required to receive reproof meekly, and parents are to offer it in a way that leaves no question about their love. At the other end of life,

---

[77]Ibid., 156ff.

[78]Ibid., 157.

[79]Samuel Willard, *The Compleat Body of Divinity* (New York: Johnson Reprints, 1969), originally published 1726, from lectures and sermons delivered beginning 1688. There is confusion regarding the pagination, as some pages were missing and/or misnumbered in the original. The material cited, from pages 598–607, is the second set of pages with those numbers, and comprises the lectures on the Fifth Commandment.

[80]Ibid., 598.

[81]Ibid., 601.

[82]Ibid., 602.

[83]Ibid., 604.

[84]Ibid., 606.

Willard observes that it is children's responsibility to take care of their aging parents, "that they not be a publick Charge."[85]

This intimate authority was to be effected, as in England, in a fairly brief time-span. Given large families and small houses,[86] children were placed out as early as age nine or ten to learn a calling and be under the authority of another, often related, master. The quality of relationship between adults and children in such a placement was to be quite similar to what it had been in the child's home (different than in England, where apprentices had no such claim on the master's solicitude), and these children did have access to their own parents—the villages, at first, being small. This passing of children back and forth furthered the knitting together of the community and allowed those with means to use larger homes to house youngsters in their service. Homes of the poor were very small, rarely more than two rooms, and were little more than shelter for sleep. Once towns developed enough so that wage labor was prevalent, most employed persons ate in the homes of their employers and worked sufficient hours that little family time was available in the limited family space.[87]

The Eighteenth Century and the Great Awakening

By the late seventeenth century the earlier colonial synthesis was perceptibly changing, strengthening the always present conservative elements and paving the way for the much sterner family theology of the First Great Awakening. At the same time, first in northwest England and Wales, and then in the melting pot of the Middle Colonies, a new Quaker theology was taking shape that would have far-reaching impact in the new republic.

The cornerstone of the Puritan commonwealth had been the tight connections between fathers and sons, first in Plymouth and Boston, then in the second tier of communities, which included the thoroughly researched town of Andover. By the 1640s settlers who had originally come from England to the coastal towns of Massachusetts were moving south to Connecticut[88] and northwest to places like Andover, twenty miles away.[89] At first they took the model for their original villages and congregations with them, but within three generations in most new settlements the tight

---

[85]Ibid., 608.

[86]See esp. Demos, 21–31.

[87]See especially Carole Shammas, "The Domestic Environment in Early Modern England and America," in Gordon, 113–35.

[88]Richard L. Bushman, *From Puritan to Yankee: Character and the Social Order in Connecticut, 1690–1765* (Cambridge: Harvard University Press, 1967), 26ff.

[89]Greven, *Four Generations,* 21ff.

combination of nuclear villages, paternal control of land, strong religious oversight of daily life, and increasing prosperity were no longer possible.

Several factors fed the passing of the synthesis. Land became scarcer. The high birth rates in the second and third generation, necessary to produce the children to get the land cleared, created an insupportable hunger for new land. Partible inheritance had enabled fathers to reward obedient sons with as much productive land as they could work for two generations, but by the birth of the fourth generation it was obvious that some would have to go into trades or professions, to emigrate, or to see their standard of living fall.[90] So increasingly fathers rewarded sons with money to set up in business, rather than with land or with education for ministry or other professions. And a growing number of fathers aided sons to buy land in new communities to the south, north, and west. Andover sons turned up in large numbers in Concord, New Hampshire, and in Windham County, Connecticut.[91] Connecticut sons moved north and west through the state, Virginia sons into the Carolinas, Pennsylvanians over the mountains and south through the Great Valley, and so it went.

Along with these pressures of population came some adventitious problems. A wheat blight in New England reduced grain production after the 1660s, increasing the economic advantages of Pennsylvania agriculture.[92] Bloody confrontations with Native Americans caused loss of life and change of attitudes after 1675 in Massachusetts.[93] And finally, New England's freedom from major health problems ended. After 1700 three severe epidemics of diphtheria and smallpox caused large-scale death throughout the colony. Birth rates declined, infant mortality increased, and the life expectancy of a person who reached age twenty-one also decreased. Death became part of daily New England experience in a way it had not been since the 1620s. Causes are not immediately obvious, but it is likely that the atrocious urban sanitation practices similar to those of England in the same period were having their effect in North America as crowding intensified. Certainly urban dwellers were much more vulnerable to disease than were farmers.

Some of the effects on families of these changes were obvious, some more subtle. Paternal authority over adult children clearly was waning, as fathers no longer had sufficient land to guarantee wealth to all obedient sons. Economic incentive alone would no longer make it to sons' advantage to work far into adulthood for fathers, which was reflected in a gradual

---

[90]Ibid., 175ff.
[91]Ibid., 156–59.
[92]Levy, *Four*, 152.
[93]Greven, *Generations*, 64–65.

drop in the marriage age. Secondary to that loss of the capacity to reward, the capacity to punish unacceptable marital choice diminished, and young adults began to exercise more authority in choosing partners. That, in turn, led to an increased emphasis on sexual attractiveness as a basis for marital choice, and more writing about feminine physical beauty as an ideal.[94]

More and more families had sons and daughters move away from the parental community, either to homesteads closer to the frontier, or to trade or professional life in the growing towns. That further necessitated a sense of independence and authority in those who moved, so that the age at which young people felt it appropriate to claim their own power decreased, reflecting their greater role in choosing marital partners. Furthermore, even adult children who remained close by their parents often had very different economic experiences, either because they were following a different vocation or farming smaller plots. Thus, parental ability to call on common experience as a source for knowledgeable advice diminished, and children's ability to trust parents for advice also shrank.

A further factor was the breaking down of nuclear villages. When New England towns were first settled, everyone lived within a few yards of the center of a circle of cultivated land. The parish church and, after a time, the school were within easy walking distance. Church attendance was compulsory and easy, and neighbors could monitor and intervene in one another's behavior conveniently. As settlements grew larger and land near the center scarcer, more pressure developed to allow people to live on their farms, far from the center of town. That became impossible to resist by thirty to forty years after the settlement of most communities, and residents began to live in widely scattered homes, immune to control from their neighbors, unable or unwilling to be part of congregation and government, and they soon competed for political power with the older and more stable settlers.[95]

Along with this increased complexity and decentralization came the growth of economic inequality. In the early settlements, wealth disparities were narrow, regulated by the size of land holdings. But as those divisions receded into memory, those whose families had been smaller in the third and subsequent generations, those who had bought more land, or those whose skill at trade was greater began to multiply their advantages over those who were gradually sinking into a hereditary lower class. By 1770 the top 5 percent of Boston's taxpayers controlled 49 percent of the taxable assets. In 1774 in Philadelphia the top 10 percent of taxpayers controlled

[94]John D'Emilio and Estelle B. Freedman, *Intimate Matters: A History of Sexuality in America* (New York: Harper & Row, 1988), 43ff.
[95]Bushman, 54ff.

89 percent of the wealth. Industry increased, class consciousness developed, and genteel deference passed out of memory.[96]

Into the turbulence of these sweeping social and economic changes came two powerful theological voices, echoing and intensifying the long-standing conservative demand for more reliance on God, less trust in human (individual, community, and familial) goodness, and more zeal in preventing and rooting out evil. Both born in 1703, John Wesley and Jonathan Edwards and their followers powerfully energized a uniquely American brand of conservative theology (though Wesley lived most of his life in England, the fullest enactment of the implications of his thought occurred in the colonial Methodist church) that called on parents to assure their children's salvation by identifying and eliminating every sign of pride of self, natural self-interest, and enjoyment of the flesh.

Both Edwards and Wesley, like colonial conservatives before them, believed in the total depravity of the human soul. Original sin corrupted even the infant absolutely. Though the moderate Puritans had believed firmly in original sin, depravity for them was partial and limited, and human effort did count for something with God. Though as strong a conservative as Cotton Mather could preach that his unbaptized child was "reserved for a glorious resurrection,"[97] the element of fear for children's souls among the Awakening evangelists was much more intense than in their grandparents' generation. Edwards wrote of infants that "all are by nature the children of wrath and heirs of hell" and that every one that has not been born again, "whether he be young or old, is exposed every moment to eternal destruction…As innocent as children seem to be to us, yet if they are out of Christ, they are not so in God's sight, but are young vipers, and are infinitely more hateful than vipers."[98] Wesley wrote, that "Man, in his natural state, is altogether corrupt, through all the faculties of his soul: Corrupt in his understanding, his will, his affections, his conscience, and his memory."[99]

The intensity of these views was due more to the conservatives', and to an extent all Calvinists', views of God than to their views of humanity. Partaking of the medieval concern for honor as the dominant ordering principle of a static society, they were enthralled with the magnificence and

[96]Stephanie Coontz, *The Social Origins of Private Life: A History of American Families, 1600–1900* (London and New York: Verso, 1988), 119–21.

[97]Greven, *Protestant Temperament*, 30.

[98]Jonathan Edwards, *The Great Awakening*, ed. G. C. Coen (New Haven and London: Yale University Press, 1972), 334.

[99]John Wesley, "The Doctrine of Original Sin, According to Scripture, Reason, and Experience" in *The Works of John Wesley* (Nashville: Abingdon Press, 1986), 9: 443.

glory of God, and the entire theological system was designed to celebrate and intensify that honor. It was an innovation (a heresy, some said) in the Calvinist thought of the eighteenth and nineteenth centuries that began to see God's salvation of humanity as the core of God's purpose, rather than God's maintenance of His glory and sovereignty as being the center. Hence, classical Christian anthropology's chief concern was to emphasize the way God's magnificence was different from human nature, and the difference was enhanced by highlighting the utter corruption of human creation by the fall. Only persons who realized their utter lack of standing before God could be expected to properly render obeisance to the God of the universe.[100]

Because of this complete submersion in sin, and especially due to the will's captivity thereto, conservative family life was organized around the breaking of the child's will—echoing the immediate post-Reformation European emphasis. "Break their wills," Wesley wrote, "so you may save their souls."[101] This produced a major, single-minded emphasis on the management of early childhood, based on the belief that if you convinced a child that it was pointless to assert its own will, it would lose the dangerous habit of consulting its own wishes and only see what was required of it by others, especially parents. Conservative writers discussed the details of this governance of children at considerable length and took it as the central piece of parental responsibility. Again, Wesley wrote, "A wise parent should begin to break their children's will the first moment it appears. In the whole art of Christian education there is nothing more important than this. The will of a parent is to a little child the will of God."[102] And further, as part of detailing the instruction, "Never, on any account, give a child anything that it cries for."[103]

The intent, as stated by Wesley and many others, was to prepare the child to accept the will of God; and the assumption was unmistakable that the child's will is always opposed to the divine will. Hence, the family's government was to be totally authoritarian. John Witherspoon wrote that parents must establish "an entire and absolute authority,"[104] in part so the authority would not have to be as severe and violent as it would if it were contested. The child is to be left in no doubt concerning the outcome of any contest of wills, so brutality isn't necessary.

---

[100]This discussion draws heavily on Joseph Haroutunian, *Piety Versus Moralism: The Passing of the New England Theology* (New York: Henry Holt, 1932), xii–xxv.

[101]Wesley, "On Obedience to Parents," in *The Works of John Wesley,* ed. Albert C. Outler (Nashville: Abingdon Press, 1986), 3: 367.

[102]John Wesley, "On the Education of Children," in *The Works of John Wesley,* 3: 354.

[103]Ibid.

[104]John Witherspoon, "Letters on Education, No. 2," in *The Works of the Rev. John Witherspoon* (Philadelphia: William W. Woodward, 1800), 3: 505.

In order to ensure this absolute authority, conservatives preferred households composed only of parents and children.[105] This was somewhat easier for conservatives than for old-line Puritans, since the former group was more mobile and often lived farther from grandparents, who were a particular enemy of this authority. Wesley noted that, "Your mother, or your husband's mother, may live with you; and you will do well to shew her all possible respect. But let her on no account have the least share in the management of your children. She would undo all you have done; she would give them their own will in all things."[106] Similarly, Wesley echoed earlier Reformation advice against letting children have anything to do with servants or servants' children.[107] Clearly, total isolation of the child with its parents was the safest course, so the child would never gain the impression that its own will was a reliable guide to happiness.

The child's role was only to obey and that for as long as the parents lived. Again, Wesley is an eloquent spokesman: "When I had lived upwards of thirty years, I looked upon myself to stand just in the same relation to my father as I did when I was ten years old. And when I was between forty and fifty, I judged myself full as much obliged to obey my mother in everything lawful, as I did when I was in my hanging-sleeve coat."[108]

Edwards also wrote of the importance of obedience to parents, assuming his own childhood as a starting-point, then noting the obligation to go positively beyond that to find creative ways of pleasing parents and, by implication, God.[109] The importance of obedience was intense for Edwards because of his focus on the undiluted sovereignty of God. He objected to the notion of covenant, the Puritans' central idea, because it appeared to limit the free will of God, and nothing could be allowed to do that. Especially, human will could not be allowed to do it. "Total submission and surrender were the only terms acceptable to God,"[110] hence the Christian should practice this submission from the beginning. Edwards is not alone on this point, however. Wesley also insisted that the natural will of human beings is to do evil on every occasion, so it must never be the guide for actions.[111]

This especially meant that the body, source of self-will and pride, had to be kept very firmly in check in ways reminiscent of monastic asceticism. Susannah Wesley wrote on the importance of never allowing the child to

---

[105]Greven, *Protestant Temperament*, 25.
[106]Wesley, "On the Education...," in *Works*, 3: 358.
[107]Greven, *Protestant Temperament*, 26.
[108]Wesley, "On Obedience to Parents," 3: 364.
[109]Greven, *Protestant Temperament*, 59.
[110]Ibid., 101.
[111]Wesley, "On the Doctrine of Original Sin," in *Works*, 9: 448ff.

choose his own food, and son John wrote that overcoming the love of the world was made easier by interfering with the pleasures of taste.[112]

George Whitefield, one of Wesley's most ardent followers, fasted regularly twice a week, trying to wean himself from earthly pleasures.[113] In a similar vein, Susannah Wesley wrote of the necessity of putting a child on a rigid schedule, again so the child would know that its own experiences would not be regulated by its wants, but by the authority of parents.[114]

Bodily functions were regarded as loathsome by many of the conservatives, with Cotton Mather, Edwards, Susanna Anthony, and Joseph Bean, among others, writing of the particular corruption of physical existence. Sexuality was especially problematic for them. Mather wrote in his diaries of intercourse as a loathsome thing.[115] Edwards' imagery often suggested a deep fear and distrust of women.[116] Wesley remained single until age 48 and was tempestuously married thereafter.

Though conservative family theology did not totally displace the more familiar Puritan and Anglican varieties, the percentage of believers following the sterner doctrines greatly increased in the middle decades of the century. Among the factors favoring the spread of the "New Light," or Great Awakening, were the scattering of families and congregations, the development of an urban artisan and entrepreneurial class, and the extension of the frontier settlements into areas where neither education nor established institutions existed. Without the familiar restraints on individual striving and the accompanying comforts of communal support, new structures that presented firm, demanding guidance and promised the constant scrutiny of God were received more warmly than they had been in a day of intensely bonded and newly settled communities. These structures reinforced the dominance of males,[117] insulated nuclear families from outsiders, and created a Godlike authority for parents, who were to provide unerring guidance for children. They, in turn, must never forget their inability to decide wisely or to live faithfully.

A New Style of Domesticity: The Quakers

As the roots of American conservative theology were first forming, a British movement with widespread implications for American family

---

[112]Greven, *Protestant Temperament,* 44.

[113]Ibid., 72.

[114]Susannah Wesley, "On the Education of her Family," in Philip Greven, *Child-Rearing Concepts, 1628–1861* (Itasca, Ill.: F. E. Peacock Publishers, 1973), 2: 46ff.

[115]Cotton Mather, *Diary of Cotton Mather* (New York: Frederick Ungar Publishing, 1957), 2: 261.

[116]Greven, *Protestant Temperament,* 138.

[117]Ibid., 127–33.

thought had been taking shape. While George Fox was evangelizing poor farmers in northeastern Wales and northwestern England, his Quakers were developing a new style of domesticity and a structure for spreading and maintaining it. Fox's teachings centered on the primacy of direct intuition of God, the communication of God's grace by few words, none of them rehearsed or written, and a rich set of nonverbal, empathic intimations of affection and concern. Since Quakerism was both banned and persecuted by the established church, and institutional structures were rare in the impoverished northwest English and Welsh hills, the family was the vessel of transmission for this new style of largely nonverbal spirituality. And women were its preeminent teachers, starting with Margaret Fell and passing through a chain of inspired "nursing mothers" of Quaker domesticity.[118]

Quakers replaced stern verbal rules with spiritualized attentiveness to the child's Seed of Truth, aimed at substituting God's calling for both physical desire and parental authority in the choice of marriage partners, and greatly increased the domestic and ecclesiastical authority of women. They developed women's meetings in which women's matters—sex, childbirth, parenting, marriage—could be discussed without men present (except for Fox or another occasional, lone male leader) and in which standards could be developed for ascertaining the spiritual integrity of a woman's motivation in choosing a husband, raising a child, or moving to America. These women's meetings spawned committees that had authority to sanction or prohibit marriages, could intervene between husbands and wives to alter marital behavior, and clearly eroded the freedom of Quaker men to govern their wives.[119]

When Quaker William Penn gained a land grant for Pennsylvania in 1674, chartered in 1681, and began recruiting colonists, poor Quaker families who were losing their children to the secular world in alarming numbers flocked to sign up. They brought their domesticity and their women's committees to the New World, and by the mid-1680s were establishing themselves on the lower Delaware River as a prosperous, pious, and family-centered economic elite. Pennsylvania quickly became the center of the richest agriculture in the Americas, and Quakers bought huge tracts of land to reward their children for following the family domestic spirituality. Their principles prohibited an established church, and that eased the way for heavy migrations of German and Swiss immigrants, many of them Anabaptists, as the Quakers were also arriving.[120] Quakers remained the

---

[118]Levy, 53–80.
[119]Ibid., 72–85.
[120]Kuhns, 62–114.

political and economic leaders of the colony until well after the Revolution.

Women were the spiritual core of the movement. Quakers had women clergy from the seventeenth century,[121] and the women's meetings continued their control of marriage and child-raising. But there was a price to this spiritual dominance for Quaker women, as their importance in governing the shape of the household was seen as so crucial that they were not to be troubled with economic affairs. At a time when Massachusetts women were gaining more economic power, gaining the right to inherit and buy and sell property and increasingly winning divorce cases on their own initiative, Pennsylvania Quaker widows were rarely free to use inherited property, to raise their children without male governance, or to establish economic independence.[122] Though Quaker women had unprecedented power over men in domestic life, and were clearly counted men's spiritual superiors, their freedom to function in the economic sphere was more circumscribed than that of the less-esteemed women in the northern colonies. They were the first exemplars of the coming cult of true womanhood that dominated nineteenth-century domestic life and theology.

---

[121]Levy, 193–228.
[122]Ibid., 197–205.

CHAPTER 6

The Creation and Erosion of the Victorian Synthesis

The decades surrounding the American Revolution were largely infertile for church, theology, and the family. From mid-century on, the growing commercial activity of the colonies increasingly conflicted with British rule, the developing middle classes agitated for change, and popular thought shifted from the sovereignty of an absolute God to the rights of free men. The English deists and French encyclopedists made Enlightenment more exciting than Awakening in the public imagination, and theories of governing the state aroused more energy than issues of church polity. Yale and Harvard, the intellectual centers of Puritan Calvinism, were temporarily dominated by Enlightenment deism and skepticism. Further, in the midst of this ferment, war broke out, was fought, and won, and brought inevitable chaos for families, commerce, and institutions.

The Decentralization of Authority

Family life in the New England and Mid-Atlantic colonies had been subtly shifting throughout the late colonial era. As villages were replaced by separated farms or growing cities, as capitalism made pursuit of gain as important to many as eternal salvation, and as pluralism and religious dissent increased, households became more spiritually and economically autonomous. The community was less intimate and less available to correct or assist. Children were increasingly raised through adolescence in their own homes. Production centered in the family, as both agriculture and manufacturing were small scale and close to home. Families were economically productive units, so men, women, and children typically worked side

91

by side during their waking hours. Leisure was rare, there was little opportunity for privacy or time for exploration of feelings and relationships, but husbands and wives knew each other's lives in detail as they struggled together to survive. Farms were smaller,[1] more farmers produced household manufactures for sale, and, after the Revolution, industrialization, economic inequity, and export production rapidly increased.[2]

The introduction of the Enlightenment emphasis on the rights of persons, coupled with growing dissent and the relaxation of standards within the churches, led to suspicion and weakening of authority. Increased population produced greater pressure on the land, leaving fathers unable to settle as much real property on sons, thereby losing the ability to govern marital choice and, in the middle classes, to assist in establishing sons in a calling. Ties among equals (brothers, neighbors, fellow tradesmen) increased in importance as the ability of the older and wealthier to advance the younger and poorer decreased. The rewards for deference diminished, and the ideology of equality grew.

This relaxation of traditional powers had implications for family life in at least the New England and Middle Colonies. In Virginia and the Carolinas, a more hierarchical arrangement persisted in the propertied classes, though without the ecclesiastical overtones. Throughout the colonies, the greater independence of young adults gave them more freedom for courtship, with sexual passion playing an increasing role in marital choice.[3] Families granted courting couples substantial privacy, and bundling was regularly part of courtship—couples slept in the same bed but were separated by a "bundling board" and were expected to keep the draw-cords on their ankle-length nightshirts tied. Premarital pregnancies, as measured by number of births within nine months of marriage, increased substantially,[4] suggesting that these rules were often eluded. At the same time, women began to enjoy somewhat greater power within marriage, as reflected in their increased ability to initiate divorce, to secure divorce on the grounds of adultery, and to manage their own property after divorce or widowhood. Their domestic productivity was more widely acknowledged, and men's traditional economic and relational power temporarily diminished. This was especially true for educated, literate women, who remained an extreme minority. They were able to raise an effective legal challenge to male adultery. Republican ideology was in their favor, targeting the traditionally freer morals of the

---

[1]Coontz, *The Way We Never Were,* 117.

[2]Ibid., 119.

[3]Ellen Rothman, "Sex and Self-Control in Middle-Class Courtship in America, 1770–1870," in Michael Gordon, ed., *The American Family in Social-Historical Perspective* (New York: St. Martin's Press, 1983), 393–407.

[4]Nancy F. Cott, "Divorce and the Changing Status of Women in Eighteenth-Century Masssachusetts," in Gordon, 350ff.

English ruling classes for disdain and requiring a higher standard for men's private behavior.

Published American religious thought in these decades focused on one overarching philosophical issue and one struggle over church polity. Philosophically the issue centered on reconciling the growing American conviction of individual responsibility with Calvinism's traditional focus on God's sovereignty. Samuel Hopkins, Timothy Dwight, Nathaniel Taylor, and Lyman Beecher all participated in the gradual shift of responsibility and power to the human side of that boundary. Revivalism from the First Great Awakening on had individualized and personalized the religious equation, diminishing the sense of community responsibility and covenant. Moral behavior, coupled with the obligatory private conversion or regeneration experience, were identified as the marks of the elect. Moralism increasingly replaced prostration before the glory of God as the indication of religious orthodoxy.[5] In these struggles to establish first principles while maintaining the appearance of continuity with the theological tradition, there was little new thought about the meaning of the family.

The other huge problem for the churches was managing independence from Great Britain. All the denominations had been spawned in England, Scotland, or Europe, and the public rejection of subservience to non-American bishops, councils, and thinkers made maintenance of those ties impossible. Decisions had to be made about new structures, bishops had to be consecrated, presbyteries established, theological education arranged, all in an atmosphere of political intrigue and the disruption that war brought to transportation and resource allocation. It required enormous energy to birth new governing bodies, maintain such ties as were allowable with the Old World, establish ecclesiastical legitimacy, elect new officials, create new offices, and determine what were the proper ties with the new republican state—all the while continuing to evangelize the always-receding frontier.[6]

The Republican Cultural Explosion

Generalizations about postrevolutionary America and most of the nineteenth century are almost as difficult as was settling and structuring the continent. At any given time, parts of the land were virtually uninhabited, others were inhabited by Native Americans, others were being wandered by traders and trappers, the advance guard of the white population, others

[5]See especially, Joseph Haroutunian, *Piety Versus Moralism: The Passing of the New England Theology* (New York: Henry Holt, 1932), xvii–110; also Sidney Earl Mead, *Nathaniel William Taylor, 1786–1858: A Connecticut Liberal* (Chicago: University of Chicago Press, 1942), and Stephen G. Post, *Christian Love and Self-Denial: An Historical and Normative Study of Jonathan Edwards, Samuel Hopkins, and American Theological Ethics* (New York: Lanham, 1987).

[6]William Warren Sweet, *Religion in the Development of American Culture, 1765–1840* (New York: Charles Scribners' Sons, 1952). See especially 2–59.

were hotly contested between the two cultures, others were being newly settled by large contingents from the East, and still others were cosmopolitan, urban, industrial cities with nearly two hundred years of history. Economic conditions, religious institutions, and family structures that were taken for granted on the Coast would be dim memories two hundred miles westward; and challenges that had to be surmounted daily on the frontier were unknown and unthinkable in the Eastern capitals. As white settlements expanded westward, various cultural syntheses moved in groups across the continent. The standards and values in the wilderness differed from those in newly settled towns, and those in turn had only distant similarities with cultural values in settled agricultural regions, which further varied from the wealthier and more sophisticated cities of the Coast. It was a migration of persons, ideas, and institutions greater in magnitude than anything in Western history since the migrations that overthrew Roman civilization and created temporary instability, large populations with little institutional structuring, and the opportunity for sudden economic and political mobility on an unprecedented scale. Since there were no law and order, no community structure, no education or congregation, self-reliance and informal, ephemeral cooperation were the qualities that made survival possible and characterized the values that pushed the frontier across the continent.

The decision to move west was almost always a male decision, and frontier culture was predominantly a male culture. Gender disproportion was very high in some areas; California was 90 percent male in 1850, though most areas didn't approach those numbers. Middle-class men were most likely to go, since the poor couldn't afford the roughly $600 cost (the 1830 figure). It was a very strained transition for women, whose supports and bases for self-esteem depended more on settled society. When wagons had to be lightened, the things jettisoned were most likely to be the things precious to women, while tools, livestock, and grain were always retained. Women took on men's work more often than the other way around, so feminine identity was weakened without a corresponding premium in privilege or status. More migrating couples were isolated, which strengthened male authority, and few women worked outside the home. Yet, following the example of the previous century's New England, a higher percentage of Western women were professionals than in the East, and both coeducation and suffrage developed earlier.[7]

Conditions in the East were also changing rapidly. In the very highest classes, men increasingly moved in predominantly male business circles,

---

[7]Coontz, *Social Origins of Private Life,* 316–21.

leaving wives and children alone at home—a trend that became more prevalent nationwide, in the upper half of society, over the next fifty years.[8]
Leisure for wives became a commodity of conspicuous consumption for
the wealthy, and wealthier women were increasingly ignorant of their husbands' property and business.[9] Women's role began to be defined exclusively in terms of motherhood, following the Quaker model, and less in
terms of production.[10]

Economic changes intensified. Export production tripled during the
Napoleonic wars of 1798–1803. Industrialization intensified in the northeastern cities, raising the proportion of free labor employed outside the
farm from 17 percent to 37 percent between 1800 and 1825.[11] The population of New York City tripled between 1800 and 1825. First canals, then
railroads brought goods and people to market much more rapidly. After
1820 industrial work moved increasingly out of homes and into factories
and shops, so workers had to come to centralized work places. Employees
and boarders lived less often with employers, and supervision of morals
and private lives by the moneyed diminished.[12] Class formation and economic inequality increased, with rapidly escalating concentration of wealth
in the upper 10 percent of the population.[13] The middle and upper classes
moved their residences away from the poor and the workers, so sharper
geographical boundaries were created around both families and entire social classes. Wage labor became more widespread, middle- and upper-class
women were increasingly separated from it, and families became responsible for regulating the boundaries between public and private life, which
was especially important in forming the identity of the largely Protestant
middle class.[14]

The Emerging Victorian Synthesis: Class and Family

Religious phenomena and religious thought played a key role in establishing both gender and class identity in the pre–Civil War era, especially in
the Northern states. Whereas the revival spirit of the eighteenth-century
Great Awakening had been populist, class-neutral, gender-neutral, and urban,[15] the nineteenth-century revivals were much more concentrated in the

---

[8]Ibid., 142–44.
[9]Ibid., 144.
[10]Ibid., 150.
[11]Ibid., 165.
[12]Ibid., 167.
[13]Ibid., 172.
[14]Ibid., 174–80.
[15]Barbara Leslie Epstein, *The Politics of Domesticity: Women, Evangelism, and Temperance in Nineteenth-Century America* (Middletown: Wesleyan University Press, 1981), 11–14.

middle and upper working classes, had much stronger female than male participation, and focused more in the open country semi-wilderness areas and in the smaller cities near the frontier.[16] Men had increasingly deserted the churches in the eighteenth century, experiencing an unwelcome tension between the economic demands for enterprise and independence and the Calvinist conviction of original sin and human helplessness.[17] But women, especially in the middle class, were expected to be religious, were highly responsive to the revivals, and became very active in attempting to Christianize their men.[18] The revivals simultaneously deepened the sense of women's spiritual and moral superiority and carried the seeds of a developing feminism, later evinced as temperance and abolitionist crusades.

This was the era of the "Cult of True Womanhood" among the Protestant middle classes. Women were urged to be pious, pure, submissive, and domestic,[19] in a time when men were increasingly away from the home and increasingly immersed in the mechanization of market economics.[20] As men were less at home, household tasks fell almost totally to women. Further, maintenance of class identity became more important, as the working class was increasingly composed of European Catholic immigrants who often had different values and life patterns. The establishment of distinctive patterns that would enable sons to develop virtues of punctuality, thrift, and self-control became a vital female responsibility. While women were more dependent on men as married adults, boys were increasingly dependent on women as creators of the character that was thought to ensure their adult economic and social success.

Protestantism and its developing theologies were central in that effort. Its foremost mid-century proponent was Horace Bushnell, whose *Christian Nurture* was first published serially in the mid-1840s. He was the son of a successful weaver, who was typical of the artisans struggling to establish themselves in the developing middle class but whose occupations didn't look promising enough to apprentice their sons to them.[21] Bushnell went to Yale. He was converted in the New Haven revival of 1831.[22] He became Nathaniel Taylor's student at the divinity school there, having left the law school upon his conversion,[23] and subsequently became pastor of North

---

[16]Sweet, 149–50, 220–29.

[17]Epstein, 24–29.

[18]Barbara Welter, "The Cult of True Womanhood," in Gordon, 372–92. See also Epstein, 48–61.

[19]Welter, 372.

[20]Coontz, *Social Origins of Private Life,* 190ff.

[21]Ibid., 187–90.

[22]John M. Mulder, "Introduction," in Horace Bushnell, *Christian Nurture* (Grand Rapids: Baker Book House, 1979). The complete 1861 edition, xvii.

[23]Sidney Earl Mead, *Nathaniel William Taylor, 1786–1858: A Connecticut Liberal* (Chicago: University of Chicago Press, 1942), 162ff.

Congregational Church in Hartford, which he served until his retirement in 1861. He was the first major Congregational theologian to explicitly challenge the belief that a sudden, dateable, dramatic conversion experience was necessary to salvation. Provoking a storm of denunciation, he argued passionately that it was sinful to raise children as though nothing important to their salvation happened before such an adolescent or postadolescent experience, and that it was equally wrong to expect explicit instruction and harsh management to inculcate Christian virtue in a child beginning in middle or late childhood.

Instead, he contended, "more…is done, or lost by neglect of doing, on a child's immortality, in the first three years of his life, than in all his years of discipline afterwards…Let every Christian father and mother understand, when their child is three years old, that they have done more than half of all they will ever do for his character."[24] It was clear to him that meaning precedes language and that what becomes habitual, even if unspoken, is never lost.

> They are now born into that by the assent of their own will (as adults), which they were in before, without their will. What they do not remember still remembers them, and now claims a right in them. What was before unconscious, flames out into consciousness, and they break forth into praise and thanksgiving, in that which, long ago, took them initially, and touched them softly without thanks.[25]

Bushnell supports this conclusion with a flood of images that are both memorable and surprisingly modern. For instance, "infancy and childhood are the ages most pliant to good."[26] And, "At first, the child is held as a mere passive lump in the arms, and he opens into conscious life under the soul of the parent, streaming into his eyes and ears, through the manners and tones of the nursery."[27] He writes of the parent exercising himself in the child,[28] of the organic power of character in the parent coming to effect in the child, and of the impressionability of the child as the strongest possible motive for parental piety.[29] Bushnell was skeptical about the possibility of teaching doctrines or behaviors to children before the onset of language but advocated instead that "first of all, they should rather seek to teach a feeling than a doctrine"[30]; "to bathe the child in their own feeling of love to

---

[24]Bushnell, 248.
[25]Ibid., 247–48.
[26]Ibid., 22.
[27]Ibid., 28.
[28]Ibid., 30.
[29]Ibid., 34.
[30]Ibid., 51.

God, and dependence on him, and contrition for wrong before him, bearing up their child's heart in their own." Ultimately, he reasons, "religion never thoroughly penetrates life, till it becomes domestic."[31]

He is not content to speak strictly of child-raising in a dyadic sense, but involves the whole family atmosphere. "And so it is with all family transactions and feelings. They implicate ordinarily the whole circle of the house...Acting thus together, they take a common character."[32] He speaks of the organic unity of the family exerting a power deeper than influence over its members, that "the bond is so intimate that they do it unconsciously and undesignedly—they must do it. Their character, feelings, spirit, and principles, must propagate themselves, whether they will or not."[33] He says the odor of the house will always be in the child's garments, regardless of the child's presumed individuality. "The spirit of the house is breathed into his nature, day to day."[34] "If the house subsists by plunder," Bushnell writes, "the child is swaddled as a thief, the child wears a thief's garments, and feeds the growth of his body on stolen meat."[35] The church's role includes gathering families into a common organism, so that their character is nurtured, since "character is a stream, a river, flowing down upon your children, hour by hour."[36]

He specifically challenges the revivalist's counsel to break the child's will, identifying the early parent-child struggles as "his feeling of himself and you, in which he is getting hold of the conditions of authority, and feeling out his limitations."[37] He holds that the struggle to break the child often results in making him "a coward, or a thief, or a hypocrite, or a mean-spirited and driveling sycophant,"[38] and urges instead that we should strive "not to break, but to bend rather, to draw the will down, or away from self-assertion toward self-devotion, to teach it the way of submitting to wise limitations, and raise it into the great and glorious liberties of a state of loyalty to God."[39]

Unlike the conservatives of the previous century, he does not see parental authority as a lifelong hierarchy. He has adopted the now more familiar view that "a wise parent understands that his government is to be crowned by an act of emancipation," perhaps more easily maintained in a time when

---

[31]Ibid., 63.
[32]Ibid., 90.
[33]Ibid., 93.
[34]Ibid., 94–95.
[35]Ibid., 100.
[36]Ibid., 110.
[37]Ibid., 244.
[38]Ibid.
[39]Ibid., 245.

parental control over marriage and parental reward through the settling of land were largely in the past. He observes that the expectation that a young person suddenly is fit for independence is naive, arguing that "pure authority, up to the last limit of minority, then a total, instantaneous self-possession, makes an awkward transition."[40] "The emancipating process, in order to be well finished, should begin early, and should pass imperceptibly, even as age increases imperceptibly."[41] He counsels that children be given reasons, which would have been anathema a hundred years previously, and that "the tastes of the child...should begin to be a little consulted, in respect to his school, his studies, his future engagements in life."[42] He goes on to argue that a parent should offer a little gospel with his law, not be known primarily as a bundle of commandments, but nonetheless be clearly the provider of government.[43] Duty, firmness, and order remain central, and he is at pains to remind readers that obedience is still required and discipline necessary, yet severity is to be avoided. "In every case of discipline for ill-nature, wrong, willfulness, disobedience, be it understood, that the real point is carried never till the child is gentled into love and duty."[44]

In all this Bushnell is an unabashed spokesperson for the prevailing cult of domesticity and its idealization of "True Womanhood." He refers to the father as the bishop of the house,[45] though in other sections he refers to the parents as a unit, suggesting they have common responsibilities. He reinforces the prevailing views of gender identity, speaking of mother "as a kind of nursing Providence."[46] She is understood as raising "the initial sense of a divine something in the world," offering the "gentlest possible beginning of authority." He then mentions the "stiffer tension of the masculine word" and "the wider, rougher providence of a father's masculine force."[47]

Like most nineteenth-century Protestant theologians, he deals with marriage almost not at all, and, when he does, it is strictly as a parenting partnership. In discussing the precondition of authority in parents, he says "they be so far entered into the Christian order of marriage as to fulfill gracefully what belongs to the relation in which they are set, and show them to the children as doing fit honor to each other. By a defect just here, all authority

---

[40]Ibid., 240.
[41]Ibid., 328–29.
[42]Ibid., 329.
[43]Ibid., 314ff.
[44]Ibid., 320.
[45]Ibid., 315.
[46]Ibid., 317.
[47]Ibid.

in the house is blasted."[48]　He cites at length a current parental self-help book on how parents should strive to give children the impression of total unity, but says nothing of the substance of their relationship that would enable such a common front. Whatever it is in marriage that empowers this saving care of children is assumed as a given or seen as an outgrowth of reason and duty.

Bushnell's theological contemporaries echoed the same themes. Alexander Campbell, leader of the early Disciples of Christ, burgeoning at mid-century, argued that the battle for the republic would be won or lost by mothers.[49] They would create the climate for the dawning of a blissful millennial age through their influence on families, being "the great agent in the grandest of all human enterprises."[50] He spoke of the wife's typical superiority to her husband "in the department of feeling, sensitiveness, promptness, decision, tenderness of affection, and self-denied devotion."[51] Her love was superior through its unselfishness, and her superiority, her mystic power, was to be protected through isolation from the world. "A mother's empire is small, but her power is immense."[52]

He followed the typical mid-century sorting of woman's life into her roles as daughter, sister, wife, and mother,[53] seeing her exercising in each relationship a civilizing, spiritualizing influence over parents, brothers, husbands, and sons. "The whole world is in her arms," he wrote, since she is entrusted with "moulding of the soft clay of humanity and forming it after her own image."[54] In an 1856 speech he extended this view of women's purpose: "The whole honor, dignity, and happiness of women is to develop, perfect, beautify and beatify man."[55]

It should come as no surprise that Campbell endorsed the inequality of the sexes, calling it part of God's design. He also followed the custom of the times by providing his two wives, though clearly designated as intellectually inferior and spiritually pure through limitation to the home, with major administrative and business responsibilities during his frequent absences.[56]

---

[48]Ibid., 322.

[49]Ralph Edwin Groover, "Alexander Campbell and the Family: Precept and Example" (Ph.D. diss., Emory University, 1982), vii.

[50]Alexander Campbell, "Address on the Amelioration of the Social State," *Millennial Harbinger,* July 1840, 320–26.

[51]Ibid.

[52]Thomas Campbell, "Brief Memoir of Mrs. Jane Campbell," in *The Memoirs of Thomas Campbell* (Cincinnati: H. S. Bosworth, 1861), 315.

[53]Groover, 47.

[54]Alexander Campbell, *Millennial Harbinger,* July 1840.

[55]Alexander Campbell, *Millennial Harbinger,* June 1856, 312.

[56]Groover, 44–46.

Campbell did directly address marriage, calling it a duty, and naming any forbidding of marriage an act of the antichrist. He repeated the traditional blessings and functions of marriage: (1) multiplication of mankind; (2) sustenance of mankind, stemming from affection of parents for children; (3) education of mankind through parental instruction; (4) sociality, comfort, and assistance of mankind, "comprehended in this word 'an help-meet for him.'"[57] There is no mention in Groover's dissertation account of Campbell's sermon notes of any direct reference to sex or affection, topics rarely spoken of by nineteenth-century theologians, though his personal letters contain a few suggestive and sexually affirming lines.[58] But in theology, reason was always to control passion,[59] and Protestant theology of this period found sexuality too passionate to be extolled in public.

Henry Ward Beecher, perhaps the most visible churchman of the nineteenth century, preached a similar gospel of industry, purity, efficiency, and family. Preaching in Brooklyn in 1849, he called family "the most important institution on earth."[60] Beecher, like other theologians of his day, relied on the institutions of church and family to reinforce the independence of the individual, the indispensable middle-class value. In conversation he asked his hearers to take the family as the model for the rule of God, an idealized commonwealth.[61] God's love for man became the core of this theology, completely eclipsing the old Calvinist emphasis on divine sovereignty. In Beecher's serialized novel *Norwood*, published in 1867, he has his hero call the family table "a kind of altar, a place sacred."[62]

The link between family, middle-class industriousness, and sexual purity was critical to Beecher's preaching, though as we shall see later, he was less successful in making it central in his life. In his oft-printed *Lectures to Young Men* he first inveighs against idleness, the absence of "the intention of usefulness."[63] He reveals his class loyalty clearly with disdain for the idleness and indolence of wealth but still extends the lure to striving, in a promise that riches are a gift of God, if justly gained.[64]

He reserves his most passionate invective for his lecture on "The Strange Woman," the prostitute. While conceding that beauty should delight us,[65]

---

[57]Ibid., 25.

[58]Ibid., 43.

[59]Ibid., 69.

[60]Clifford E. Clark, *Henry Ward Beecher: Spokesman for a Middle-Class America* (Urbana: University of Illinois Press, 1978), 84.

[61]Ibid., 190.

[62]Coontz, *Social Origins of Private Life*, 227.

[63]Henry Ward Beecher, *Lectures to Young Men* (New York: Newman, 1851), 15.

[64]Ibid., 80.

[65]Ibid., 188.

he warns that he who follows the artful woman will never return: "Trust not thyself near the artful woman, armed in her beauty, her cunning raiment, her dimpled smiles, her sighs of sorrow, her look of love, her voice of flattery."[66] And no sin, he writes, is worse than impurity, the Victorian euphemism for masturbation.[67] Those who follow these twin evils are inescapably dragged through the five wards of the strange woman's house: pleasure, satiety, discovery, disease, and death.[68]

The young Beecher's theme of reason over passion was further elevated and elaborated by a group of Christian medical thinkers throughout the middle fifty years of the century, linking the dangers of food and sex. Sylvester Graham, a New Jersey Presbyterian minister and self-styled physician,[69] was the first to gain wide attention. He became a vegetarian and temperance lecturer and is best remembered for inventing the whole-wheat flour and cracker that bear his name. He argued the general health advantages of a vegetarian diet and at one point had several New York hotel kitchens following his regimen.[70] Graham argued in his 1834 *Lecture to Young Men* (a common title in this era) that the excitement of sexual arousal "induces a greater or less degree of debility and diseased irritability in the nerves of organic life."[71] Insanity, he said, is "generally attended with excessive sexual desire," and is aggravated and confirmed by self-pollution.[72] The key to his argument was the belief that stimulating and heating substances, especially excessive, highly seasoned, and fleshy food, increase "concupiscent excitability" and increase its influence over judgment. In turn, inflamed desire disturbs all the systems of the body, especially inflaming the brain.[73] The excess of excitement produces first irritability, then debility, then death. He argued that nondepraved men would have sex only about as often as animals and that too much marital sex produces "an immeasurable amount of evil."[74] Once a month is maximal for the young and healthy. But "by far the worst form of venereal indulgence, is self-pollution."[75] The only remedy is to "subsist on a plain, simple, unstimulating, vegetable and water diet."[76]

---

[66]Ibid., 191.
[67]Ibid., 184.
[68]Ibid., 200–206.
[69]Gerald Carson, *The Cornflake Crusade* (New York: Rinehard, 1957), 48.
[70]Ibid., 52.
[71]Sylvester Graham, *A Lecture to Young Men* (New York: Arno Press, 1974, Weeden and Cory's 1834 reprint), 17.
[72]Ibid., 18.
[73]Ibid., 19–20.
[74]Ibid., 34.
[75]Ibid., 39.
[76]Ibid., 76.

Bushnell was obviously impressed with this thinking. He devoted several pages of *Christian Nurture* to the dangerous overfeeding of children and its damaging effects on character.[77] The next major crusaders on the subject were John Harvey Kellogg and Will Kellogg of the famous Seventh Day Adventist Sanitarium in Battle Creek. Dr. J. H. Kellogg graduated from medical school in 1875 and was soon expounding vegetarian dogma, teaching homeopathic medicine to Adventist doctors, and offering rest cures to the wealthy and faithful in Michigan. His 1884 *Plain Facts for Young and Old* continued the crusade against stimulating food and its dangerous sexual effects. Corn Flakes and Grape Nuts were direct results of his effort.

Kellogg argued that normal children have no sexual feelings or ideas, and that the onset of sexual precocity shatters the constitution.[78] Sex, he wrote, was the most exhaustive and destructive human act, so dangerous that every indulgence after the age of fifty hastens death.[79] Overindulgence was the reason the American race was dying out and being replaced by immigrants. But, again, the worst vice was masturbation, doubly damnable, beyond "illicit commerce between sexes."[80] It causes a score of deadly diseases, he wrote, and can drive one to "driveling idiocy from this vice alone."[81] He also condemned contraception, intercourse during menstruation and pregnancy, intercourse after menopause, and any conditions that could lead to learning to masturbate. He advocated circumcision without anesthesia as a punishment for masturbation[82] and suggested a mild electric shock to the genitals as a good preventive for nocturnal emissions.[83]

In addition to constant supervision, prevention of privacy, and avoiding the mixing of sexes after the age of five, the primary preventive for undue sexual desire was diet. "Flesh, condiments, eggs, tea, coffee, chocolate, and all stimulants have a powerful influence directly upon the reproductive organs," he wrote.[84] They increase the supply of blood in the abdomen, which arouses passions. Late suppers are particularly dangerous. He warned especially against feeding clergy richly, because clerical vice is doubly reprehensible.[85] (It should be remembered that he was a physician, not a minister.) He did marry, but he and his wife claimed to have always lived without sex to prove that it wasn't necessary to health.

---

[77]Bushnell, 272–79.
[78]J. H. Kellogg, *Plain Facts for Young and Old* (Burlington: I. F. Segner, 1884), 117–20.
[79]Ibid., 134.
[80]Ibid., 315.
[81]Ibid., 321.
[82]Ibid., 385.
[83]Ibid., 409.
[84]Ibid., 103.
[85]Ibid., 184.

A further element in the Victorian synthesis was its intensely anti-Catholic thrust, a response to the huge flood of European immigrants after 1830. By 1850 one-third of American factory workers were immigrants. There had been a 30 percent drop in the native-born birth rate between 1800 and 1860,[86] and the specter of becoming the minority in the country that was supposed to be Protestantism's showplace was unacceptable. Class phenomena were at work here as well, since the bulk of immigrants were factory workers and Roman Catholic, and the Protestant middle classes were frightened of what they perceived as the immigrants' undemocratic political loyalties to European rulers and their more accepting attitudes toward emotionality, sexuality, and alcohol.

One of the most widely known attacks on Catholic immigration was by Henry Ward Beecher's father, Lyman Beecher. His 1835 *Plea For the West* was originally a lecture given in several Atlantic cities as a fundraiser for Lane Seminary in Cincinnati. He begins by citing Jonathan Edwards' claim that the millennium would begin in America, endorses it,[87] and says it will only happen if we supply the West with education. The lack of education is especially dangerous because of immigration, he contends.[88] He argues that immigrants constitute 37 percent of the population,[89] (he may have meant 37 percent of the population in the West) and that

> three-fourths of the foreign emigrants whose accumulating tide is rolling in upon us, are, through the medium of their religion and priesthood, as entirely accessible to the control of the potentates of Europe as if they were an army of soldiers, enlisted and officered, and spreading over the land; then indeed, should we have just occasion to apprehend danger to our liberties. It would be the union of church and state in the midst of us.[90]

He observed that the new pope, Gregory XVI, was an Austrian subject, and that at his orders loyal Catholic immigrants could make the West slave to the Austrian chancellor, Metternich. He alleged the antirepublican sentiments of the Catholic faith,[91] noted the substantial contributions being made by European Catholics to missionary Catholic schools in the American West, and challenged the Protestants to give handily to outcompete them.

---

[86]Coontz, *Social Origins of Private Life*, 190.
[87]Lyman Beecher, *Plea for the West* (Cincinnati: Truman and Smith, 1835), 9–10.
[88]Ibid., 49.
[89]Ibid., 50.
[90]Ibid., 54.
[91]Ibid., 85.

Challenges to the Victorian Ethos

Though Beecher's fears of the immigrants' political loyalties and behaviors, and the fears of many Protestants well into this century, were unfounded and damaging, there were important differences between the immigrants and the dominant middle-class Protestant culture. Many, if not most, of these differences concerned attitudes and practices surrounding marriage, family, and sex.

At a time when Protestant theologians were arguing for an ideal of womanhood totally without sexual feelings, and a manhood that subsumed sexual passion to reason in every case, the Roman Catholic bishop of Philadelphia wrote in 1843 that a married woman had a right to bring herself to orgasm by her own touch if intercourse had failed to produce it.[92] He also wrote, in a widely used textbook in moral theology, that a husband sinned if he did not remain active in sex until his wife had orgasm, and that a woman sinned mortally if she distracted herself during sex to avoid having orgasm. This last decision was inherited from Alphonsus Liguori in the eighteenth century, when folk wisdom said that avoiding orgasm prevented conception, but Kenrick (the bishop of Philadelphia) affirmed this pleasure without reference to contraceptive intent.[93] Kenrick specifically linked sex and love, writing that fostering love was a legitimate reason a husband might seek intercourse.[94] Catholic love was more unambiguously physical, and Protestants were frightened of it.

Further, this love was embedded in a working-class culture with unsettlingly different attitudes and behaviors. Working-class people were much more tolerant of drinking and drunkenness, which perpetuated European and earlier American patterns of very high alcohol consumption. Prerevolutionary estimates of consumption vary widely, but tax records show a sharp increase between 1790 and 1830, a period that saw a wave of European immigration. Consumption rose from 5.8 gallons of alcohol per adult (over 15) per year in 1790 to 7.1 gallons in 1830.[95] Germans, the largest group of early-century immigrants, were often especially enthusiastic about their drinking.[96] Churches and other community groups had been comfortable with drinking, as long as it didn't lead to drunkenness, throughout colonial days, and the typical work break at 11 a.m. and again at 4 p.m. had typically revolved around an employer-provided glass of whiskey.[97] This

---

[92]Peter Gardella, *Innocent Ecstasy: How Christianity Gave America an Ethic of Sexual Pleasure* (New York: Oxford University Press, 1985), 9.

[93]Ibid., 17.

[94]Ibid., 23.

[95]Epstein, 91.

[96]Ibid., 99.

[97]Coontz, *Social Origins of Private Life*, 181.

pattern was defended as a right by the working class far into the nineteenth century; hence, those who aspired to middle-class status saw avoiding drink as a way to achieve it. The prevalence of drink in heterogeneous residential neighborhoods was one of the factors leading to the development of separate, more expensive residential areas, occupied primarily by the middle class.

Coontz points out a particularly critical distinction that began to emerge in the newly settled communities of the 1830s and was extended westward each decade as new communities developed. With class boundaries still fairly fluid, those from artisan and laboring backgrounds who preferred drinking on the job, sociability, spontaneity, and loyalty to the colonial or European cultures that favored them, increasingly developed class consciousness as workers. Those who favored punctuality, self-control, saving, and economic advancement increasingly saw themselves as middle class.[98] Protestant revivalism in the Second Great Awakening was often the decisive act for recruiting men, typically through their wives, into the more genteel and orderly middle class life, and teetotaling was a strong value in those communities. Between 1830 and 1840, in response to these efforts, national per capita alcohol consumption fell by more than half.[99]

In the remaining working class, though women might prefer not to work outside the home, economics forced them to. In one New York district in 1855 only 22.5 percent of male artisans supported a family on one income. By the Civil War 25 percent of factory workers were female.[100] By the full development of working-class culture at the end of the century, there was a strong class consciousness, fueled in part by American management's more aggressive use of labor. (English mill workers operated two looms; in Massachusetts four was the norm.) Immigrant girls started work in the mills early in adolescence, and families were larger for both economic and religious reasons. Forty percent of industrial workers were below the official poverty levels. Men's earnings peaked in their twenties, and with no Social Security and income declining as the ability to do heavy work declined, multiple children was the main method of avoiding abject poverty. Working class families had less space, so there was less privacy and less boundary between family and street life but, on the other hand, more of a boundary between an alienated work life and social life. Young adult and adolescent peer groups outside the family were tolerated, even encouraged, as space to contain youngsters at home was lacking. The broader community took on some of the supervisory functions played by mothers

---

[98]Ibid., 195–6.
[99]Ibid., 196.
[100]Ibid., 197–202.

in the middle class. As long as people saw no way to protect themselves from the rapid economic oscillations, solidarity was intense.[101]

In working-class communities, privacy was neither a possibility nor a value, so family boundaries were fluid. Boarding and lodging with non-relatives was a way of life for 15 to 20 percent of the population. Most men lived within a mile or two of work, so most people walked to work, and much socialization was in the streets. The gender segregation for leisure time that marked middle-class life did not exist. In this setting there was little support for personal ambition or individual mobility, since extended family had a prior claim on money. Money often went back to the country of emigration, either to support aging relatives or to pay passage for new immigrants. And the churches (largely Catholic) were strongly supported, in turn playing an important role in undergirding the values of working-class culture.[102]

But Catholics were not the only laborers in the working class vineyard. Methodism, termed by Richard Niebuhr in 1929 (prior to the burgeoning of Pentecostalism in this century) "the last great religious revolution of the disinherited in Christendom," was expanding from its base among small farmers and urban artisans, remaining attractive to that population, and carrying many of its adherents into more middle-class habits and occupations.[103] But it kept its ardent emotionalism and moral demandingness.

One of its most effective revival preachers during and after the Second Awakening in New York, New England, and southern Canada was Phoebe Palmer, a physician's wife who followed the old Methodist tradition of lay and female preaching.[104] Mrs. Palmer received the gift of holiness at a meeting conducted by her sister, Sarah Worrall Lankford, who had been discussing Wesley's doctrine of perfection.[105] From this event in July 1837,[106] she quickly moved into leading classes and conducting her regular Tuesday afternoon meetings,[107] which became the most productive crucible of religious thought for the developing Holiness and Pentecostal wings of the Methodist church.

Her relevance to this study lies in her development of a doctrine of human fulfillment with intense emotional and physical components.[108] In these meetings, men and women together (a rarity for Victorian times)

---

[101]Ibid., 290–301.
[102]Ibid., 305–9.
[103]H. Richard Niebuhr, *The Social Sources of Denominationalism* (Cleveland and New York: World Publishing, 1929), 72.
[104]Gardella, 86ff.
[105]Ibid., 87.
[106]Phoebe Palmer, *The Promise of the Father* (Salem, Ohio: Schmul Publishers, 1981), 202.
[107]Ibid., 227ff.
[108]Gardella, 87.

discussed the most intimate details of emotional experience relating to holiness and perfection. She seized on the biblical phrase urging the believer to "glorify God in your body and spirit which are his."[109] Though she specifically denied that emotional exaltation was the substance or proof of holiness,[110] she did see feeling as the fruit of faith, and detailed a way of evoking the experience of holiness in the believer that emphasized the shedding of intellectual defenses and the direct encounter with both God and the messenger, who was often Phoebe.[111]

She called the hearer to identify the physical components of "breaking through to holiness." She repeated over and over the plea to the supplicant to lay "body and spirit"[112] on the altar of God, so that God could accept the sacrifice and repay the believer with the experience of certainty, typically in the form of intense emotional release and the compelling urge to demonstrate the possibility of this holy joy to others.[113] She spoke of a present salvation,[114] of eternal life already begun,[115] and of the urgency of believing that it is possible right now. To claim it now one had to promise to leave the sacrifice on the altar forever.[116] Though there is nothing explicitly sexual in her language, and her moral claims were unambiguously orthodox, her choice of words suggests to the Freudian reader that ecstatic religious fulfillment and sexual fulfillment were not antagonistic to each other. Phrases such as "virtue came out of Jesus,"[117] "endearingly attached to the division of Christ's body," "he purchased all, body, soul, and spirit,"[118] "surrendering all to the Redeemer,"[119] and "lean so entirely, with naked faith on a naked promise"[120] speak to the perhaps half-conscious awareness of the parallels between the apparently distinct sexual and spiritual modes of experience.

Palmer's Tuesday meetings went on for thirty-seven years, becoming a model for perhaps two hundred others that spread across the country by 1886.[121] She published a monthly magazine, *The Guide to Holiness.* She continually taught that perfection could be dated to a specific, identifiable experience of God's Spirit and that that experience had unmistakable physical

---

[109]Ibid., 88.
[110]Phoebe Palmer, *The Way of Holiness, with Notes by the Way* (New York: Palmer, 1871), 39.
[111]Ibid., 220–84.
[112]Ibid., 126.
[113]Ibid., 235.
[114]Ibid., 149.
[115]Ibid., 159.
[116]Ibid., 243.
[117]Ibid., 56.
[118]Ibid., 66.
[119]Ibid., 68.
[120]Ibid., 99.
[121]Gardella, 89.

components. "Palmer contended that God neither destroyed human nature nor left the body as it had been; rather, the grace of perfect love accepted all bodily drives and turned them into holy channels."[122] Happiness was a religious duty for the sanctified.

By the last quarter of the century this type of religious ecstasy had led to the formation of dozens of camp meetings, a combination of religion and entertainment that enlivened the summer scene throughout the late-Victorian era and is still evident in programs like the Chautauqua Institute.

Three years before Palmer's death, and only a few miles from the site of her Tuesday afternoon meetings, Andrew Ingersoll was developing a more specifically physicalized and sexualized view of Christian salvation.[123] Ingersoll, a Presbyterian physician at Corning, New York, published in 1877 the case of a seventeen-year-old girl with chronic head and back pain and an unceasing cough. He wrote that "her prostration was caused by the suppression of sexual life by the will,"[124] and he used her story as the exemplar for a doctrine of sexual salvation.

With a mindset that anticipated Freud by fifteen years, but saw Christianity as an ally rather than an enemy, Ingersoll argued for "an entirely different view of sexual life."[125] He wrote that the sexual life is the sustaining of every organ of the body, hence "We should not seek to suppress sexual life, but should desire Christ to redeem it."[126] It is condemnation of the sexual life, Ingersoll wrote, that turns it into lust, and the strength of the sexual life that immunizes against disease. "The more we are in harmony with Christ's spirit and subject to His will, the greater power will the life of the body, which is sexual, have for its sustenance, and for the overcoming of disease."[127]

He writes of one healing in a manner quite reminiscent of Palmer's methods, on the one hand, and of modern Gestalt therapists, on the other. The woman suffered from dysmenorrhea.

> I never saw greater anger in any human face than hers, when first called to see her in one of these attacks. I told her the spasmodic action was caused by her anger with God for creating her a woman, and thereby subjecting her to menstruation; that her anger must cease, for she was beyond relief until she became reconciled to this function. She insisted that she could not control herself, and that

---

[122]Ibid., 91.
[123]Ibid., 68.
[124]Ibid.
[125]Andrew J. Ingersoll, *In Health: Sex, Marriage, and Society* New York: Arno Press, 1974), 4. Originally published as 4th edition, revised (Boston: Less and Shepard, 1899, first edition, 1877).
[126]Ibid., 21.
[127]Ibid., 55.

she was not angry. Finally, however, my convictions of her state prevailed over her own, her will relaxed, and the spasmodic action and pain passed away.[128]

Ingersoll, like Palmer, saw the conscious will as holding the sufferer away from the saving force, God's love expressed through physical as well as spiritual manifestations.

He attributed hysteria to the attempt to consciously crush out sexual feeling, causing constriction of muscles, particularly the *constrictor vaginae.* "All who thus suffer should desire sexual life, and reverence and gratitude for every consciousness of it, trusting in Christ to overcome their fear. Then the muscles will relax and the suffering cease."[129] Ingersoll directly contradicted those who thought they were doing God service by condemning the sexual nature and urged women to reverence their husbands' sexual nature and thereby "obtain a stronger influence over him than any other woman."[130]

The acceptance of pleasure was central to Ingersoll's thought, as it had been to Palmer.[131] He taught a method of relaxation that centered on breathing and touch,[132] learned from his mother (one wonders if she may have gone to Phoebe Palmer's meetings), and a resignation of the will to Christ, producing a relaxation in the nervous and vascular systems.[133] "Hanging the head cured psychosexual disease by releasing, in the moment of ecstasy, that free movement of breath which hatred and suppression of sex had restricted. After their breathing became free, patients not only lost their hysterical symptoms, but also became capable of finding physical ecstasy and spiritual meaning in sexual relations."[134] Married couples should yield to every sexual impulse in marriage, he wrote, seeing it as God's attempt to make their love cleansing of both soul and body. He saw sexual redemption as linked to perfection, adding the explicitly sexual to the physical liberation that Palmer had outlined.[135]

Growing respect for sexual feeling was eroding the high Victorian Protestant synthesis of rationalism and romanticism, and the struggles to hold it together were nowhere more evident than in the scandal surrounding Henry Ward Beecher's sexual life. The events around these controversies are explored in a fine book by Altina Waller,[136] who illuminates the

---

[128]Ibid., 62.
[129]Ibid., 91.
[130]Ibid., 104.
[131]Ibid., 69.
[132]Ibid., 72.
[133]Ibid., 71.
[134]Ibid., 72.
[135]Ibid., 74.
[136]AltinaWaller, *Reverend Beecher and Mrs. Tilton* (Amherst: University of Massachusetts Press, 1982).

sociological and ideological forces that surrounded Beecher and Brooklyn, as well as the detail of the relationship.

When Beecher left Indianapolis for Plymouth Church, Brooklyn, in 1848, he was coming to a brand-new congregation in a rapidly expanding city.[137] Businesses were booming, population increasing rapidly, fortunes being made and lost in a weekend. Beecher was recruited by two men, Henry Bowen and John Howard, who had left the newly established Church of the Pilgrims. Its pastor was more suited to the educated, established leadership of the older Brooklyn business families and insufficiently emotional and flexible for the new urban migrants, largely younger, less educated, and intending to be upwardly mobile.[138] In response to the longings of this group, Beecher elaborated what he called the "Gospel of Love," a less cautiously conservative theology than described in his earlier writings. It celebrated individual initiative, dyadic relationships based on "affinity," and emotional intensity. Though his congregation relished its Congregational polity, it clearly preferred personal loyalty to institutional continuity and the meeting of strongly felt personal needs over rational deliberation.[139]

Beecher arrived in Brooklyn with an often sick, openly unhappy, and complaining wife, accompanied by occasional rumors of adulteries in his Indianapolis ministry at Second Presbyterian Church. He was apparently a lonely, emotionally needy, narcissistic man, with a flair for attracting attention and a thirst for the personal loyalty and unquestioning approval of his congregants. He drew crowds, and Plymouth was quickly a thriving congregation, the largest in the city.[140] He particularly attracted young men, who seemed drawn by his ability to dispel the loneliness of the anonymous city and to rationalize the striving necessary to survive there. He often preached on one of the major concerns of young men, sexuality, in one memorable sermon condemning seducers and bemoaning the fate of their victims, while remaining deeply sympathetic with the snares in which both found themselves entangled.[141] At about the same time he was apparently involved in an affair with Bowen's young wife and was openly hosting free-love advocate Stephen Pearl Andrews in meetings at his home.[142] Though very sympathetic with Andrews' views, he ultimately held that these reformers were unrealistic, "because they assumed all men were perfect, when in reality most men still required external law to keep them from a plunge

---

[137]Ibid., 65–68.
[138]Ibid., 93ff.
[139]Ibid., 33–37.
[140]Ibid., 67.
[141]Ibid., 36–38.
[142]Ibid.

into utter ruin."[143] Waller goes on to note that Beecher apparently reserved the right of those on a higher plane to act upon their romantic intuition.

Economic ambition and sexual ambition worked together in intricate ways. Bowen learned of the affair, but by that time his manufacturing businesses had failed and his only secure income was from his newspaper, for which Beecher's columns provided the primary readership. There was an agreement to keep the sexual matter private. In the meantime, Beecher performed the wedding of Theodore and Elizabeth Tilton in 1855.[144] It was a troubled marriage, troubled in ways that were characteristic of the times. The couple lived first with Elizabeth's mother, who ran a Brooklyn boarding house, while Tilton worked for Bowen, functioning as Beecher's secretary, and often ghostwriting his columns. Tilton was drawn to the intellectually stimulating life of the people whom Beecher attracted, the cream of the New York political and cultural community. He was embarrassed at his own family's rural manners and increasingly unhappy in Elizabeth's family's uncultured household, where boarders and relatives felt free to criticize his marital conduct.[145]

After one false start in rented quarters and a return to the family, Tilton was finally able to buy an elegant home in 1866 and worked to separate Elizabeth from her relatives. He overextended himself financially, contracted to make lecture tours to pay the mortgage, and found himself facing the same loneliness and temptations that Beecher had faced.[146] He complained bitterly to and about Elizabeth, wrote often of his depression and loneliness on the tours, and both had and confessed several affairs in the late 1860s.[147]

Following Beecher's preaching on the "moral affinity" of spouses, Tilton resolved to plunge himself into what he called in his letters the "new marriage," an intense focus on domesticity, privacy, and independence from extended family (especially his wife's). Like many of her contemporaries, Elizabeth experienced intense loneliness, loss of function and identity, and psychosomatic illness. Though their letters explored romance and professed the attempt to be romantic, their time together was increasingly strained and unpleasant. Since their lives had little in common and represented strongly variant values, as did those of thousands of similarly upwardly mobile late Victorian couples, the pain is not surprising. Beecher's preaching and writing provided the spark that ignited the conflagration. He, by

---

[143]Ibid., 37.
[144]Ibid., 38.
[145]Ibid., 44–45.
[146]Ibid., 46ff.
[147]Ibid., 51–53.

this point, was preaching "passionless love," which should replace duty as the basis for marriage.[148]

The comparison of the love that was preached and believed and the reality facing the Tiltons was agonizing. She wrote Theodore at one point in 1867, "When, my sweet, will you talk to me as you write? Pretending always that you think I am the best and loveliest of little wives."[149] There was an agreement, by letter, to raise their children to revere spouse more than parents, an important culture-wide shift during this period. But the pain became inescapable after their fourth child died in 1868. Theodore blamed, Elizabeth alternately defended and grieved. Waller writes that "they had constructed a perfect, imaginary marriage, centered on one another. And yet, it was painfully obvious that every time they were together for more than a few days…the old demons reasserted themselves with excruciating regularity."[150]

Waller argues convincingly that this illusion of perfect togetherness, spouses "as sole providers of a meaningful identity," was a widespread and precarious situation. This generation, she writes, "was caught in a limbo between a time when an individual's identity was provided by the combined social institutions of the family, community, and church, and the era when identity would be found in profession or social class." This produced the "formalized but illusory romanticism of a Victorian marriage," where an apparent relational calm provided an antidote to the external insecurity and instability. But it was a calm based on mutual ignorance and relational distance, hence one with a limited life expectancy.

Beecher continued to preach the gospel of love, including a focus on the higher and lower spheres, with men still bound by rules living on the lower plane. He emphasized the difference between being legally married and spiritually mated and claimed the preeminence of the latter. Tilton picked up Beecher's rhetoric, arguing in his own writing that mutual affinity should transcend legal sanctions; when love prevailed, a marriage existed.[151] Beecher argued in an 1872 sermon, "Whoever loves rightly loves upward…and…loving that object, loves God." In the fall of 1868 the affair between Beecher and Elizabeth apparently began, ending or at least being interrupted when Elizabeth confessed to Theodore in the summer of 1870.[152] The business and ecclesiastical entanglements kept knowledge of the affair limited to Plymouth church insiders until 1872, when Victoria

---

[148]Ibid., 50.
[149]Ibid., 58.
[150]Ibid., 61–62.
[151]Ibid., 116.
[152]Ibid., 122–27.

Woodhull, an infamous advocate of free love and a friend of Theodore Tilton, publicly accused Beecher of both the affair and of failing to make his secret support of the doctrines of free love public. There ensued confessions (by Elizabeth), retractions, accusations, threats, new confessions, and finally a church trial in 1874 and a widely publicized civil trial in 1875.

Beecher was exonerated on all counts. Tilton, and Bowen, who sided with him, were financially ruined. Elizabeth, who ultimately reasserted her confession, was stripped of her membership in the church and lived the remainder of her life a poverty-stricken recluse. Beecher continued as pastor of Plymouth church until his death, but his great political influence and literary following were lost. The acquittals appear, at least to Waller, to be less a result of jurors' belief in his innocence than of their choosing to excuse his guilt, finding his adultery less damning than the disloyalty and naked ambition they attributed to Tilton and Bowen.[153] The verdict represented the height of the acceptability of romanticized personal loyalties as the governing norm of Victorian life, even as those responsible for the acquittal moved back toward more institutionally protective norms for the remainder of the century.

The Great Feminist Crusades

The battles between men and women, between social classes, and between alternate views of the family continued in the major social crusades of the last decades before the Great War: temperance, social purity, contraception, and suffrage.

As Elizabeth Tilton had discovered, and millions with her, the increased emphasis on domesticity in the mid-century middle class had increased women's dependence on men. If marriage didn't succeed, women were in a very difficult position.[154] The leading marital guidebooks of the day demanded that wives concede in all differences of opinion and prefer being at home over all options, regardless of their competence either there or elsewhere.[155] This made a woman extremely vulnerable to her husband's success or lack of it, a reality that provided significant fuel for the temperance movement and related crusades.

The temperance movement was "largely a female drive against the intemperance and irresponsibility of men, a campaign against the masculine culture that these women saw as supporting such irresponsibility," according to Barbara Epstein. It exploded into the public eye with the Woman's Crusade, a mass female assault on saloons of Ohio, Indiana, and Michigan

---

[153]Ibid., 141–45.
[154]Epstein, 67.
[155]Ibid., 78.

in 1873 and 1874, took institutional shape in the Women's Christian Temperance Union (WCTU), and had its greatest success and its greatest failure in Prohibition.

As Epstein writes, "It was men who drank and women who suffered from men's drinking."[156] She points out that most of the crusaders were Protestant and middle class and that the crusades occurred after per capita alcohol consumption had already decreased by half since the beginning of the century. These militants dramatized the child abuse and poverty created by drinking,[157] and in the process found an arena for sharing their experience of vulnerability and passivity in the face of their husbands' unpredictable socioeconomic mobility.[158] Their attacks on saloons, often quite violent, let them vent their wrath on "the symbol for the larger issue of the exclusion of women and children from men's lives," and of their dependence on men whom they could not control.[159] Women had found a way to talk about their isolation and loneliness and to take power against the institutions and men whom they held responsible for them. If evangelical religion was often a boost up the economic and class ladder, whiskey was often a fall down it; and a man's fall would take a whole family with him. This was a middle-class crusade, since it was typically the middle-class woman who had something to lose. Working-class men actively opposed the effort, and working-class women typically ignored it.

The organization of the WCTU, coupled with the emergence of women who were powerful in many church organizations, began to produce a women's culture with power to influence the broader society. Frances Willard, president of the WCTU from 1879 to 1898,[160] urged the union to take an aggressively prosuffrage stance. She also pushed the union toward an active antiprostitution campaign, seeing prostitution as another sign of an irresponsible masculine culture.[161]

Prior to mid-century, prostitution had been a small-scale and part-time activity for a few working-class women who preferred it to domestic service, but that situation changed with the combination of rapid Eastern urbanization, the Civil War, and the expanding frontier. Huge numbers of independent single men, a population this society hadn't seen before, clustered in cities, army camps, and frontier towns.[162] Prostitution as a full-time occupation surfaced in response to this available market, largely among

---

[156]Ibid., 51.
[157]Ibid., 103.
[158]Ibid., 104.
[159]Ibid., 106.
[160]Ibid., 116.
[161]Ibid., 125.
[162]D'Emilio and Freedman, *Intimate Matters,* 132–38.

women of working-class and immigrant backgrounds, and worked to re-
cruit clientele wherever demand and money coincided.

Opposition surfaced with vigor in the last decades of the century, with
former abolitionists central to its leadership. The catalyst was discussion in
several American cities about adopting European-style licensing and regulation of prostitution, and this policy became law in St. Louis in 1870.[163] It
was under serious consideration in Chicago, Washington, Philadelphia, and
New York; clergy, religious women, and former abolitionists joined against
it. Those favoring regulation cited the danger to public health and the lost
opportunity for civic revenue posed by unrestricted prostitution.[164] Social
purity was the battle cry of those opposing, committing themselves to the
attempt to eradicate this expression of sin, rather than managing it. During
the 1870s local social purity committees stopped attempts to legalize and
regulate prostitution in several major cities, coalescing around the ideal of a
new kind of man-woman relationship. Where those on the regulationist
side saw prostitution as a protection for the virtue of middle-class women
in danger from the newly liberated hordes of single men, the social purity
movement stood for a more spiritualized sexuality modeled on the moral
standards of Victorian women.

The strongest institutional expression of this crusade were the White
Cross and White Shield societies, which joined the independent social purity committees as a program wing of the WCTU in the late 1880s. YMCAs
and YWCAs were intensely involved, as were the major denominations.
Young men and women were asked to pledge themselves to a pure life,
essentially the objectives of the developing, though still fragmented, women's
movement;[165] and very much the social program of middle-class Protestant
religion.

One of the wings of the antiprostitution movement was a group of
female physicians headed by Elizabeth Blackwell, who was deeply concerned
about moral education and described a physiological basis for sin. Her book
The Moral Education of the Young aimed at inspiring the preservation of
innocence but offended so many by its frank discussion of sexual topics
that she was unable to find a commercial publisher. The women physicians
as a group challenged some ideas about sexuality widely held in the women's
movement, with Dr. Blackwell ultimately scandalizing many leaders by
publicly proclaiming that women did indeed have a sex drive.[166] This

---

[163]David Pivar, *Purity Crusade: Sexual Morality and Social Control, 1868–1900* (Westport: Greenwood Press, 1973), 52.
    [164]Ibid., 60–62.
    [165]Ibid., 114.
    [166]Ibid., 156.

outrageous challenge to Victorian reality caused a rift in the movement for a time and illustrated the power of antiphysical idealism and gender antagonism in the Gilded Age.

Obviously, the social purity movement did not eliminate prostitution, but it did have significant effects. It effectively stopped legalized and regulated prostitution, except for some isolated Western states, and obtained a few antiprostitution ordinances in Eastern cities. More substantially, it achieved age-of-consent legislation in many states. Previously, in sixteen American states[167] there had been no age at which a female could not legally have sex, and the majority of states that had legislation set the minimum at ten years of age. That had made it possible for poor parents to legally sell pre-adolescent daughters into prostitution, and there were widespread reports of twelve- to fourteen-year-olds in the prostitution ghettos around logging camps and mining towns. A measure of the power of this movement is that by 1895 every state had such a law, though in Delaware the age was still seven and in half the states the age of consent was above fourteen.

An important player in the overall attempt to purify society of male profligacy was Anthony Comstock, who was outraged over the attempt to import what he considered indecent French literature and art. He was successful in 1873 in obtaining federal legislation prohibiting use of the mails to convey discussion of sexual material or transmission of sexually explicit art and in achieving local purity legislation in several states. He was America's first politically powerful censor and understood himself to be representing Protestantism's right to purify and privatize sexual life. Probably the most damaging and revealing aspect of the Comstock Act was that it specifically designated the mailing of birth control information as a federal crime, a situation that lasted into the 1960s. This placed the Federal Government over against the birth control movement and tacitly on the side of a status quo that included secret and illegal population restriction for those who could afford it, and involuntary pregnancy, huge families, and frequent death by septic abortion for those who couldn't.

Into this combat came Margaret Sanger, the radical nurse who James Reed, the historian of American birth control, says "had a greater impact on the world than any other American woman."[168] This incredibly effective woman didn't invent contraception—it had been practiced for thousands of years—but she did lead the movement that made it widely available,

---

[167]Ibid., 141–43.
[168]James Reed, *From Private Vice to Public Virtue: The Birth Control Movement and American Society* (Princeton: Princeton University Press, 1978), 67.

legal, and morally intelligible within American society; and in the process she pounded the final nail in the coffin of the Victorian understanding of marriage and family, while providing much of the spiritual rationale for the evolution of a new theology of marriage.

Before Sanger's birth in 1879, contraception was a well-established fact of American middle-class life. American birth rates had fallen by half since 1800 and by more than that among those above the poverty level. Though some of that drop can be explained by the Victorian attempt to relegate intercourse to the times when a child was desired, more is traceable to withdrawal (practiced for centuries), douching (which has some contraceptive effectiveness, and was developed by mid-century), the pessary (a close relative to the diaphragm, in wide use by 1875), the cervical cap, and the rubber condom (animal skin condoms had been in use for centuries, but were expensive and unreliable; vulcanization produced a rubber condom that could be made widely available). American physicians, however, were not trained in contraception, medical books and marital manuals skirted the religious sensitivity on the subject, and finally the Comstock Act essentially ended public discussion on the subject for two decades. The prevailing Protestant view was that contraception was a means of circumventing the need for male sexual self-limitation and as such a sinful indulgence of unhealthy lust.

Margaret Higgins Sanger was born to a Roman Catholic mother and free-thinking Irish father, in Corning, New York, the same community where Andrew Ingersoll practiced his Presbyterian brand of sexual salvation. (There is no evidence that they ever knew of one another.) She was the sixth of eleven children. Her father's monument business was financially productive until he offended the community by organizing a local speaking opportunity for the famous atheist Robert Ingersoll. The Catholic Church owned the hall, someone barred the door, and others subsequently attacked the Higgins children in the parochial school as children of the devil.[169]

That led to Margaret's being enrolled at Claverock College,[170] a Methodist preparatory school, one of the first coeducational schools in the country. It was strongly influenced by Phoebe Palmer's Holiness movement, and though it regularly produced candidates for the Methodist ministry, it was congenial with Margaret's father's views that all religious viewpoints should be heard and examined. Margaret gave her first speech for women's rights in the college chapel and imbibed the Holiness gospel of human perfectibility and emotional power. One of the texts regularly used at Claverock

---

[169]Margaret Sanger, *My Fight for Birth Control* (Fairview Park: Maxwell Reprint, 1969. Originally copyrighted, 1931), 6–9.
[170]Gardella, 131.

was Francis Wayland's *Elements of Moral Science,*[171] in which Wayland argued that sexual pleasure was the will of God, that passion was not unnaturally strengthened by sin, and that sex was required to be enjoyed to its fullest while also being managed by conscience and self-love.[172] These views are remarkably similar to those that Sanger propounded in her adult life.

After Margaret had been at Claverock three years her mother died, having been severely weakened by eleven births and at least one miscarriage, and Margaret returned to Corning to help her father and raise her younger siblings. She left home a year later after an argument with her father and ultimately entered nursing school at White Plains. After some years in nursing and as a suburban wife and mother, Margaret and her artist husband, William Sanger, moved to New York City and involved themselves in the radical community. The combination of friends like William Haywood of the International Workers of the World, novelist Neith Boyce, and Charles Hawthorne,[173] and her daily experience of nursing among the poor of New York's Lower East Side took her established capacity for independent thought and pushed it into explicit commitment to the radicals' series of causes. She sensed the connection between the labor-management struggles of the IWW, the poverty of the immigrants, the constant pregnancy of their women, the deaths she witnessed following cheap abortions, and the pleas of these women for information about contraception.[174]

She sought to educate herself on the subject, found there was almost no publicly available information, and resolved to accompany her artist husband to France, where the discussion was more advanced. She returned in 1914 "armed with French pessaries, formulas for suppositories and douches, and new determination to defy the Comstock laws."[175] In March 1914, with the help of her radical friends, she published the first issue of *The Woman Rebel,* a magazine urging women to "raise more hell and fewer babies." The post office declared it unmailable; she evaded the prohibition by mailing it in small batches from different locations in the city and was indicted after the August issue. She quickly prepared a pamphlet on birth control, *Family Limitation,* took a train to Montreal and then a ship to Europe. From shipboard she wired her friends to release the pamphlet, which went through ten printings in a few months.[176]

---

[171]Francis Wayland, *Elements of Moral Science* (Cambridge: Harvard University Press, reprint of 1837 edition).

[172]Gardella, 131–32.

[173]Sanger, 59 ff.

[174]Ibid., 48–52.

[175]Reed, 85 ff.

[176]Ibid., 87–88.

Sanger returned to this country in 1916, opening the first American birth control clinic in Brooklyn on October 16.[177] It lasted ten days before a police raid, which resulted in thirty days in jail for her and her sister, Ethel Byrne, for violating the law forbidding giving or selling information on contraception. Shortly after the war she opened her first doctor-staffed clinic, and the publicly accessible work of the birth control movement was underway. The remainder of her life's work will be considered later in this volume.

Sanger's ideas came out of the prewar period, though many of them weren't published until the 1920s and 1930s. Her commitments included women's right to control their own bodies, their right to sexual satisfaction without the fear of pregnancy and its resulting threat to health, the right of couples to focus their child-rearing energies on a small number of highly invested children, and those same couples' right to intensify and sexualize their relationships without the fear, exploitation, and hatred that came from unwanted pregnancy.

She was practically mystical in her celebration of sexuality and its role in marriage. She spoke regularly of sex as a sacrament. Arguing against the standard belief that the purpose of the sexual act is reproduction, she said, "Sex intercourse is the greatest sacrament of life. It may be the most beautiful sacrament between two persons who have no desire for or thought of having children."[178] "All that has to do with sex is sacred, holy and reverential."[179] "Sex expression, rightly understood, is the consummation of love, its completion and its consecration."[180]

In her 1926 *Happiness in Marriage*, she specifically rejects the belief that the body is an enemy of the spirit, then argues, "More than any other bodily act, sex expression is a sacred gift which awakens men and women to the innate beauty of life."[181] She argued for the conventional premarital abstinence and counseled young women not to marry men who were not physically appealing to them. She observed that this mutual satisfaction not only deepened the marriage relationship, but "releases...those hidden vital energies that are so essential to the peace and security which create those values so essential for creature living."[182] She strayed toward an idolatry of marital love in advice like "Make the love you have found and which means so much to both of you your religion. For it can be the noblest of

---

[177]Ibid., 106.
[178]Margaret Sanger, *What Every Boy and Girl Should Know* (New York: Maxwell Reprint, 1969 reissue of 1927 edition), 78.
[179]Ibid., 12.
[180]Margaret Sanger, *Happiness in Marriage* (Garden City: Blue Ribbon Books, 1926), 19.
[181]Ibid., 20–21.
[182]Ibid., 119–20.

religions"[183] and in the process anticipated the direction of much twentieth-century thought, capturing the essence of the ideas that ended the domination of the nineteenth-century separation of sex and love.

During the years when Sanger was developing her thought, major changes were already afoot in Victorian relational life. Premarital sex and pregnancy, which had been declining from 1800 until the 1870s, began an increase in the '70s, which still continues.[184] The marriage rate increased, with the growth in number of marriages exceeding the growth of population by about one-third between 1867 and 1929.[185] People were marrying younger and younger, the average age falling from 26.1 for men and 22.0 for women in 1890 to 24.6 and 21.2 in 1920.[186] But the biggest change was the skyrocketing divorce rate, increasing from 1.3 divorces per thousand marriages in 1870 to 7.7 per thousand in 1920. These are very small numbers in comparison with those of the 1980s, but they represent the greatest acceleration of divorce rates in U.S. history to that time.

Elaine Tyler May's careful research of two samples of Los Angeles County divorcing couples, one from the 1880s and the other in 1920, and another from New Jersey in 1920, produce important insights into these changes. The occupational differences were particularly illuminating. The only group of men overrepresented in the divorcing sample from the 1880s is that of proprietors of businesses, especially smaller ones.[187] By 1920 this had changed markedly. Large proprietors' representation in the divorcing sample was the same as in the population at large, small proprietors were overrepresented by 3 to 1, and semi-skilled workers were overrepresented by a factor of 4 to 1. Significantly, the percentage of the total male work force in Los Angeles who were proprietors of their own businesses dropped during the interim from 22 percent to 8 percent.[188] May observes that this parallels a major shift in the economy. Corporations were increasing and outcompeting smaller proprietary concerns and essentially driving small artisans and merchants out of the proprietary class and into wage labor. That this population was already under severe stress in the 1880s was evident from the high divorce rates among small proprietors in that sample. But apparently some restratification had occurred by 1920, as large proprietors' divorce rates had leveled off, suggesting that those who had firmly made it into the upper levels had more comfortable lives. But the pressure

---

[183]Ibid., 225.
[184]Elaine Tyler May, *Great Expectations: Marriage and Divorce in Post-Victorian America* (Chicago: University of Chicago Press, 1980), 94.
[185]Ibid., 2.
[186]Ibid., 167.
[187]Ibid., 171.
[188]Ibid., 171, 176.

was increasing both on those who were barely holding on to their own businesses and those who had failed.[189]

This is corroborated by two additional factors: the increase in the percentage of wives who were employed over this period, and the increased number of divorces filed by wives who cited husbands' failure to provide as a major factor in their marital dissatisfaction. The proportion of working women doubled in this period, and among divorcing women the employment rate was about double that in the population as a whole. May suggests that these women were working largely because they were dissatisfied with their husbands' incomes. Of the two hundred six divorcing, employed, Los Angeles wives in 1920, ninety claimed that their husbands did not adequately provide, and thirty-seven said they were forced to go to work. In May's 1920 New Jersey sample, 66 percent of the working divorcing women said they had not wanted to go to work.[190] The picture that emerges is of a shrinking entrepreneurial class, in which small businesses often survived by use of family labor at the cost of freedom for the spouse and children and of intimacy for both. Those forced out of their own businesses often suffered significant financial setbacks, precisely at a time when consumerism was escalating. Financial ambitions were increasing, the ability of many families to meet them on one income was decreasing, but the social expectations that husbands should provide adequately had not changed. Hence wives, who outnumbered husbands as petitioners by 2 to 1, were frustrated and chose to leave their marriages in larger numbers than ever before.

May points out a number of other changes, largely based on the differing grounds for divorce across the research period. In 1880 marriage was still largely seen as a relationship based on duty and sacrifice, with the husband's responsibility being to provide food and lodging, to be content with a relatively infrequent and uninvested marital sex life, to protect his wife's chastity, and not to bring his vices home.[191] His wife's duties were similarly clear: to keep the house, be unquestionably chaste, provide a minimum of sexual satisfaction, and refrain from spending too much money. Men were allowed discreet involvement in prostitution or drinking in a largely male world of amusements, and women were to meet their social needs through church, family, and voluntary associations.

But by 1920 these responsibilities had become much less clear, and those that were clear were quite different. Suburbanization, advertising, and corporate production all posited conspicuous consumption as norms.

---

[189]Ibid., 49–51.
[190]Ibid., 120.
[191]Ibid., 47.

Feminine beauty became a much more visible standard of worth, urged on by the proliferation of the cosmetics industry. Marital relationships were increasingly expected to provide happiness, as the society increasingly proclaimed the general right to have one's wants satisfied, and particularly of relational and material ones. Hence, appearance began to show up in divorce complaints by both sexes, complaints of sexual dissatisfaction began to come from women as well as men, and women who were accused of frequenting bars and dances were not automatically assumed to be whores.

The worlds of amusement and employment were both much more open to women, though not on the same terms as men, and in ways that were often very frightening to both men and women, who could no longer control their spouses' access to the opposite sex. Women were demanding the right to have fun, though they were still only able to afford much of it if they could count on a man's financial support. Men, and to an extent women, were increasingly able to count on society's support of a right to an enjoyable marital sex life, though contraception was still largely class-bound.

The one thing that remained constant was the expectation that men would provide, but there was much less clarity about what that meant. It clearly extended beyond food and lodging now, and with the sudden increase in alimony settlements it clearly extended beyond the marriage itself, but how far and by what principle had not been established.

The marital relationship was beginning to get as much attention as was child-raising, but the ability to make marriage a more equal relationship or to envision a link between marital satisfaction and child-raising were still far in the future.

The decades before and after the turn of the century were obviously filled with explosive change for American society. Wealth was multiplying for the upper classes, national power and prestige were booming, consumerism was intensifying. Women's political agenda was becoming clearer and assuming greater power, at the same time as (and largely in response to) men's triumph over geographical and economic barriers. Class advantage was being exploited more powerfully than at any time in American history, while at the same time some of the Victorian boundaries between men and women on the one hand, and immigrants and native-born on the other, were being broken down. This was beginning to erode the apparent certainties of earlier middle-class role assignments, the structure of middle-class marriages, and the predictable course of middle-class life.

A Partial Theological Response

American theology was struggling to keep up in response to this. The pace of change was so rapid in economic, philosophical, and ecclesiastical circles that such theological writing as was done gave little attention to microeconomic realities like family. Struggles over the theories of evolution, the realities of economic change, and the growing split between fundamentalists and modernists occupied most theological energy. Yet there were some indicators, almost between the lines of these more dramatic struggles, that theology was responding to shifting concerns about the family with recognition at least, if not with creative new explorations.

Church historian Martin Marty calls Theodore Munger one of the founders of the New Theology movement.[192] Following on the pre–Civil War work of Horace Bushnell, this movement sought to unify religious thought with intellectual currents in contemporary science and philosophy. In this era that meant adopting a fairly naive social Darwinism, picking up the prevailing nineteenth-century developmental optimism, and extending it into the life of faith.

In his most ambitious theological work, *Freedom of Faith*, Munger sounds classically Victorian but offers very little directly about marriage, family, sexuality, or the other major topics of this study. He does, however, echo Bushnell in his respect for the immense power that the environment has over persons.[193] His debt to Bushnell is also evident in his discussion of the perfectibility of character, which he calls a "unique feature of the Faith."[194] He anticipates the Social Gospel's critique of the rampant individualism of this era, observing that Jesus spoke for the solidarity of the race, and in his observation that divine justice would set limits on the accumulation of wealth.[195]

His views on the family are more evident in his occasional writings. In *On the Threshold*,[196] a series of lectures to young men, he wrote some blandly class-bound advice. Character, he wrote, depends to a major extent on establishing a home of one's own, neither boarding nor renting, in which one can control one's environment—only possible to people in perhaps the upper third of the economic spectrum.[197] He assumes that all young men will, or should, marry, which is particularly valuable to them because it brings them into contact with feminine virtue, the essence of which is its ignorance of evil.[198] He urges young men to have money: "The great factor in society is money." He doesn't bring that under criticism, rather pointing out how to

---

[192]Martin Marty, *Righteous Empire: The Protestant Experience in America* (New York: Dial Press, 1970), 190.

[193]Theodore Munger, *Freedom of Faith* (Boston: Houghton-Mifflin, 1883), 202–3.

[194]Ibid., 197.

[195]Ibid., 187.

[196]Theodore Munger, *On the Threshold* (Boston Houghton-Mifflin, 1884).

[197]Ibid., 22–23.

[198]Ibid., 46.

achieve it. He calls Anglo-Saxon blood "the best in the world,"[199] because "the main quality of this blood is force." Hence, only the physically robust can succeed, and he lauds the moral value of a broad back and round chest. And he objects to popular amusements, not primarily because of their content, but because they involve mingling "socially in company that is open to all on payment of money—a doorkeeper and a ticket the only introduction and barrier."[200] The importance of the Victorian boundaries between classes and races and the identification of keeping those boundaries and Christian acceptability is unmistakable here.

In his sermons the class-blind naiveté continues, coupled with his optimism about the human project. One sermon is titled "Man the Final Form in Creation," arguing that the creation of the individual person is the objective of nature.[201] "Man is already a perfect creature—the image of God, as near and like to God as a created being can be."[202]

This untroubled optimism diminishes in the works of Washington Gladden, the first theologian clearly allied with the Social Gospel movement. Gladden, while agreeing that the production of wealth is good,[203] observes that this nation's wealth is benefiting the poor very little and concludes that "the wage-system, so long as it rests wholly on competition, is fundamentally wrong."[204] He does show noticeable ambivalence, evident in statements such as "property is the raw material for the development of character."[205] Following Hegel, he says that it is in the power to manage property that one demonstrates and develops moral strength. He criticizes much current religion, and by implication both Bushnell and Schleiermacher, by pointing out that a religion that is based on feeling (like most American revivalism) is intrinsically selfish and that its economic correlates are that "individual rights count for everything, and social obligations for little or nothing."[206]

Gladden does speak directly of the family, though in terms indistinguishable from Bushnell's. He calls the monogamous family the structural unit of society.[207] Such a family is most favorable to stability and peace, best accommodates the physical needs of children, and allows the

---

[199]Ibid., 104.

[200]Ibid., 187.

[201]Theodore Munger, *The Appeal to Life* (Boston: Houghton-Mifflin, 1887), 294.

[202]Ibid., 297.

[203]Washington Gladden, *Applied Christianity: Moral Aspects of Social Questions* (Boston: Houghton, Mifflin, 1894), 8.

[204]Ibid., 31.

[205]Washington Gladden, *Ruling Ideas of the Present Age* (Boston: Houghton, Mifflin, 1895), 77.

[206]Ibid., 65–66.

[207]Gladden, *Applied Christianity,* 187.

development of character. "It is for the cultivation of the moral qualities that fit men for association with one another that the family is indispensable."[208]

His description of family is the prelude for his sounding the alarm, since "the proportion of our population who do not live in families is steadily increasing."[209] He cites Massachusetts statistics, notably variant from the national statistics earlier presented by May, to support his argument. Perhaps New England's ratio of divorces to marriages, and of both to population growth, was much gloomier than those of states in other regions. He reasons that a smaller percentage of people living in families, and the smaller size of families, means "less discipline of the young; less self-restraint among young and old…greater exposure of the young and the weak to temptation."[210] He cites the increase in illegitimacy and blames the whole accelerating disaster on the economic system and its abuses. People can't afford decent housing or to stay together as families, which portends a decline in moral standards and a loss of both national and Christian purpose. Gladden accepts at face value the Victorian assumptions about families but differs from Munger, his older contemporary, in his unmistakable conclusion that turn-of-the-century social conditions were undermining the family's ability to be what it was created to be.

The Social Gospel movement reached its height in the immediate pre–World War I work of Walter Rauschenbusch. His powerfully written, economically sophisticated, and biblically informed work has a similar starting point to that of his predecessor Gladden, but he has seen the effects of another fifteen years of uncompromising capitalism. He is passionate and persuasive in his indictments of the early twentieth-century system and includes more previously invisible awareness of the nature of marriage and family in his arguments. They do not become central, but they do suggest that the theological community was broadening its awareness of this set of relationships.

He echoes Gladden's description of the family as the structural cell of society, calling it the "source of nearly all the real contentment among men."[211] He presents an interesting combination of Victorian and non-Victorian views. He echoes the traditional belief that the ideal spatial relationship is one family to one house,[212] repeats Gladden's concern about population loss and the absence of children, but in a radically non-Victorian

---

[208]Ibid., 190.
[209]Ibid., 192.
[210]Ibid., 193.
[211]Walter Rauschenbusch, *Christianity and the Social Crisis* (New York: Macmillan, 1910), 272.
[212]Ibid., 276.

way advocates financial and social equality in marriage.[213] There is no view here that men are intellectually, or women morally, superior; nor that it is proper that only men manage the money or only women manage the house. He also acknowledges that women have sexual desire: "The girls themselves have the womanly desire for the company and love of men."[214] And while some of his opinions are unquestionably characteristic of his social class, such as his lament that the fertility of Harvard and Yale graduates has decreased below the replacement level,[215] at other points he reveals a very non–middle-class Victorian willingness to consider the humanity of immigrants and factory workers as equal to that of bank presidents and judges.

In his 1911 book *Christianizing the Social Order* he combines very Bushnellian Victorian statements, such as "The home is God's country" and "Christianity and the home have constituted an offensive and defensive alliance," with very modern comments on marriage, such as "The natural friendship of two human beings is diversified by the play of sex difference and intensified by sexual love."[216] He places these views in close proximity to statements such as "In the home the primal sex passion is bound up with all that is noble, with loyalty, self-sacrifice, child life, common memories and hopes. Outside of the home it becomes predatory, marauding, piratical, a destroyer of existing homes instead of a builder of new homes. Unless we can give the people homes, they will have vice."[217]

He repeats the Victorian Protestant certainty that the home, especially the private, single-family home, is the bulwark of faith. But he enriches his view of the relationships that exist within that home, allowing women to be seen as sexually vital without losing virtue, seeing men and women as comparably dignified in intellect and spirit, and understanding sex as part of the God-given vitality of family life. He does not dwell on any of these arguments at great length, often stating them in passing as though they were commonly understood and needed no argument. It appears he is saving energy for his more central thesis, that all these values and hopes are in danger of being overwhelmed by the social misery that rampant capitalism is creating. That argument is forcefully stated: "If the home is the institution of love, and if love is of God, then the forces that cripple home life are an invasion of God's dominions."[218] The other possibility is that these views, hitherto absent from theology, had gained such currency in the society at

---

[213]Ibid., 248.
[214]Ibid., 278.
[215]Ibid., 275.
[216]Walter Rauschenbusch, *Christianizing the Social Order* (New York: Macmillan, 1912), 262.
[217]Ibid., 265.
[218]Ibid., 270.

large that the theological community was the last to notice. But the opposition that Sanger and the suffragists were meeting suggests that this was not the case, that Rauschenbusch was indeed on the leading edge of the society's awareness of sexuality and marital meanings, and that his early death—coupled with his urgent preoccupation with macrocosmic social injustice—deprived us of important advances that then had to wait for a less chaotic time. His peculiar blend of awarenesses—social justice, biblical rootedness, and the link of sexuality and the energy of the home—provide a precursor for the theologies of the twentieth century. But Rauschenbusch died, and a world war had to be endured and assimilated before this promise could be fulfilled.

CHAPTER 7

The Twentieth-Century Revolution

When World War I ended, an American cultural era ended with it. Continental expansion had been completed, industrial productivity had skyrocketed, American prestige was at an all-time high, immigration had slowed, and it began to be realistic to speak of a national, or at least a national urban, culture. The accelerating changes of the immediate prewar era in contraception, falling birth rates, sexual experimentation, divorce, public education, temperance, women's suffrage, and class structure were coalescing into a societal form powerfully different from that of the late nineteenth century. It was a dynamic and unstable mix, soon to pass from the Roaring Twenties into the Depression, from there to war, then to the massive postwar prosperity that spawned the Baby Boom, giving way again to the social turmoil of civil rights, Vietnam, and feminism in the 1960s and 1970s. Each of these societal undulations had powerful and different impacts on family life and thought, as did the Reagan rollback of social programs and the re-sorting of class structures in the 1980s and early to mid-1990s. Factor in the powerful emergence of gay and lesbian ideologies, the huge upsurge of women in the workplace and of single-parent families, the still mushrooming impact of the AIDS epidemic, and you have a fascinating and unpredictable background for contemporary theological thought.

Contraception and the Declining Birth Rate

American birth rates have been declining almost constantly since before 1800.[1] At the beginning of the nineteenth century American women

---

[1]Susan Householder Van Horn, *Women, Work, and Fertility, 1900–1986* (New York: New York University Press, 1988), 2.

bore one hundred eighty live infants per one thousand women aged fifteen to forty-four per year. By 1900 the rate was down to slightly over one hundred twenty, bottoming out in 1936 at just under ninety. In 1936 a gradual increase began, exploding into a boom after World War II and reaching 122.9 per thousand in 1957.[2] The largest number of babies was born in 1960, though the rates had already begun to fall,[3] the drop continuing gradually until 1965, then precipitously, reaching subreplacement levels in 1973[4] and remaining there until a modest upturn in the late 1980s and early 1990s. This had again been reversed by 1995 and 1996 with a return to the levels of 1973.[5] There were more babies born in 1990 than in any year since 1961, and the birth rates were the highest since the early 1970s. They did not, however, approach the Baby Boom level and only slightly exceeded population replacement requirements.[6]

The native-born Protestant middle class led the decline in births immediately following World War I. Fertility at that time was quite different in different sectors of the population. Urban white fertility was much lower than that of rural whites, immigrants, and blacks.[7] All rates were falling, and those of urban whites had reached between ninety-two and eighty-eight from 1875 to 1925. In 1875 immigrants and blacks were having twice as many children per adult woman, giving rise to fears of the middle class being reproductively outcompeted. Immigrants' fertility was still 30 percent higher than that of urban natives in 1925, slightly exceeded by that of blacks and rural whites. In the Eastern cities in 1920, over 40 percent of couples who had completed their families had two or fewer children. This was long before many prosperous married women were working outside the home and during a period when per capita income was rapidly increasing.[8] It appears to have been a response to a decline in death rates, the closing of the frontier, and the emerging preference of middle-class couples for a style of marriage in which child-rearing was not the central satisfaction.

The availability of contraception enabled this decline. Eighty-eight percent of Kinsey's sample of women born before 1899 reported using some form of family planning. These were women who finished their peak childbearing years before 1930.[9] The diaphragm, which Margaret Sanger and

²Ibid., 85.
³Ibid., 150.
⁴Victor R. Fuchs, *Women's Quest for Economic Equality* (Cambridge: Harvard University Press, 1988), 1.
⁵*Family Therapy News*, May–June 1989, April 1991, June, 1991.
⁶*Family Therapy News*, December 1991.
⁷Van Horn, 15.
⁸Ibid., 35–36.
⁹Reed, 124.

her followers had made widely accessible, was their major technological aid. It was used frequently by 24 percent. Condoms were used by 36 percent, with the traditional methods of douching and withdrawal at 24 percent and 23 percent. Kinsey's figures were probably somewhat skewed, due to a bias toward college-educated Protestant women. Prior to 1925 diaphragms had to be smuggled into this country from Europe. Arrests were common. But in 1925 Sanger's second husband, J. Noah Slee, financed the company that started manufacturing diaphragms domestically.[10]

Poor women continued to have less access to contraception. The Clinical Research Bureau, Sanger's agency for contraceptive research, reported that working-class women knew less about contraception than the rest of the population did and were more likely to use withdrawal or periodic abstinence.[11] The famed Middletown study also documented the class difference in contraceptive usage: The Lynds reported that all the business-class wives in their sample used birth control in some form, while only thirty-four of seventy-seven working-class wives used any, and almost half of that thirty-four used methods with little reliability.[12] Twenty percent of the working-class women were unaware of any means to control their fertility. Working-class women were more likely to be immigrants and Catholic, so their higher birth rates over the next twenty years were predictable.

With the crushing impact of the Depression, fertility patterns changed again. Child labor laws had removed the economic incentive for urban families to have children,[13] and the deepening unemployment made children an expensive luxury. By 1936 one quarter of the work force was unemployed, and that same year the birth rate dropped to 75.3 per thousand women,[14] the lowest to that point in American history (again reached and surpassed in 1978). Young people in that decade, those most seriously impacted by joblessness, produced fewer children than any group in modern times. Gallup Polls indicated that people were having fewer children than they wanted to have, and for a brief period the declines were most severe among the poor. Only the prosperous could afford children. For the poor, marriage was delayed and childless periods after marriage lasted longer than in any previous epoch.

Another significant shift was that differential fertility diminished as 1940 approached. All groups in the population moved toward the previous

---

[10]Ibid., 114.

[11]D'Emilio and Freedman, *Intimate Matters*, 246.

[12]Robert S. Lynd and Helen Merrell Lynd, *Middletown: A Study in Contemporary American Culture* (New York: Harcourt, Brace, and Company, 1929), 123.

[13]Van Horn, 34.

[14]Ibid., 33.

middle-class standard of two children per family. Urbanization has always brought fertility down, and urbanization plus poverty reduced the differences between Protestant and Catholic, native born and immigrant—though immigration had significantly decreased by this time.

As income inched up after 1936, fertility followed. Women of all income and education levels, of all ethnic groups, participated in a twenty-two-year rise in reproductive rates. Practically all important demographic variables shifted. The marriage age fell, and the marriage rate increased.[15] Size of families grew, with more third and fourth children being born in 1957 than any other year this century.[16] Contraception was still being used, so the five- to ten-child families common a century earlier did not return. Further, the spacing of children was different from that of noncontraceptive societies. In the previous century women had borne children every two years until menopause to achieve very large families, but during the Baby Boom child spacing was intensified, children being born much closer together than could have occurred in a society where breast-feeding and sexual continence during lactation were practiced. It was a period of very close spacing of births, very young women having many children in a few years, focusing intensely on mothering for a decade or more, but ending their child-bearing careers by the age of thirty. These same women largely avoided paid work while their children were young but started the move into the work force after they had raised their families. And their children, the famous Baby Boomers, have had even fewer children per capita than their Depression-era grandparents.

The birth rates turned downward in 1960, though more babies were born that year than any year in American history.[17] The shift in birth rates coincided with the Food and Drug Administration's 1960 approval of Enovid, the first oral contraceptive,[18] following a thirty-plus–year research effort spearheaded by Sanger's connections. Her associates funded much of the work of Gregory Pincus, who ultimately produced the pill for Searle Corporation.[19] By 1970, 58 percent of married couples reported using either the pill, the intrauterine device, or sterilization for birth control. All were newly available in the previous twenty years.[20] Fertility rates of all population groups had converged by 1970, with even 68 percent of Roman Catholics reporting the use of artificial birth control.[21] By 1996 white

[15]Ibid., 89.
[16]Ibid., 90.
[17]Ibid., 150.
[18]Reed, 364.
[19]Ibid., 322–40.
[20]D'Emilio and Freedman, 251.
[21]Ibid., 252.

fertility rates lagged behind African American and and other non-Caucasian groups by about 10 percent.

The shrinking of families and decline of fertility continued for more than twenty uninterrupted years, reversing and undoing many of the trends of the 1940s and 1950s. Between 1960 and 1980 the marriage rate itself dropped by fully one quarter, and the median first marriage age for both men and women increased by about two years.[22] By 1995 the average marital age for American men was over twenty-six years, for women over twenty-four. Those who were married were delaying childbearing, with more than a quarter of married women in their late twenties remaining childless in 1980.[23] In that year more than half of American households had no children at all. By the mid-1980s there were almost twice as many house pets in America as children under age eighteen.[24]

There had been major increases in the financial costs of child-rearing with the inflation of the 1970s,[25] but a major change in tastes had already affected the desire for children. A group surveyed while still childless in 1961 had indicated preference for fewer children than their parents had had, and by 1977 this group had actually produced 27 percent fewer children than they had earlier indicated they wanted. Rising costs may have further diminished their eagerness for children. Unemployment was higher for young couples in the 1970s than it had previously been, partially a result of the huge number of people seeking to enter the labor force at the same time.

Birth rates continued to fall through most of the 1980s,[26] possibly in response to the continued economic difficulties of young families. The real mean earnings of men twenty to twenty-four years of age, a figure that always correlates strongly with marriages and births, were one-quarter lower in 1986 than in 1973. Real median income of families headed by men in that age group fell 27 percent in that period, home ownership among married household heads under twenty-five fell 10 percent during those years, and the proportion of twenty to twenty-four-year-old males able to support a family of three above the poverty level dropped by almost a quarter. Poverty rates among African American males were more than double those of whites.[27] There was a roughly 10 percent gain (in constant dollars) for African American median household income between 1986 and 1997, while

---

[22]Ibid., 330.

[23]Ibid., 331.

[24]Fuchs, *Women's Quest,* 102.

[25]Van Horn, 161.

[26]Dana Vannoy-Hiller, and William W. Philliber, *Equal Partners: Successful Women in Marriage* (Newbury Park: Sage, 1989), 51.

[27]*Family Therapy News,* January/February 1989.

the white median remained almost constant over that ten-year period. This suggests that the substantial per capita income gains of the early and middle 1980s were disproportionately limited to workers born in the early Baby Boom, and that maintenance of middle-class status was much more difficult for those born at the end of the Baby Boom than it had been previously.

By 1988 birth rates had begun an upturn that was sustained into the early 1990s before leveling off.[28] More babies were born in 1991 than any year since 1970, but that figure has dropped slightly in subsequent years. Speculation about the reasons has centered on the postponing of births that would have been expected in the early and mid-1980s if economic conditions had been better, or if marriage ages had been as low as during earlier decades. Further, the supply of young adults is thinning out, so competition for positions in the labor force is not as intense as a decade earlier. Employed young adults are more likely to marry and have children, but this slightly higher birth rate is being produced by a smaller population of childbearing age, so the total number of babies born is not reaching earlier levels.

Marriage rates have also gone back up, after a period of decline beginning in the early 1970s. There were more marriages in 1984 than there had been for two decades.[29] The rate fell again in 1985 but was gradually increasing again by the end of the decade and has maintained that increase into the 1990s as well. It peaked in 1992 and has declined slightly since.

Though a hundred years ago a large segment of the society would have said that the purpose of marriage was primarily to have children, the bearing and raising of children has occupied less of American families' energy and financial resources in the last half century than at any time since the colonial period. Though the birth rate has stopped sliding, there is no hint of a return to the family sizes of the Baby Boom generation, let alone those of a precontraceptive America. The meaning and purpose of marriage have clearly changed. The rest of this chapter will be devoted to exploring other aspects of the shift and attempting to locate the new center of motivation to form families.

Women in the Work Force

American women, like women the world over, have always worked. In agricultural societies, including the early United States, women shared management, grew and preserved vegetables, spun yarn and sewed clothes,

---

[28] *Family Therapy News,* May/June 1989; December 1991.
[29] *Family Therapy News,* July/August 1988.

helped with harvesting, and cared for animals. In early American cities, as in most third world cities today, there was little separation between home and shop, production and sale. All family members were typically involved in all aspects of the family's economic life. The husband may have made the shoes or sold the harnesses, but at the same time he might be supervising a child; and his wife would typically be negotiating with a supplier, bringing materials to his work area, keeping the fire burning, and watching the stew out of the corner of her eye.

As indicated in the previous chapter, these patterns changed with the Industrial Revolution of the late eighteenth and early nineteenth centuries. Work locations typically moved a distance from homes. Cottage industries were outcompeted by mass production, farms increasingly counted on cash commodities and less on small-scale kitchen gardens and egg production, and men's and women's lives were increasingly lived in separate spheres. Young single women began taking factory jobs, children's work supplemented family incomes, and economically marginal married women took in boarders, did laundry, and cleaned houses to keep their families out of poverty. But the leisure of wives was a commodity for conspicuous consumption, so families who could afford it kept wives home tending the class boundaries between themselves and those women who had to work. With few labor-saving devices available, and little public education, even with the shrinking families of the nineteenth-century middle class, there was plenty for women to do.

In 1880, women had made up 14.7 percent of the work force. By 1920 the figure was 18.8 percent, but again the increase was primarily among single women.[30] Nine percent of married women were working outside the home. Most of their jobs involved providing the care and oversight of persons and property consistent with women's domestic role and were typically sought only by married women whose husbands were disabled, absent, or impoverished.[31] There were strong ideological barriers against women working if they had a choice. Those married women who did industrial work clustered in the cigar factories and textile mills, for very low wages. There was also a smattering of professional women, physicians, professors, and so on. Almost no women worked in the middle occupational levels, though the skills required for these levels were often used in a myriad of volunteer activities.[32]

The impact of these factors was intensified by huge increases in life span and major decreases in other claims on women's time. For women, life

---

[30]Van Horn, 24.
[31]Ibid., 26.
[32]Ibid., 26–27.

expectancy rose from 48.3 years in 1900 to 65.2 years in 1940 (it remained about two years lower for men throughout this period).[33] As obstetrical conditions improved and women bore fewer children, their exposure to the risks of childbirth diminished; and as children more often survived infancy, child-rearing became less an anxious attempt to prevent death and more an investment in the individual development of each child. But since children were absent at school much of the time, the total time consumed by their care was going down. Further, as more foods and household appliances were industrially produced and as advertising created a perceived need for them, the social prestige of women's domestic production dropped. Women's time at home was less full, but in 1940 there were still few paid outlets for it. There had been small increases in women's employment during the 1920s, especially in mid-level sales and clerical jobs, but that was reversed during the Depression, during which women were often fired so a man, who "needed it more," could have the job.[34]

By 1940, 36 percent of workers were women, with the increase over the 1920 figures occurring largely among married women,[35] primarily those whose children were grown—an effect of the lengthening life span. Six million additional women joined the work force during World War II, and women over forty constituted half the total of employed persons in 1943. Young married women continued to stay home. With the unavailability of young men, a wide range of occupations were opened to women. By 1945, 22 percent of the workers in heavy industry were female, up from 9 percent in 1939.[36]

In 1946 there was a huge surge in marriages (and divorces) and a mass exodus of young women from industry. But the middle-aged were protected by union membership and seniority rules, and in large measure they remained at work, though they were often demoted. Other changes were more lasting. Women were being employed in sales positions, their numbers in those jobs increasing from 25 percent in 1940 to 40 percent in 1947. The number of women dentists doubled in the 1940s. Women engineers increased sixfold.[37] Greater diversification in professional employment occurred, with the percentage of professional women who were teachers or nurses declining from 70 percent to 65 percent during the 1940s. Yet men's participation in professional groups increased even more, so the percentage of women in male-dominated professions declined until 1960.

---

[33]Ibid., 46.
[34]Ibid., 63.
[35]Ibid., 59.
[36]Ibid., 140–42.
[37]Ibid., 128.

Another important shift during the years of escalating birth rates was the economic level of working women. Prior to World War II, married women whose husbands had good incomes rarely worked. But by 1960 the likelihood of a married woman's working was completely independent of her husband's income, following a progressive decline in the historically inverse relationship between husband's income and work force participation.[38] The factor that most strongly influenced the likelihood of a married woman's working was participation in child-rearing. The highest entry rates were for women over fifty and for younger married women who had not yet begun having children.[39]

By 1960 the older Baby Boom families were raised and most of the younger ones were already born. One in three married women was working already,[40] and the total number of women working would double in the next twenty years.[41] By 1980, 65 percent of married women in their prime child-bearing years, twenty-five to thirty-four, were employed,[42] exceeding for the first time the work rates of those over forty.

Economic reasons for this explosion of women workers are hard to find. Women's wages did not keep pace with men's.[43] Women workers were often channeled into uninteresting and unpromising jobs, with little chance for advancement or challenge. Absolute economic need cannot be claimed, since the average husband's real income was higher in 1987 than in 1960.[44] A new stratification of age and class levels appears to be involved. Between 1968 and 1987 the average husband's real income was increasing, but during the same period the average twenty-five to thirty-four-year-old husband was experiencing a 13 percent drop in real income.[45] Older married men were able to provide more than the previous generation, while younger married men could not do as much. Younger married women were under real economic pressure to help provide, though that wasn't the case for their older sisters.

Other factors must also be explored. First, with the profusion of consumer goods and the proliferation of advertising, couples were increasingly presented with the opportunity to own and enjoy products that hadn't existed in their parents' generation. To be without central air conditioning, home computers, or microwave ovens was not a mark of low social status in

---

[38]Ibid., 132–33.
[39]Ibid., 134.
[40]Ibid., 124.
[41]Ibid., 166.
[42]Ibid., 167.
[43]Fuchs, *Women's Quest*, 3.
[44]Ibid., 11.
[45]Ibid., 100.

1960. To be without them in the mid-'90s raised questions about one's financial success, though they were by no means necessary for life. The inflation of the 1970s meant that two incomes were required for young families to continue increasing real income.[46] The combination of the availability of new goods that made life easier or more enjoyable, with the decreased earning power of husbands' incomes, lured many women into the work force. This was especially the case among young families in the white-collar sector, where incomes rose more slowly than among blue-collar and upper-management workers.

A second factor, as we will see below, was the doubling of the divorce rate within twenty years. Women who thought a 1960 marriage to an affluent husband made them financially secure for life were nervously aware by 1980 that their lack of marketable skills made them vulnerable to a catastrophic drop in their standard of living.[47] They needed an established skill level and record of productive work.

Third, housework is not fun. To quote Rebecca West, "The great enemy of feminism is that men don't like housework and women don't like housework."[48] Not only don't they like it, but a constant diet of it makes them sick. As Jessie Bernard has written in one of the classics of modern sociology and the feminist movement, "Housework is a dead-end job; there is no chance of promotion. One cannot grow in it…Not only does the wife not grow, but the nonspecialized and detailed nature of housework may have a deteriorating effect on her mind."[49] Bernard documents with stunning thoroughness that marriage is much better for the health of men than for that of women and that marriage is much worse for the health of women who do not work outside the home than for those who do. The isolation and lack of intellectual stimulation in the housewife role produced an increase in eleven of the twelve psychological symptoms she studied, when compared with married women who worked outside the home and with single women. Though it may be convenient to have the extra money, it is lifesaving to have something to do with other people, something that makes a discernible contribution and requires some exercise of the mind.

Accordingly, by 1985 over half of the married mothers of children under six in this country were working outside the home. By 1996 these percentages had increased further. Clearly the home as a haven and sanctuary, the place that women longed to keep safe from the encroachment of

---

[46]Ibid., 173.

[47]Ruth Sidel, *Women and Children Last: The Plight of Poor Women in Affluent America* (New York: Penguin Press, 1986), 16–20.

[48]Fuchs, *Women's Quest*, 74.

[49]Jessie Bernard, *The Future of Marriage* (New Haven: Yale University Press, 1982), 44.

outsiders, had lost much of its allure.[50] Van Horn argues that this is a response to the removal of meaningful work from the home and women's demand to have something useful to do with the hours not required by direct, hands-on child-rearing. Even child-rearing had lost some of its satisfaction, since television had made it impossible to shield children from knowledge of the outside world, and made it unnecessary for parents to carry as high a proportion of the child's education about that world. By the 1970s research results consistently showed that parents were happier with their lives when they had fewer children. Parental satisfaction dropped with each additional child.[51]

Both Van Horn and Fuchs observe, however, that women have not rejected the importance of the home. They continue to spend, on average, twice the time their husbands do in its care and cleaning, so that their total (paid and unpaid) work requirements have risen about 20 percent in twenty years, while their husbands' time has diminished by about the same amount.[52] That suggests a huge investment in creating a domestic environment, though a domestic environment different from their mothers'.

In half of American marriages in 1986, both spouses worked outside the home, a figure that has continued to increase. Increasingly, professional and other high-status men are marrying women in similarly high-status jobs.[53] As the proportion of service or information-related jobs increases, requiring intellectual and emotional dexterity more than physical strength, women increasingly have access to a wider spectrum of well-paid work.[54] It is increasingly possible for a person of either sex to be economically independent. Fuchs's research has demonstrated that young, well-educated single women have begun to show major economic gains relative to men,[55] and as these women marry, they appear to be avoiding some of the economic pitfalls that have historically kept the wage differential so wide—failure to get advanced professional education, dropping out of the workforce for years, working part-time, and so forth. As women delay childbearing, and they are doing that, their power to influence the shape of their marriages increases,[56] as does their overall power vis-à-vis men.

Yet another problem surfaces. The more educated a woman is, the more income she makes, the less likely she is to marry, and if married, the more

---

[50]Van Horn, 187–90.
[51]Ibid., 192.
[52]Fuchs, *Women's Quest,* 76–78.
[53]Ibid., 16.
[54]Ibid., 48.
[55]Fuchs, *Women's Quest,* 76.
[56]Vannoy-Hiller and Philliber, 52.

likely she is to divorce.[57] The suggestion is that these healthier, less isolated, more interesting women are less willing to accept marriages to men with traditional role expectations and highly competitive orientations. To fully understand this development we must explore the mushrooming of (now receding) divorce rates and the role of marriage in the lives of women and men.

The Divorce Explosion

After rising gradually since the founding of the republic, then rising abruptly after World War II, divorce rates in this country fell between 1950 and 1968. But as Van Horn points out, when the large families (always a predictor of marital dissatisfaction) of the Baby Boom generation reached adolescence, the divorce rate began to climb. It doubled between 1965 and 1975, then grew more slowly and reached an all-time high of 22.8 divorces per thousand married women in 1979. Between 1960 and 1980 the number of divorced Americans increased by 200 percent.[58] The rate itself has declined very slowly ever since,[59] reaching the levels that had been passed in 1975 by 1988,[60] dropping 10 percent between 1980 and 1989. The 1996 rates were the lowest since 1970.[61]

The change in the likelihood of divorce was most marked between the group of women born 1941–1945 and those born the following five years. By age thirty-nine more than 30 percent of the latter group had been divorced, a jump of almost 10 percent from the 1941–45 group. The 1951–55 cohort showed a smaller jump, and the 1956–60 group, after showing a substantial increase in its younger years, had almost merged with the rates of the 1951–55 group by the age of thirty. Another change brought on by this upheaval is the point in marriage at which divorce most often occurs. In the 1960s the average duration of a marriage ended by divorce was about three years, whereas it had risen to 7.1 years by 1988. This may reflect the tendency to delay childbearing, as well as the greater likelihood that a woman who marries will continue working, thus diminishing the disorientation that comes from too many massive life changes at one time.

So the first answer to the question, "Who gets divorced?" is that the Baby Boom generation does, at a far higher rate than any previous one. The divorce rates rose for Baby Boom women as adults at almost the same rate as the birth rate had for them as infants. To say it differently, the peak in

---

[57]Ibid., 133.
[58]D'Emilio and Freedman, 331.
[59]Fuchs, *Women's Quest,* 18.
[60]*Family Therapy News,* August 1991.
[61]*World Almanac,* 1995.

divorce rates (1980) came almost precisely twenty years after the peak in birth rates. It appears that the same youngsters who grew up in families with three to five siblings in the late 1940s and early 1950s, when their mothers were generally at home with them and experiencing the marital frustrations of large families, are those who were marrying later, having fewer children, and divorcing more often in the 1970s and 1980s. They were also the young people who encountered the glutted labor market during the inflation of the 1970s and who suffered the lower real incomes of young wage-earners in the 1980s.

This squares with the long-established finding that men in lower occupational levels are more likely to divorce than higher-status men.[62] Though this differential diminished during the last two decades, laborers are still three times as likely to divorce as are professional or business people. Even that figure probably understates the reality because of the greater prevalence of desertion and unofficial separation among those with little property. Higher-income men have divorced more frequently since 1960 than before, but not nearly enough to close the gap. Among women the figures are less clear. If a woman does not work outside the home, her chances for divorce decrease as her family's income rises. On the other hand, if she does work for pay, her likelihood of divorce increases as personal income grows, though again that gap is diminishing in more recent decades.[63]

Further demographic variables are important. Urban people are more likely to divorce than rural ones, though that may reflect a tendency of maritally unhappy persons to move to the city before a separation. Westerners, especially Californians, are more likely to divorce than easterners. On the other hand, Roman Catholics are no less likely to divorce than are Protestants, and regular church attenders are reported as only slightly less likely to divorce than nonattenders.[64] Childless couples have a higher divorce rate than those with children,[65] though childless couples also report a higher rate of marital satisfaction. Apparently many unhappy couples do stay together to provide a home for children. Finally, those who marry in their teens are much more likely to divorce, by a factor of two to four times, than those who marry in their twenties.[66] And the divorce rate declines gradually with age, with no sharp drop-off at any point.[67] Thousands of people in their later sixties divorce every year.

---

[62]Morton Hunt and Bernice Hunt, *The Divorce Experience* (New York: McGraw-Hill, 1977), 15.
[63]Ibid., 16.
[64]Ibid.
[65]Ibid., 17.
[66]Ibid., 19.
[67]Ibid., 14.

The impact on those who divorce is massive. It creates, among other things, huge financial dislocation. One oft-cited California study reports that in the first year after a divorce the average woman's income declines by 73 percent, while the average man's increases by 42 percent.[68] Reports indicate that no more than half of court-ordered child support is actually paid.[69] Only one noncustodial parent in five pays all that is ordered throughout the minority of his or her child. As a result, the disorienting stress level for single parents, usually mothers, is intensified by financial uncertainty.

The period immediately after the separation is typically a chaotic one for both partners. There is an upsurge of rage, and couples that have never been violent with each other often lash out physically, especially in the presence of children.[70] There are at least three powerful contributors to this upheaval. The first is the very common experience that money is short, that new patterns for using it have to be learned, and that each partner is perceived as depriving the other of funds needed to handle a flood of transitional expenses: lawyers, apartment deposits, child care payments, and so forth.

Second is the blow to self-esteem, particularly in the sexual area. Often the fears and hopes about continuing sexual attractiveness produce experimentation with new partners, which foments outrage and woundedness on the part of the ex-spouse. Further, marriage itself, even a painful marriage, contributes to the regulation of emotional life. When its structuring influence disappears, there are fewer secure points of reference to determine behavior, fewer automatic limitations or opportunities provided by the presence of the other.

Family boundaries are more porous during this stage, as one partner leaves and some of the space is taken up by friends, relatives, new lovers, and new child-care workers. Often a previously unemployed wife and mother leaves the home for work. Many families will be forced to move at least once. It's a very difficult time for the adults and a dangerous one for children.

Wallerstein and Blakeslee report that it takes the average man two to two and one-half years to establish a sense of external order after a marital separation, and the average woman a year longer.[71] At the five-year mark, half the men and one-third of the women report that their lives are less enjoyable than before the divorce.[72] Since women more often seek the

[68]Lenore J. Weitzman, "The Economics of Divorce: Social and Economic Consequences of Property, Alimony and Child Support Awards," *UCLA Law Review*, no. 28, November 1981.

[69]Hunt and Hunt, 164.

[70]Ibid., 8.

[71]Judith Wallerstein and Sandra Blakeslee, *Second Chances: Men, Women and Children a Decade after Divorce* (New York: Ticknor and Fields, 1989), xii.

[72]Ibid., 17.

divorce, it would appear that a significant majority of those most dissatisfied with the marriage are satisfied with the divorce, but for the non-initiating spouse there is a strong residue of bitterness and unhappiness. Ten years after the divorce half of the women and a third of the men report still being intensely angry at their former spouses,[73] suggesting that many who are satisfied with the present are still angry about the past.

Men remarry more quickly, on average, by a difference of about a year, and more men do remarry.[74] Women typically wait longer, with the odds against a custodial woman's remarrying increasing with each child and with each additional year of her age. The more income and education a divorcing man has, the more likely he is to remarry. The more income and education a divorcing woman has, the less likely she is to remarry.[75] Second marriages have a somewhat higher divorce rate than first marriages, and each subsequent remarriage has an even greater probability of ending in divorce. Problems dealing with step-parenting are most often cited as the cause.

With divorce such a painful and disorienting trauma, what accounts for its upsurge in the 1970s and 1980s? A key influence is that isolated by Vannoy-Hiller and Philliber: "In today's marriages husbands and wives are not bound to each other by strong exchange relationships; each is capable of providing or securing basic goals and services without the other. The important element is emotional gratification, and emotional gratification depends on the quality of the interaction."[76] Because it is possible for women to be economically independent, even though at a more marginal and less rewarding level, they can now insist that the quality of their relationships be gratifying enough to outweigh the costs.

But why are marriages so often not gratifying and why in the particular decades we have noted? A possible explanation lies in the spacing of the generations. As we have seen, the post-1968 upsurge in divorce only intensified two centuries of increase that had been interrupted by the remarkable anomaly of the postwar orgy of domesticity. In that celebration, young women reverted to a homebound status and a focus on mothering multiple children on a scale that the society had never seen. And as Bernard, Friedan, Van Horn, and others have pointed out, it was dangerously toxic for many of them. Friedan's chapter in *The Feminine Mystique* "Housewifery Expands to Fill the Time Available" dramatized the makework nature of this domestic

---

[73]Ibid., 29.

[74]Marilyn Ihinger-Tallman and Kay Pasley, "Divorce and Remarriage in the American Family: A Historical Review," in Pasley and Ihinger-Tallman, *Remarriage and Step-parenting: Current Research and Theory* (New York: Guilford Press, 1987), 11.

[75]Ibid., 12.

[76]Vannoy-Hiller and Philliber, 87.

activity. Household appliances had increased women's efficiency, so an advertising blitz was necessary to convince them to greatly raise the standards of homemaking.[77] Sheets suddenly needed to be ironed, shirts shed their detachable cuffs and collars and had to be washed after every wearing, germs had to be rooted out of lairs in which they had been previously undisturbed. All these changes were occurring while formerly indispensable female domestic activities were being absorbed into the marketplace—making soap, preparing food, sewing—and the time requirements of others were shrinking due to dependable refrigeration, plumbing, and electricity. As Van Horn points out, women had always had economically necessary roles, but during the Baby Boom years these roles were vanishing, and artificial ones were being made socially mandatory.

In response they had more babies, more symptoms, and more dissatisfaction. They turned to the children they were raising for a disproportionate share of their personal meaning, their husbands being absorbed in very separate occupational spheres. Their homes could only occupy a limited share of their creative energies. They were bored. My contention is that their children, the Baby Boomers, sensed the emptiness these isolated parents had conceived them to remedy, resolved en masse to reject that model of life, but learned little of the skills required to erect a new one. Simultaneously, by their sheer numbers they created an economic disaster for each other, so that their young adulthood was marred both by the horror and disillusionment of Vietnam and the "stagflation" of the 1970s economy. They refused the only model of marriage they knew how to create; they lacked the skills and attitudes to create a new one; and they faced political and economic obstacles that made supporting a family more difficult and marital stress inevitable. They responded by delaying marriage, avoiding childbirth, and divorcing each other in record numbers. Their pain constituted a challenge to the existing understanding of the roles of marriage and child-rearing in American life, a challenge that is beginning to produce revolutionary and revelatory change.

The Changing Nature and Purpose of Marriage

Marriage has fulfilled multiple purposes in American history. In the early years it peopled a continent, provided a religiously sanctioned setting for sexuality, and created the goods and services its partners and children needed to survive. In the nation's adolescence it stabilized class boundaries, domesticated, evangelized, and sobered up a boisterous frontier, and taught

---

[77]Marcia Lynn Whicker and Jennie Jacobs Kronenfeld, *Sex Role Changes: Technology, Politics, and Policy* (New York: Praeger, 1986), 87–100.

the young to be decorous, competitive, and loyal. More recently it has become the bearer of romantic hopes for emotional fulfillment, the center of consumption, and a major problem for the culture. What is it trying to become? Is God seeking to lead us somewhere through the transformation of this institution?

The struggle over the institution's postpatriarchal shape was under way publicly before the Depression. A remarkable 1927 book by Denver judge Ben Lindsey argued for a new set of marriage structures and proposed revolutionary ideas concerning what marriage was about.[78] He suggested there be two legal forms of marriage, the first called *Companionate Marriage,* childless, requiring birth control (illegal then in most states), and permitting divorce by mutual consent. The other form, which he called *Family Marriage,* would only be available to couples who had been together in Companionate Marriage for a period of years, had the financial resources to support children, and would commit themselves to a union much more difficult to end.

The judge reaped a firestorm of controversy, much of it from the church community, which he held responsible for producing marriages destined to end in divorce.[79] He assailed the linking of sexual impulse and sin, the demand that sex only take place in marriage, and the importance that this very restriction gave to sex in the church's view of matrimony. He sounds much like John Milton almost three hundred years earlier. For both, the core of marriage was spiritual, not sexual; and for both, affection and sex were crucial in developing that spiritual closeness.

"Sex is a spiritual thing," Lindsey wrote.[80] "Sex is a hunger, a spiritual hunger, healthful to feel and healthful to gratify. It is simply idiotic for society not to recognize this and provide adequate social regulations for its healthful, fearless, unashamed expression. We have, in many quarters, the orgy of sex that these Puritans fear; and they are the people who have created it. What I want to do is to end it."[81]

Lindsey was a strong advocate of monogamy and argued that it is the natural condition that most humans seek. His proposal was an attempt to make divorce in Family Marriage less probable by legitimizing other sexual outlets than procreative marriage. "I am for monogamy and against divorce," he wrote,[82] explaining that divorce is a great social evil.

---

[78]Ben B. Lindsey and Wainwright Evans, *The Companionate Marriage* (New York: Boni and Liveright, 1927).
[79]Ibid., 274.
[80]Ibid., 156.
[81]Ibid.
[82]Ibid., 267.

Marriage, properly undertaken, is a vital good for the society, Lindsey held. "It has value, constructive and creative value, in people's lives, even when it is not, superficially speaking, a success."[83] It creates a community of interest, a "spiritual profit," a discipline that makes it valuable even if it doesn't bring happiness.

> Marriage, in short, is beneficial and profitable and of supreme importance because it is difficult, because it is a creative art, because it is not primarily happy, and because it calls upon every nerve and sinew of the soul for the utmost effort and fidelity of function if genuine happiness is to be created out of the stubborn stuff of human nature male and female.[84]

He goes on to say that "in marriage two lives unite themselves to the creation…of a new spiritual reality, which grows from that union as a child grows from the union of two cells."[85]

Though he had a hearty respect for the pleasures of sex, he claimed that we endanger marriage when we give sex the central position in it. We perpetuate the fiction that sexual attraction is enough to sustain marriage and the parallel fiction that sexual attraction for another is enough to dissolve it. He emphasized spiritual fidelity and monogamy, arguing that they are much more important than—and not always identical with—physical fidelity, and that dissolution of a marriage on the basis of a physical act is foolish and immoral. Divorce, he argued, "is a crippling; it is transplantation; it delays growth, and may kill the plant."[86] Marriage requires a lifetime to do its work, and it should require a spiritual, not merely a physical defection, to abort it.

Many of Lindsey's arguments are consonant with Sanger's praise for the sacredness of sex and the spirituality of marriage, which both considered dependent on reliable birth control and woman's control of her body. Lindsay alluded to the importance of such unions in the raising of children, though he didn't treat the link in detail.

He did argue for the equality of men and women in marriage but did not discuss the economic and social factors blocking the creation of equal marriages. Serious attention to those issues awaited the passing of Depression and war and the emergence of the women's liberation movement in the late 1960s and early 1970s.

---

[83]Ibid., 271.
[84]Ibid.
[85]Ibid., 272.
[86]Ibid., 274.

Jessie Bernard's research into the effects of marriage around 1970 was the next pivotal contribution. She established that marriage, at least the marriage of the late 1960s, functioned differently for, and had different effects on, men and women. For men it was a very effective protective institution. "There are few findings more consistent, less equivocal, more convincing than the sometimes spectacular and always impressive superiority on almost every index—demographic, psychological, or social—of married over never-married men." [87] Married men live longer, have better physical and mental health, make more money, commit fewer suicides and fewer crimes. She cites Paul Glick's demographic findings: "Most men profit greatly from having a wife to help them to take care of their health." When men lose their wives, they remarry quickly. If they don't, their mortality skyrockets.[88] Twice as many married as never-married men reported themselves as very happy.[89] Bernard reasons that when the marriage rate goes up, men less and less qualified for marriage are being recruited into the institution of marriage. This is a factor in the elevated divorce rates of the '70s and '80s, following a period of unprecedentedly high marital rates.

The protective effect of marriage, however, does not extend to women. "More wives than husbands report marital frustration and dissatisfaction, more report negative feelings; more wives than husbands report marital problems; more wives than husbands consider their marriages unhappy, have considered separation or divorce, have regretted their marriages, and fewer report positive companionship."[90] Married women, furthermore, showed more mental health symptoms than unmarried women, commit more crimes, and have less of a life expectancy advantage over men than do single women.

Single women are radically healthier than single men. Far more healthy and successful women remain single than healthy successful men. Hence, when marriage rates increase, they increase by luring the cream of the female crop into the marriage market to meet the bottom of the male barrel. And those rates increased to such levels in the 1950s and 1960s that there were essentially no qualifications one had to meet to be able to marry, especially for men.[91] As Bernard has suggested, "Marriage is a cheap way for society at large to take care of a lot of difficult people. We force individuals—a wife or a husband—to take care of them on a one-to-one basis."[92] From

---

[87]Bernard, 17.
[88]Ibid., 19.
[89]Ibid. 21.
[90]Ibid., 26–27.
[91]Ibid., 112.
[92]Ibid., 161.

her perspective, most of those who need to be taken care of in marriage are men.

The puzzling thing for her is why so many women marry, and why, in the face of all the problems they report, they describe themselves as happy. Her conclusions were both alarming and widely shared by the women's movement: that society had designated the married role as the only acceptable one for a woman and penalized her so severely if she didn't accept it that she could not be happy. Yet her symptoms showed that the costs of that subjective happiness were alcoholism, depression, and isolation.[93] Bernard likened our shaping of women's characters to the ancient Chinese deformation of women's feet.

> To be happy in a relationship which imposes so many impediments on her, as traditional marriage does, a woman must be slightly ill mentally. We therefore 'deform' the minds of girls...in order to shape them for happiness in marriage. It may therefore be that married women say they are happy because they are sick rather than say they are sick because they are married.[94]

She goes on to document the now widely noted awareness that we have, or at least had, a double standard of mental health. "We incorporate into our standards of mental health for women the defects necessary for successful adjustment in marriage."[95] She ultimately asked if we should not find a way to structure marriage that's not so costly to women, and she has become a major influence on a movement that has sought, with some success, to do so.

In her continued study of marriage, she focused heavily on the development of egalitarian or companionate relationships and their ambiguous ability to produce happiness. Studies in the 1930s and 1940s showed egalitarian marriages as happier than similar studies in the 1950s and 1960s, reflecting the change in values between the two periods. In both periods the quality women valued most from marriage was companionship. Yet, by the 1960s, research was showing that men who were competitive and motivated by power were not happy in these more equal, more companionable marriages. Studies identified a tension between companionship and sexual satisfaction, suggesting that men, especially those most motivated by status and power, linked physical domination and sexual prowess so closely that their sexual functioning diminished as gender equality was approached. Apparently defining sex and power as strongly linked, as men in this society

---

[93]Ibid., 48–51.
[94]Ibid., 51.
[95]Ibid., 52.

had traditionally done, creates a barrier to men's participation in the companionship that women especially crave in marriage.

Bernard's followup research in 1982 is particularly enlightening. During the period 1957–1976 household size diminished, the number of women working increased greatly, both women and men married later, and there was a reported increase of almost 10 percent in marital happiness among both genders. Wives still were more negative than husbands about marriage and were more likely to complain about husbands than husbands were about wives. A new factor that appeared in this research was work overload, as women increasingly worked outside the home, but men did not increase their share of housework and child care. Women were less likely than men to say that they found support in their marriages. But as divorces increased in the 1970s, those marriages that survived were reported as happier, though not unambiguously.[96]

In Bernard's later findings, marriages were gradually increasing their ability to provide companionship, though not without difficulties. They were moving men and women increasingly toward a shared world at both home and work, though not yet toward egalitarian roles in that shared world. But most importantly, women were finding the ability to survive outside marriage. Single status was becoming a realistic economic alternative to marital structures that they had found intolerable.

By the late 1970s researchers were finding that most couples were enjoying marriage more and that one of the long-standing sources of dissatisfaction, differing preferences for sexual frequency, had almost disappeared. D'Emilio and Freedman reported an upsurge of published sexual material from women's points of view in the 1970s and with it an increase in women's interest in marital sex. Both men and women reported increased agreement about desired sexual frequency and satisfaction with their sex life at levels of three or more occasions of intercourse per week.[97] In the same decade, Blumstein and Schwartz reported that all varieties of couples they studied, married, nonmarried, lesbian, gay, reported that "a good sex life is central to a good overall relationship, and that sexual dissatisfaction will undermine relational quality for both genders." They also report, as did Bernard, that those marriages that survive are happier, because those that don't meet minimum standards are ending in divorce.

By 1980 it appeared that marital power was equalizing and that women's working outside the home was improving their overall health. A new and more affirming consensus was emerging about the importance of marital sex. What was not yet clear was whether role and work overload would

---

[96]Ibid., 297–301.
[97]D'Emilio and Freedman, 338.

outweigh the gains, or if wives' increased mental health and sexual satisfaction would be purchased at the cost of physical exhaustion and a continuingly unjust domestic division of labor.

More contemporary research suggests that the trends that Bernard saw are continuing, but that clear resolution of the strains in marital structure continues to evade us. Vannoy-Hiller and Philliber's 1989 book *Equal Partners* reports the finding that the 50 percent prevalence of two-job couples is widely seen as highly stressful.[98] Conflicts between work and relationship are expected by almost everyone, and the statistics indicate that the more successful the wives in such relationships are, the higher the divorce rate. Their contention is that such marriages will continue to increase and that it is crucial to identify the factors that make their success more likely.

They cite a troubling but widely known set of facts that must be accounted for in any view of marriage. Women rarely marry men who are shorter than they are, weigh less than they do, have less education than they do, whom they perceive as less intelligent than they are, or who get paid less than they do. Both men and women seem to choose partners that make it appear, at least superficially, that the man does, or at least could, take care of and protect the woman.[99] At least unconsciously, our present visceral feeling for what it means to be male and female appear bound up with these protective–controlling-providing functions, despite the changes that make physical force less a factor in maintenance of safety and income. The summation of these individual choices suggests that equality, in and of itself, does not attract.

In looking for a mate, single respondents indicated that someone who was compatible (25 percent of the men) and/or kind (17 percent of the women) ranked right behind finding someone whom they loved and someone of good moral character, the highest values. All of these outranked physical attractiveness and potential as provider or homemaker, suggesting that we see the former variables as crucial to what we hope for from marriage. Married respondents reported that the single most influential variable for marital quality is the sensitivity/supportiveness of the husband. The more sensitive he is, in terms of indicating awareness of the difficulties in his wife's and others' lives, the more both spouses like the marriage.[100] The more competitive he is with his wife, the worse the marriage for both. "The simple conclusion most consistent with these data is that one partner's need to be better than his or her spouse is incompatible with the emotional bonds that produce high-quality marriages."[101] Expectations, and spouses'

---

[98]Vannoy-Hiller and Philliber, 9–17.

[99]Ibid., 18–20.

[100]Ibid., 121.

[101]Ibid.

perceptions of them, are also critical. The more traditional a wife's expectation of marriage, the higher the overall marital quality; and the less traditional a husband's expectations, the higher the marital quality for both.[102]

A final factor that Vannoy-Hiller and Philliber measured was marital balance, the spouses' sense that they are or are not contributing equally to the success of the marital venture. The more tasks the husband shares with the wife or does himself, the higher the overall marital quality.[103]

In terms of influencing marital quality, differences in husbands' expectations, attitudes, personality, and role performance are more powerful than any shifts in the wives'. This suggests that contemporary marriage is changing in directions that wives as a group are more able to accommodate. Husbands seem to enjoy marriage, at least dual-earner marriage, and are themselves enjoyable in such marriage, when they have integrated shifts in gender identity that enable greater sensitivity and supportiveness of their wives, less competiveness, and more balanced sharing of domestic duties. Men who hold to a more traditional view of male identity are neither enjoying the model of marriage that contemporary America is creating, nor are they being greatly enjoyed as marital partners. They are contributing in major ways to the still unacceptably high divorce rate.

Over the twentieth century marriage has shifted in much of our society from what Scanzoni and Scanzoni termed the owner-property model, through the head-complement model and, for most Americans, to the senior partner/junior partner model. Many have taken the additional step to the equal-partner marriage.[104] The relationship has largely dropped the functions of providing social control for wives, of providing women's only income and protection, and of providing the sole acceptable sexual outlet for both genders at all points in the life span. It has become a setting for companionship, for mutual character formation, and for shared work. We are not very good at these tasks yet, especially the men among us, and that lack of skill creates severe pain and confusion for adults and threatens to be catastrophic for a whole generation of children.

The Impact on the Young

"Compared with their parents' generation, children today commit suicide at a higher rate, perform worse in school, are more likely to be obese, and show other evidence of increased physical, mental, and emotional distress. The poverty rate among children is almost double the rate for adults—a situation without precedent in American history," writes Victor

---

[102]Ibid., 142.
[103]Ibid., 114.
[104]Ibid., 14.

Fuchs.[105] Fuchs documents an alarming decline in the quality of life and level of achievement of children. In the early 1980s the suicide rate for fifteen to nineteen year olds, arguably a reflection of teenagers' estimate of their future prospects, was two and one-half times higher than it had been twenty years earlier.[106] Scholastic Aptitude Test scores fell on average fifty points on the verbal, thirty points on the math,[107] between the peak in the early 1960s and the nadir in the early 1980s—and the drop was true of all socioeconomic groups, all kinds of schools, and all parts of the country. The lower average scores are not the result of a difference in the sample, but of actual poorer performance among students of comparable percentile rankings.

Childhood obesity rose 50 percent between the early 1960s and the late 1970s, with super-obesity almost doubling in the same period.[108] Maltreatment of children seems to be increasing, though there is widespread uncertainty about how much of the statistical difference is due to difference in reporting. Neglect and abuse cases reported almost tripled between 1976 and 1984.[109]

Poverty among children has expanded very rapidly, reaching 20 percent of all children by 1986 and continuing to climb through the early 1990s. Large families are especially vulnerable to poverty—average household income for households with four children was 8 percent below the mean household income in 1986.

Throughout the population poverty is more widespread. The official poverty figures computed by the government rose 30 percent between 1979 and 1984, despite computation techniques designed to minimize the appearance of difficulty.[110] There was no increase in constant dollar median income levels for families between 1984 and 1996. The poverty rates in 1982–1984 were the highest since 1966, and the gap between rich and poor was the greatest since the Census Bureau began keeping these statistics. The median income for families in the poorest 40 percent of the population was $470 lower in 1984 than in 1980, whereas the median for the top 40 percent was $1800 higher. The poorest 40 percent of U.S. families received 15.7 percent of the national income in 1984, the lowest percentage since this record keeping began in 1947. In 1984 the poverty rate for female-headed households was 34.5 percent, five times that of families

[105]Fuchs, *Women's Quest*, 94.
[106]Ibid., 104.
[107]Ibid., 104–5.
[108]Ibid., 109.
[109]Ibid., 110.
[110]Sidel, 10.

including a married couple.[111] Over half of children living in female-headed households were poor by official standards.

These statistics report the overall picture. If you look at African American or Hispanic poverty figures, they are much more severe, and the condition of their children is much worse. The income gap between white and African American households continued to grow until 1989 and has narrowed only slightly since.

Summary

By the late 1990s much of the avalanche of change that marked the 1970s and 1980s had slowed or stopped. Divorce rates had been flat or slowly receding for almost a decade, though they appeared to be stabilizing at much higher levels than before 1970. Birth rates, after falling to an all-time low, crept upward until the early 1990s, then receded again. Most women are already in the workforce, so there is little room for further increase in those figures. Women's average pay is inching toward 70 percent of that of men, and that of young, well-educated, single women was nearing equity. That in turn was producing later, and more egalitarian, marriages for them, which may enable those women to avoid the slippage in relative earnings traditionally brought on by time out of the labor force during their twenties and thirties.

The function of marriage, the shape of family, and the quality of child care were changing drastically. At the beginning of the twentieth century marriage was a multifunction relationship, centering on economic production and consumption and labor-intensive child care, with the companionship needs of both men and women being largely met in same-sex occupational or extended family networks. By mid-century marriage's economic functions had been stripped away, and a mother-intensive child care had replaced them at the center of the family. Romantic love had become the norm, but men and women still functioned in relatively isolated gender-specialized spheres. Almost everyone married, family size increased, birth rates soared, women's economic dependency increased. But by the 1980s and 1990s a powerful reaction had set in. Marriage became one of many options, women could earn enough to live independently (though not comfortably), and marriage was increasingly viewed as requiring companionship and emotional intimacy. Households were much smaller, single people lived alone and together, and female-headed households became nearly as numerous as those headed by couples. And although the rhetoric, and to

---

[111]Ibid., 3.

an extent the economic reality of egalitarian marriage, was intensifying, men (with the emerging exception of very young men) did not significantly increase their percentage of child care or housekeeping tasks. The need for a new view of maleness, emphasizing less competitiveness and more sensitivity, was widely discussed.

In the midst of this, a troubling re-sorting of class structures was emerging. It was harder for young men to earn enough to support a family, and a gulf was widening between those whose fortunes had been aided by the Reagan prosperity of the middle and upper classes and those who suffered the loss of tax-subsidized social supports during those years. Income seemed to be shifting from the young to the elderly, and the nation was said to have the poorest children and the richest old people in the developed world. Children were neglected and abused at a higher rate than ever recorded; domestic violence appeared to be increasing; drug use, pregnancy, AIDS, and poverty were epidemic among the young. This was bad among the female-headed households of the white majority, and significantly worse among blacks and Hispanics.

It appears that we are crafting a family significantly different from that which anchored American society fifty years ago and are in the early stages of learning the skills it requires. It remains to be seen if we can stabilize the upheaval, establish the needed intimacy, and learn the new gender identities and relational roles before the casualties of the transition undermine our ability to maintain a society.

For the church to wield influence in the emerging society, it must attempt to discern what God is doing in this shift of family forms. We cannot believe it has escaped God's attention or that God is uninterested in the outcome. So far the church's efforts have been thin and slow. We now turn our attention to identifying the theological questions that must be addressed in order for the Christian community to be a faithful witness to and for the families that are coming to be.

CHAPTER 8

Conclusion

The Basic Questions

We have explored nearly three millennia of religious community, family life, and theological reflection. We have seen an enormous range in human organization of kinship structures. We have seen a variety of normative sexualities. We have seen several patterns of organizing households within their broader societies. And we have seen first the Hebrew community, the synagogue, and, more extensively, the Christian community arrive at strongly opposing views of what God is seeking to accomplish through intimate human associations, how God would have us act with those closest to us, and what the consequences of various forms of action are likely to be for our spiritual lives.

Very little is consistent throughout these centuries. What seems holy in one epoch is anathema in another. Ideas that have not yet been invented in one decade are obligatory for everyone a few decades later. Only one thing seems dependably consistent: God is understood as caring about, having a passionate concern for, our sexuality, our family structures, and our child-raising in every generation. There is a secondary theme that can also be discerned: Even at times of dramatic change and perceived crisis, serious theological thought about family and sexuality lags decades, if not centuries, behind the changes in practice and circumstance that have brought new behavior to the fore. Things change much faster than the church and its theological thought can keep up with, and we don't notice the changes until they've been in place for quite a while.

Two conclusions can be drawn from these realities. At any given point in Christian history, the church (at least in some visible section) has proclaimed as the will of God behaviors or structures that were unknown or hated fifty years earlier or later; and, second, that the sociohistorical realities that support, even necessitate, any given theology of family are always passing out of existence before that theology is fully coming into focus. It seems that, at our best, we are at least a step behind. That is probably true of this effort as well.

There are a number of implications we could draw. We could conclude that God is capricious in these matters, wanting first one thing and then another, according to whim. But it would be impossible for us to accept that and continue to believe in a God we can trust. We would have a paranoid-schizoid God, with no sense of continuity or historicity, one who awoke every morning to a new world, having no commitments to any line of influence or development from the moment or the month before. This would be the God of Luck, to be seduced by the proper offering to magically bring divine power to bear on circumstances, depending on the superior manipulative bribe. Neither Christian nor Jewish faith is consistent with such a God, and we must reject this possibility if we are to continue holding the notion of a God who reveals Godself in a way that makes divine-human relationship possible.

A further possibility, less theologically unacceptable though uncomfortably humbling, is that the church is always wrong to some extent about God's action. We could easily accept the idea that the church's knowledge of God is always partial, never fully up-to-date, always limited by human finitude. These propositions seem to me appropriate recognitions of the difference between what is knowable to God and to us. Another version, however, of "the church is always wrong" would be less acceptable. It would hold that the church's conclusions about God's hopes for our sexual and familial lives (and everything else) are completely unrelated to the divine reality. There is no communication through any means that offers more accurate knowledge of God's intent than a random guess. God may have a consistent will for and action in the family, but it is utterly unknown to us—as is everything else about God's will and action. To believe that, we would have to believe that our claim to know God through Jesus Christ, or in any other way, is false. We would have to disavow our belief that the Holy Spirit offers any useful leading to human deliberations on this or any other subject and that a study of the scriptural canon would be useless in informing us about God's hopes and fears for our intimate lives. Since such a position would disqualify all Christian faith, it must be excluded here.

We are left with a church that is always wrong about God in the sense of completeness or timeliness of knowledge, but that does receive God's leadings, can hope for some education at God's hand, and can expect to gradually gain insight into God's will and action; but the church may be perpetually figuring out what God was doing fifty or a hundred years ago and only partially able to grasp what is coming into being today.

Because of this time lag in grasping God's action and our inability to resolve the ancient riddle of God's infinite power and goodness, we can believe in a God with power, love, and knowledge, but only with power and knowledge that are limited. There are other influences, not governed though influenced by God, that contribute to historical outcomes. Physical givens, the whole of past history, present social organizations, values, ideas, and resources, all establish hard realities that every force, including God, must deal with. God is at work making the best, in God's eyes, of the circumstances that the world makes possible at any given moment, in competition with other forces that are also seeking to achieve their objectives. As God works by persuasion, not by force, the free subjective aims of concrete, existing beings are free to choose between God and other sources of possibility. We hope to be allied with God in the effort to transform the world, but we are sometimes wrong and always, at least in part, evil. Part of God's work is to transform us into better, more reliable, allies, but the obstacles are real.

This God, then, does not simply will that things will be a certain way and zap them into existence in that form. Were that the case, there would be no history—God would simply have decided that some configuration of human relationships was the desired one and set it in place, perhaps to be repeated over and over as in the movie *Groundhog Day*. Life itself, which implies change, would be unnecessary, even unthinkable. The patriarchal extended family of early-monarchy Israel, or Origen's perpetual virginity, or Luther's father-dominated nuclear household would have been the only family we found anywhere or at any time.

Since that is not the case, I conclude that God, by preference and/or by limitations on the divine power, has a greater investment in the direction and quality of processes that unfold in human structures and relationships than in specific outcomes. The hallmarks of God's activity are in the nature of relationship between a process at any given level of complexity and inclusiveness and the other processes with which it connects. It is a matter of the contribution a structure or relationship makes to its context, that context being either historical, structural, or spiritual. A contribution to the historical context allows the future to benefit from a past or present movement. A change in the structural context alters one level of inclusiveness by virtue of a shift at another level. An example is the way that noble families relate in a society and how that relationship increases or diminishes the safety of wives from domestic abuse in their husband's castle. A change in the spiritual context is one in which a shift in the function or structure of a human institution influences the depth and intimacy between a person or an institution and God. God works unceasingly to bring about a situation in which contributions within any of these levels will positively influence transmission from one historical context to another, from one structural context to another, and from one spiritual context to another. And ultimately God works for the maximum mutual influence of each of these contexts on one another in the grand adventure that is the life of God.

Hence, there is no set of rules that applies at all times and places, because the same actions (were exact identity possible) that would maximize that mutual influence under one set of circumstances would not be precisely the right ones under many, perhaps all, different sets of circumstances. It is consistent to argue for biblical authority and still notice that God appeared to prefer sexual joy and fecundity in the garden of Eden accounts, divorce of the foreigner under Ezra and Nehemiah, a more restrained sexual expression in the Pauline epistles, and tight restrictions on divorce in the gospels and pastoral epistles. In their contexts, if the Hebrew community and the church were right (always debatable), those sets of actions would maximize the transmission of divine love from societies to families to individuals to God, and vice versa. But this would not be so in other contexts, in which other actions would have been required. Times change and with them what is right in relationship also changes.

This leaves us with critical methodological questions as well as a plethora of specific issues that must be addressed if we are going to consider a constructive statement of family theology. I advocate a specific methodological principle: The decisions and conclusions that must be reached regarding most if not all substantive theological questions around family life are subject to the same canons of knowing that apply in other areas of human inquiry. They are never solely theological concerns, bound only by prior theological judgments.

An illustration of the importance of this distinction follows. I have concluded, on the basis of the historical data, that it is meaningless to talk of the human person, hence of any human institution, as though the terms meant the same thing throughout human history. I note the different assertions made, for instance, by Augustine, who argued that sex between a man and a woman introduced lust into the relationship and thus destroyed the friendship that God hoped for between them; and by Sanger and Lindsey, as cited in this volume, or contemporary writers like Mary Hunt[1] or Jim Nelson,[2] who suggest that sex, under the right conditions, intensifies both the friendship and both parties' love for God. It is possible that these are flatly empirical differences: that human individuals, societies, and relationships were structured in such a way in North Africa at the end of antiquity that precisely the same acts would have different effects then than they would in twentieth- or twenty-first-century North America. To believe that, one would also have to believe that societal growth and learning made human beings different in some essential way over that fifteen-hundred-year gap. Simply to name this an empirical question does not resolve all the problems, because it is an empirical question that does not yield an immediate answer—since it is hard to dissect many fifth-century relationships today.

But to affirm that there might be data that would give one a right to answer the question is to take a profoundly different position than to say that God made sex to be a certain kind of thing and to have certain kinds of effects, and it had those effects when the claim was made, and in Davidic Israel, and in twentieth-century North America, and that is the end of the discussion. Hence, to claim that some theologian's, or some biblical translator's, use of a word for a set of structures and relationships, like "family," "marriage," "virginity," "adultery," "divorce," and others, means that our use of the same word obligates us to understand it as the same thing, is to make a theological claim that is vulnerable to empirical challenge, unless one rules out such challenges altogether on theological or philosophical grounds.

It will not surprise the reader to learn that I believe such a claim to be absurd. Human beings are, in very profound ways, different (not necessarily better or worse) from those one hundred or one thousand years ago. Thus marriage, child-raising, families, sexual choices, and the relation of all these to the broader society and to God, are also and must also be different. We are, and humans always are, stuck with the necessity of discerning whether the principles that we believe rightly governed life in some prior age are the ones that we can safely follow now. We cannot relax into the security of being certain that the way our grandparents, or Thomas, or Paul did it will please God today. We must risk being right or wrong for ourselves, though simply to say that doesn't relieve us of the necessity of dialogue with those who have gone before, as this volume has attempted to demonstrate.

---

[1]Mary Hunt, *Tenderness: A Feminist Theology of Friendship* (New York: Crossroad, 1991).

[2]James B. Nelson, *Embodiment: An Approach to Sexuality and Christian Theology* (Minneapolis: Augsburg, 1979).

They also were seeking to be open to God as they thought, prayed, and lived, and we ignore their witness at our peril. But we are bound by it to our certain disaster, because it was not designed by God to decide for us, even if those who first said it thought it was.

Because I believe these things to be true, I believe there are many areas of contemporary Christian sexual, marital, familial, and cultural life that we must revisit and rethink if we are to discern God's actions and intents in those areas. I further believe that such discernment is required if we are to make appropriate ethical choices at the personal or societal levels. Among those questions are the following: (1) How does God use human sexual fulfillment as a vehicle for spiritual development? (2) Can and does God use such fulfillment outside the boundaries of legal marriage for our spiritual benefit? (3) What are the qualities of such relationships that God most loves and that most prepare the way for spiritual development? (4) How does divorce affect the achievement of God's aims for human marriage? (5) Does God use relational happiness in marriage to affect the lives of children growing up in that household? (6) How does God utilize the interplay between same-generation relationships in a family and the ties between succeeding generations? (7) How does God use the relationships between any one household and the structures of the broader society, especially church, class, and state? (8) What is the most fruitful relationship between (sexual, economic, physical) power and marital and family relationships? (9) How does God view individuality and aloneness and their various alternatives? (10) How does God view the tendency of human beings, in many ages, to differentiate themselves into distinct men's and women's cultures? and (11) How does God see and use the relationship between work and the intimate lives of persons and families?

The answers to many of these questions, of course, overlap with the answers to others. Much of the same data would have to be consulted for several of them, and any one of them is worthy of elaboration into at least an entire chapter, if not into many volumes. What we can do here is flesh out some of the questions, so the reader can begin to consider what might be involved in generating a constructive theology of family life.

Sexual Satisfaction and the Spirit

The crucial question here, perhaps for the whole inquiry, is how God views sexual satisfaction for its own sake. With human beings as they are presently constituted, living the kinds of lives they actually live, is our sexual fulfillment a joy to God? Is it God's preference that all human beings have access to this special way of enjoying their bodies and one another? Or, conversely, is there something about the fact of sexual enjoyment that interferes with a person's fitness for union with God? If the latter is the case, is the interference a matter of competition for time and energy, or some additional and substantial impediment that sexual satisfaction itself produces?

There are crucial empirical questions that may shed light on the answers to the above questions: How is the spiritual life of persons who routinely experience sexual pleasure different from that of persons who do not? Is that different if the partners are married? heterosexual? if there are partners at all? Are persons who regularly experience sexual pleasure likely to be more effective parents and by what measure? Are they more likely to be economically productive, and how important is that? And, conversely, are persons with certain qualities of spiritual life more or less likely to be sexually satisfied than persons of a different sort of spiritual life? Is it likely to make as much difference to persons with one kind of spirituality than another? Are persons who are satisfied with their work life more likely to be sexually gratified or gratifying? persons who are enjoying their parenting or their experience as grown children of their parents?

If one has decided, as I have, that the answers to these empirical questions should make a difference to one's theological conclusions, then informing ourselves about these empirical variables is a key part of the methodology used in seeking the answers.

Another critical part of that methodology would be dialogue with the historical record, much of which we have already done. To refresh our memory, this wasn't much of an issue in the biblical Hebrew community. Individual spiritual fulfillment wasn't a major priority until late in Israel's history and was seen as stemming from definably religious acts: following the law, being faithful to the covenant, praising God—though one does get some hints from the Song of Solomon that some connections were beginning to be discerned by Hellenistic times. For most of the Old Testament epoch, the main connection was that if one had the wrong kind of sexual fulfillment, one could be struck down by God or stoned to death by the community.

In the New Testament world, sex was more of a problem, but in a different way. It was beginning to be seen as an attraction that competed with devotion to God. While satisfying the desire for it in marriage was seen as spiritually more sound than adultery or fornication, if one could get along without any of them, one would have more time to give oneself to God. On the other hand, such satisfaction was not seen as a bar to spiritual fullness until a century or two later. By the end of antiquity, the combined force of Ambrose, Jerome, Augustine, Origen, the Stoics, and the Epicureans, not to mention numerous popes, had established that the holiest of lives were those altogether and forever without sexual feelings or pleasures. They had decided that neither Christ nor Mary had experienced either one and that those pledged to virginity and celibacy were spiritually superior to those who married. Though this was occasionally challenged by rebels and heretics and began to soften in lyrical work like Bernard's, it only met effective, direct opposition in the Reformation. Luther argued that celibacy cannot have been such a widely granted vocation, and Bucer and Milton celebrated the spiritual elevation of marital love. We can see the expansion of these ideas in the Romantic preaching of Beecher, and we can see their corruption in his self-indulgence. The early twentieth century saw the sacramentalization of sex in the work of Margaret Sanger and Ben Lindsey, and we can find more fully developed theological thought in the same vein in the last two decades. We can also find the consequences of the exploitation and trivialization of sexual pleasure all around us, with its artifacts in unwanted pregnancies, abused children, and casual infidelity.

In a thoroughgoing methodology, our task would be to place each of these theological positions in its context, showing how it might have been more or less appropriate to the times in which it was uttered. We would then need to show how changes in circumstances altered what religious thinkers understood to be God's will for their times and make a judgment on the adequacy of their thought for their own age. Then we could assess which of their ages and theologies was most comparable to our situation and our needs, partly through a comparison of broad historical trends, and partly through seeking answers to the empirical questions described above.

Once that historical dialogue was completed and the empirical questions answered as fully as possible, our attention could turn to the theological subquestions that are part of arriving at an answer to the category's overarching question. My contention is that God does use a wide variety of sexual expression, which honors both partners and makes provision for the consequence of their acts, to give persons an experience of the goodness of creation and the mercy of God. In gratitude, thankfulness and praise are probable, and adoration of God is likely to bring the celebrant closer to the divine as well as to the beloved. Such occasions are the very substance of spiritual fulfillment.

Must Sex Be Marital?

If one has reached the conclusion that God does, in at least some situations, take joy from the simple fact of human sexual pleasure, then the question of the status of nonmarital sex becomes relevant. Even to address it reveals a striking gap between popular religion and theological reflection. Theologians typically have a complex and somewhat gracious set of views on the matter, while popular religious feeling (and, particularly, official church pronouncements) has held during much of Christian history that any sexual relationship outside of marriage was a one-way ticket to hell.

This tension brings a set of questions into focus that tests our earlier methodological principles. If we were to discover that persons who experienced various levels of nonmarital sexual expression had spiritual lives as rich and powerful as those who had not, would it make any difference to the theological answer one should reach? If one believes it should, much data could be collected. It would concern the ways in which persons who had been involved in nonmarital sex were different from those who had not. It would consider a variety of differences: the intensity of their subsequent prayer lives, their explicit religious involvement, their ethical fruitfulness, the durability of their marriages, and the health of their children. Admittedly this would be difficult research to conduct, but fully possible in principle. If its findings were clearly negative, it would not remove the theological questions, but it might make them less pressing than if we were to find that the "sinners" in this sample lived noticeably more fruitful lives than the sexually pure.

Theological questions might begin with how "marriage" was defined. Is a church wedding required? Must the marriage be legal? Do legal, common-law arrangements suffice? How is God's pleasure under each of these conditions different from the others and, further, how different from the divine satisfaction over the sexual encounter of an engaged couple, over the first discovery of sexual pleasure in the life of a profoundly lonely introvert, over the rediscovery of connection for a previously despairing middle-aged widow or widower? If God is not pleased, what is the source of the displeasure? Is it disobedience, exploitation of the vulnerable, the possibility of unwanted conception, the trivialization of deep sexual communion? How much does God's displeasure depend on the actual likelihood of unfortunate temporal consequences, and how much on the fact of the transgression itself?

Consulting the tradition would yield a dependably confusing mix. The Old Testament wasn't much concerned about sex that did not violate a marriage or parental covenant. In fact, in some instances such extramarital sexual unions seem to be celebrated by God and the community (especially Tamar in Genesis 38, Ruth, and Esther). The New Testament church was much more judgmental about all sexual expression, particularly fornication. As the church moved out into the Mediterranean basin, it encountered a style of legal marriage, at least for those with property, that seemed much less humane and loving than did the same epoch's equally legal concubinage. Yet the church called such marriage sacred and such concubinage licentious, for reasons that appear to be connected with its distrust of sexual pleasure and its endorsement of what it discerned as a Jewish style of marriage. As we move into medieval times, the church was more interested in establishing its control over legal marriage, clerical and monastic sex, and political opponents than it was in trying to condemn or prevent the sexual exploits of younger noble sons or of the poor. By the Reformation both Protestant and Catholic communities were strongly motivated to establish their authority, which included authority over sexual expression, but that was more intensely focused on violation of privileges of power and control than on the spiritual dangers of nonmarital sex.

The American combination of the First Great Awakening evangelists, with their deep suspicion of the willfulness involved in the seeking of any physical pleasure and their widespread distaste for body processes, and the sexual purity crusades developing out of the nineteenth-century's Second Great Awakening produced the fullest appeal for the limitation of sex to marriage in several hundred years. This combination occurred in the midst of a sexual political struggle that privately allowed discreet indulgence for Victorian men outside their marriages, if they didn't insist on their wives' being enthusiastically sexual within the marriage. But even as that tension was being sharply drawn, it was dissolving in the Ingersoll-Beecher-Sanger-Lindsey movement for a type of sexual salvation that was not convinced that sex had to be marital to be redemptive.

This history has brought us to a present in which a very high percentage of couples are openly sexual before marriage, where unmarried pregnancy no longer carries significant social stigma, yet most public church statements still contend that all sex outside of marriage is against the will of God. It creates the odd situation in which most people outside the church appear to believe the church is very repressive sexually, but most Christians and certainly most theologians would concede that there are situations in which nonmarital sex is holy (though they might disagree about which situations). The church as public institution, however, cannot make that statement. This sabotages the church's ability to be in conversation with a culture that desperately needs sexual norms, norms for decisions that it will refuse to make simply in order to obey principles it sees as profoundly uncharitable.

What God Loves about Sex

Though this is not the first question, it is in many ways the central question. If we conclude that God enjoys our sexual satisfaction under some conditions and that it is not simply a matter of all marital sex being good and all other sex being evil, then what is the nature of the sexual contact that God loves?

This again is a question that tests the methodological relationship between the theological and the empirical. We could probably determine, if we decided it was relevant, the causal links between certain kinds of sexual situations and their effects on the lives of the participants, their broader families, and the society. We can say with some certainty, at least under twentieth- and early twenty-first-century conditions, that father-daughter incest is terribly destructive of the psychic integrity of daughters and the structural integrity of families. We can measure the effect of premarital intercourse or premarital cohabitation on marital longevity and various qualities of marital interaction. Given a long enough time line, we can measure its effects on the lives of the children of those marriages. We cannot, of course, empirically determine which of these outcomes measured matter to God. That is a theological judgment, inextricably linked with how we understand God's priorities. More specifically, is God more concerned about God's honor, hence our obedience (as a New Light Conservative would have contended), than about humanly discernible indicators of the welfare of women and men? If God is more concerned about human welfare, or even the welfare of all the ecosystems in which humans are resident, is it possible that God has knowledge of what constitutes our welfare that we have not understood? So God could disagree with us about what constitutes our welfare, without making a plea for simple obedience. But we have to come down somewhere with reference to the empirical variables that may be important, and that specificity requires theological decision.

In this area, an exploration of theological tradition will produce much data. The Hebrew tradition, as we have noted, saw God as most interested in whether the sex served the covenant community. If it did, God liked it. The first few Christian centuries were uncomfortable with the notion that God valued sex at all, but could find the best warrant for such valuing when the sex was marital and served to domesticate lust. "It is better to marry than to be aflame with passion," as Paul writes in 1 Corinthians 7:9. The church in these years was more focused on understanding the sacred status of celibacy and virginity than of marital sex, which was the only kind it could see as possibly free of sin. By medieval times it was clear that sex that "paid the marital debt" was acceptable to (not celebrated by) God, and that sex that was enjoyable though not sought for the sake of pleasure was similarly acceptable. But seeking sex for pleasure—even within marriage— was sinful, and the prohibition of sex for much of the year was a clear indication that it was seen as compromising spiritual purity.

The work of Bucer, the Anglicans, and the Puritans marked the next major shift in these questions in the English-speaking world. Matrimony could be holy, companionship itself was sacred, and sex could be part of that. "It is not good for man to be alone." It was clear in this stream of Protestant history that God had an investment in the kind of sexual connection that helped persons experience themselves as part of the human community, as neither abandoned nor oppressed. The Puritan attitude was particularly complicated, combining a deep reverence for the beauty of relationship and a suspicion of seeking physical pleasure for its own sake. Perhaps the key here was the distinction between the relational and physical aspects of the pleasure. If the physical supported the relational, it was blessed. If it was independent of or outranked the relational, it was suspect. Much of this attitude was elaborated in the early Quaker movement, where the holiness of specific relationships was weighed, and the community (especially the female community) was seen as a shared source of wisdom about it.

The nineteenth century saw a confluence and contrast among American Christian views on this subject. Catholics saw God as loving sex that was aimed at conception and as seeing woman's orgasm as critical to that. Protestants, for much of the century, were denying that women had any sexual drive at all, so the best thing about sex would be that it was disciplined (how exciting!). But late in the century it began to be seen in a growing minority of circles as physically healing and contributing to the bond between married partners. By early in the twentieth century it was coming to be understood as linking couples together so they were more likely to care for their children.

In my lifetime we have been sensitized to the impact of power on sexual relationships, and one of the questions a constructive theology would have to address is that of the necessity (or lack thereof) of relatively equal power in a redemptive sexual relationship. That in turn brings us around to questions of physical abuse, of economic security, and of contraception and abortion. It could be argued that all the questions named earlier in this chapter are really subheadings under this question of power.

God loves human sexual sharing that intensifies the relationship between committed and mutually redemptive partners and through intensifying that relationship clarifies for each participant the beauty and graciousness of God. That divine love is greatest when the sexual bond deepens the links among the historical, structural, and spiritual contexts, and is undertaken with reverent responsibility for the outcome of the physical acts at all levels.

Divorce

The enormous surge in divorce rates in the 1940s, and again in the late 1960s and 1970s, forces us to consider the theological importance of these ruptures. Does God always hate divorce? Is a bad marriage (if there is such a thing in God's eyes) better than a good (same question) divorce? Is woman's (more than man's) frequent choice to put asunder what God has joined together always sinful? If the answers to these questions are "Yes," then we need to ask why that is. Is it a facet, again, of obedience? Is there something about the act of the church in sanctifying the marriage that makes it so precious that no human suffering can justify its loss? If so, is that because of an intrinsic blessedness for the partners that accrues from their loyalty to the institution, some actual good it confers, or is the reward only an eschatalogical one, conferred for obedience?

Here again there is rich and ambiguous empirical data, and the same nagging methodological question. We know that the lives of children are disrupted in major ways by a parental divorce, causing at least short-term declines in academic performance, increases in psychological and physical symptoms, disruptions of their relationships, and so forth. We know that the severity of those dislocations seems to be diminishing as divorce becomes less of a stigma and as the society becomes more skilled in dealing with its consequences, but there is no prediction that the disruption will disappear. We know less about long-term effects, with the political motivations of researchers on both sides being unclear enough to cast doubt on the currently available conclusions. We know that the partners themselves go through a period of acute distress, financial and relational disruption, sexual experimentation and tentative repartnerings that traditionally have been seen as wildly sinful. It is also clear that it takes a number of years after a divorce before the former partners can report being happier than they were before it. But it is also true that the much greater availability of divorce and the ability of women to survive it economically have corrected much of the power imbalance in marriage as an institution and possibly made it a more powerful vehicle for spiritual growth.

Conclusions here must be reached with considerable care. The very prevalence of divorce, with its attendant disruption, has intensified the society's move toward a lower quality of child care, more frequent relationship-disrupting residential moves, increased pressure on women to work outside the home, and greater pessimism among children and adolescents about the security of their own relational prospects. All this raises the possibility that the societal fragmentation may lead to further crisis—such as the escalation of violence—that will interfere with our ability to continue the relational learning that seems to be contributing to recent modest declines in divorce. It could be argued that God is participating in a societal gamble: risking the often stultifying and oppressive stability of the marriage forms of the late nineteenth or mid-twentieth century in hopes of generating the "intact, equal-regard, public-private, sexually invested family" that the Browning study proposed. Or it could be contended that our corporate impatience, greed, and individualism have sinfully overwhelmed our covenant faithfulness and launched a process of relational dissolution that undermines everyone's security for generations to come. I believe that both are true to some extent and that it will be several decades, perhaps a century or two, before the progress of theological discussion and empirical assessment makes consensus on these questions possible.

Marital Joy and Child-Rearing Success

While the status of sexual satisfaction, and possibly even of marital happiness (clearly not identical phenomena), remain ambiguous in the historical and theological record, there is no such uncertainty about the welfare of children and families. From the very beginning of Old Testament covenants, God is described as decisively committed to the survival and success of a particular family lineage—Abraham's.

Theologies from that day to this have emphasized God's investment in raising up heirs to the covenant. Contemporary theological argument over the status of marriage and sexuality has asked whether excessive focus on the joys of adulthood, particularly the relational and sexual joys of marriage, compromise the welfare of children and families.

Here the methodological uncertainties of previous questions become less intense, though they do not disappear. The focus on the well-being of and faithfulness to children and their families is prominent throughout scriptural and theological history. The argument for the theological import of children's connection to faithful families has established a prima facie case. A critic could contend that God wills us to continue experimenting until we find a way to guarantee children's welfare and holiness without depending on the quality of parental marriage, but surely the burden of proof would be on the critic.

As we can see from chapter 7, the data do not yet support unambiguous conclusions. The research shows, for instance, that it is quite possible for children to be relatively happy in marriages that their parents regard as unhappy: if the conflict is explicit and focused within the couple, if they do not frighten the children by displaying it openly between them, and if they do not triangulate the children into taking sides in it. Those are very difficult tasks for human beings, achieved in a minority of unhappy couples, but clearly achievable by some. I suspect that something important for children is lost in such unhappy but safely structured marriages that would be available in families containing a richer pair bond, but that argument is still to be made and must be supported by new research. The something lost will probably turn out to be a sense of joy and hope in their own future marital relationships, which may be a concrete help in creating such relationships. But the space is not available here to make that argument, and the research on such couples has not yet been done. Such an argument would be the task of future constructive family theologies.

Other factors that would have to be accounted for include the danger to the whole societal fabric, including family life, of many of the current excesses of the search for individual and couple happiness. It could be argued that the overestimation of the importance of marital happiness has set an impossibly high standard for marriage as an institution, so that people hope for more from the relationship than it is structured to provide and run to the divorce courts when it fails in the impossible task. Contemporary conservative theologians, both Protestant and Catholic, make that argument, contending that we have substituted what can be had from marriage for what should be had from a relationship with God, with extended family, and with community. These are arguments subject to some empirical evidence, such as the relationship between a given level of marital expectations and happiness within marriage. Also relevant would be the extent to which a couple's sense of what provides adequate reason to end a marriage correlates with specific average durations of marriage. Certainly it would be possible for couples to expect so much of marriage, and of life in general, that the sheer weight of the expectation would make all relationships, by comparison, dissatisfying. This may be an artifact of the focus on individual fulfillment at the expense of community and relational bonds, an instance of our reputed narcissism. These arguments need to be reviewed, counter-arguments for the greater hope in marital happiness provided, and all of this subjected to the test of research.

As with the discussion of divorce, I believe that it will take a few more decades of living, researching, and reflecting under social conditions largely like the present ones before answers to these questions can be conclusive. I suspect that God is at work elaborating a way of being married that inseparably links spousal happiness and childhood hope, stability, and well-being. But this argument remains to be made.

Does God Prioritize the Horizontal or Vertical Axis?

Since the beginning of Christian history (it wasn't so much an issue for either the biblical or postbiblical Jewish communities), there has been tension in the church and community over whether the most important bonds in families were those between husbands and wives or those between parents and children. Jews have always made a theological choice for the parent-child bond, as noted in chapter 2, but Christians have been less firmly settled. Twentieth-century changes, particularly the great increases in geographical mobility—always more an American phenomenon—and the rapid growth in life expectancy, have fueled increased emphasis on the marital pair. But it is far from clear how the optimal balance can be determined empirically, and the theological questions also persist.

It is clear that both God and persons value the continuity of cultures, nations, and families. No choice for a marital priority can stand if it is prejudicial to these broader loyalties. The broad conviction that God acts in history has been taken to mean that the divine will is invested in the health of the church across the ages, of the Jewish community from the time of the patriarchs, and of particular cultures within which the church and Judaism are located. The life of no individual or marital pair can be intelligible and viable if these contexts are shattered. But it is clear that couples are in a stronger position to contribute as a unit, now that those that do not divorce last far longer after all children have left home than any child typically lives with a parent. This is such a dramatic shift that it gives God a new situation to work with, one in which rich, satisfying marriages are more a resource for achieving the divine objectives than they have been in any previous century, and one that could open previous divine priorities for reconsideration.

History is not unanimous on this subject, though the leaning has been toward the lineal ties in most epochs. That is clearly the situation that the church inherited from Judaism, but two factors challenged it immediately: the expectation of the coming parousia, and the struggle with Roman society over the inheritance of wealth. Neither factor elevated marriage, but both raised suspicion about the sanctity of the emphasis on the lineage, substituting the church as candidate for the top loyalty of both married person and celibate alike. Emphasis on lineage would have strengthened the monarchic dynasties at the expense of the church, which was a political if not a theological obstacle.

Following the Reformation, the national state grew in influence, and the Protestant churches reeled loyalty back into the family and the congregation and away from the church universal. Lutheran countries emphasized paternal rule, hence parent-child relations, more strongly; Reformed ones, the marital pair. As time passed, the more conservative elements within Calvinism and the Anglican tradition placed more emphasis on the lineage, but as the urbanization and mobility of the Industrial Revolution proceeded, marital pairs became more independent without great challenge from the church. In North America, however, an unusual contrast developed. The original colonists were largely young adults, typically here without parents, who thus had few loyalty conflicts for their nuclear households. Very quickly, however, economic necessity favored extended families, as sons were needed to clear the land. Within the evangelical church, the independence of child-rearing couples from their parents in some ways was emphasized, while the in-household focus was on the parent-child tie. As the frontier expanded and couples were more often far from their parents, when the church spoke on these issues, it spoke of the mutual obligations of spouses, with little reference to the older generation.

Discussion in the twentieth century followed similar lines, though the picture has been enriched by our longer life spans. Evangelicals still talk much more about duties of parents to children and children to parents, and the more liberal churches of the relationship between spouses. But it has become necessary, as older generations live into and beyond retirement and increasingly live apart from adult children, to look at what middle-aged children do and do not owe to their aged parents. It is not as simple as saying that the marital bond is more important, because there are aspects of being a spouse that involve supporting the other in the care of parents. And if a person loses self-respect through failing an obligation to parents, she or he also becomes less of a resource for the spouse.

It is important to remember that God loves our communities, and our communities include all generations. This is an area in which establishing clear rules about priorities is doomed to failure, because the contexts change yearly, and when they change, they offer different opportunities for growth, sacrifice, challenge, and learning. A critical task for a constructive theology of family is to explore the conditions under which a couple's focus is most faithfully on the parenting task within their own home, when it is on their pair bond, when it is on caring for their aging parents, and when it is on supporting one another in their work in the broader world. For everything there is a season, and the church needs to consider what God is doing with each season of our lives.

The Family and the Broader World

One of the crucial questions for the current church and family debate concerns how the family relates to the society as a whole, to its economic, religious, cultural, and political life. This is the "public-private" in the

Browning study's norms, the balance between the ways the family provides "a haven in a heartless world," and the ways it is resourced by and is a resource for a world that is a mixture of stimulation and deprivation.

This is an issue that depends more on the theological and ethical tradition than on empirical data, though some of the latter is relevant. The family has long been described as a subunit of the church, at some points quite explicitly, as in the Reformation and contemporary evangelical thought. It is a pillar of traditional Christian thought that the family will take structural forms and moral precepts from church teachings and offer back to the church service and participation. That remains the expectation across the spectrum.

What is less widely agreed on is the extent to which the family should be permeable to and proactive regarding the political, economic, educational, and entertainment structures in the world beyond the church. This is a huge point of difference between liberals and evangelicals. Liberals are more likely to claim a "Christ transforming culture" stance, while being accused by conservatives of giving way to a "Christ of culture" position.[3] The closer to the right-hand end of the spectrum, the more one is in the territory of "Christ against culture." Different elements in the church differ intensely on issues like home schooling, parents' rights, government aid to day care, levels of taxation, abortion, and censorship. The differences typically come down to the question of optimal permeability of family boundaries and responsibility to maintain those boundaries. The liberal church, typically emphasizing the importance of the marital bond, also typically sees that bond as more connected to the world of work, the assistance of government, support for and from public education, and involvement in pluralism at multiple levels. More conservative segments of the community typically choose the primacy of cross-generational bonds; regularly prefer a less permeable family with tighter parental control over education, entertainment, financial resources; and place a higher emphasis on policy and theology that urge parents, especially mothers, to devote a large segment of their energy to maintaining those family boundaries. There also are typical differences about how much the family owes the broader world in economic productivity, political participation, and community advocacy and charity.

Over the centuries the church has taken divergent positions on this issue. The pre-Constantinian church saw itself as opposed to the public world, and the period from Constantine to the High Middle Ages was more interested in the relations of church and political power than in issues

---

[3]H. Richard Niebuhr, *Christ and Culture* (San Francisco: HarperCollins, 1986).

of family versus broader community. By the time feudalism was well established, the church and the society were all but coterminous, and family life could serve both equally, though neither as well as could monks and nuns. In Reformation Europe and colonial North America, church and state were closely aligned, and for a few generations there was no discrepancy. But as separation of church and state began to emerge as an American ideal, and as conservative Christians began to stand against more cosmopolitan political and religious authorities, this separation became a point of faithfulness for them to be independent of the increasingly secular society and state. Today it is often a controversy with life and death intensity (note the abortion and gun-control issues) and cries out for theologically serious discernment.

Empirical variables take less prominence here, but there are some data that would be helpful. We know, for instance, that child abuse is more common in more isolated families, at least in the United States. If it were demonstrated that other forms of restriction, either to the interior of one's family or to a group of very like-minded persons, produce demonstrable differences in ethics, spirituality, or health, it would contribute to this discussion. Are families that have connections across wider sections of the society more or less likely to commit crimes, to pray, to attend church, to have lasting marriages, to raise Nobel laureate children, and so on? Some of this data exists, some does not. Such data, and reams beyond it, would aid in the discernments to be made here.

The differences to be explored are deep and passionately held and create the sort of chasm across which theological discussion is difficult. Yet a discussion that takes more seriously both theological norms and empirical data and is less reliant on political preference and ill-focused public sentiment could do tremendous service to churches on both sides of the typical divide. I believe that the typical American family, including my own, is probably a bit too permeable to the marketplace of goods and images, but I doubt that I have the knowledge to establish what the criteria should be. Careful, informed theological thought is necessary to arrive at them. The answers do not appear to lie in a separatism, a refusal to use and address the emerging resources and options, but do require a more proactive challenge to capitalism's temptation to reduce us all to consumers of ideas and products.

Relational Power in the Eyes of God

Our attention turns now to the "equal regard" term in the Browning norms. Feminist political and theological thought has established that theological convention and family practice have created and/or preserved men's power advantage over women in most family relationships. It has also demonstrated that whole groups of women have found that profoundly alienating, troubling their relationship with God, church, employment, mothering, heterosexuality, and their own bodies. Theology must find a way of describing and celebrating an equality of gendered power in intimate relationships or, failing that, a new and creative way of making sense of inequalities that persist. Once we have reordered theological thought on gender power, there are other arenas of power imbalance that must be addressed: adult-child, knowledgeable-ignorant, rich-poor, human-nonhuman, white-black-Hispanic-Native American, and so forth.

None of these are simple to resolve at the practical level, and many have profound conceptual complications. Some power imbalances—parent-child, for instance—are inescapable and highly useful. It probably makes sense for people with more knowledge in a certain area to have power in that area over those who actually have less (though we must be very careful in adjudicating claims concerning which knowledge is most important). Care for the earth is an important human responsibility, carrying with it some inevitable power, which is often severely exploited.

A rationale for the maintenance of power, particularly within family relationships, must be elaborated. It must be context-specific, spelling out the circumstances in which the temporary exercise of power on behalf of another individual or the broader system is appropriate. It must establish criteria that determine when that power ceases to be appropriate. It must honor the principle that all stakeholders have equal worth and dignity, though they cannot all simultaneously carry the authority to accomplish specific objectives.

And it must do these things without much help from the tradition, which in its explicit utterances assumes the power imbalances in almost every age as normative. There are some principles that can be deduced from historical practice as described in scripture or theology, though they are not apparent on the surface. Power that is sanctioned is always deployed on behalf of some community as a whole, not for the individual pleasure of the powerful: husband over wife, parents over children, clergy over laity, king over commoner, humanity over the natural world. This principle is worth retaining, even if the specific incarnations of it may not be. There were stirrings of a concern for equal power in the Reformation, but that equality did not exist within families. The Quaker movement began to argue for equal power in intimate matters, but at the cost of women's economic power. It is only in the last thirty years that significant portions of the church, and that not unanimously, have been clearly in favor of a theology that supports equal gender power in families.

A constructive theology for the next decades must articulate a nuanced care for the reality of some power imbalances, in and out of family, and the elimination of others, and present a clear rationale for the difference. That theology must link these developments with scriptural and theological tradition, looking behind the overt hierarchies to find the statements of equal regard that underlie the overt differences, so that the present possibility of economic and social equality is resourced by the constant themes, however submerged they are, in Christian and Jewish history.

What Remains to Be Done

This brief overview of a few issues that a constructive theology of the family would address draws together some of the threads of the previous chapters and helps us see the shape of work that is yet to be done.

My first observation is that many of the same themes come up from epoch to epoch, but all are transformed by the historical and theological developments of recent decades. Some of the recurrent themes are those discussed in the last several sections of this chapter. Others extend beyond that list: contraception, family violence, inheritance, civil authority, implications of the typical life span in a given century, match of families to the primary economic structures, and so forth. A constructive theology of the family must determine what themes must be treated to give a comprehensive view of God's action in contemporary family life. The items mentioned above give us a start on that list.

A constructive theology must articulate the key theological questions suggested by a given theme and relate those questions to one another in an ordered way. If one takes a particularly troubling area, such as family violence, one quickly notes that the way one phrases the questions shapes and is shaped by the political ethos of the discussion. To ask, "What is God achieving through family violence?" is different from "Are there situations in which family violence is consistent with the will of God?" One might see the first question as blasphemous, and the second as requiring an affirmative answer, if one's definitions do not eliminate the relevant areas of discussion (emergency prevention of dangerous behavior, for instance). Arriving at the questions to be explored, once the key variables are identified, is critical to an evenhanded discussion.

Once the questions are identified, the implications of overall methodological decisions relating empirical and theological norms must be established. If one's overall judgment is that there are areas in which human knowledge is both possible and relevant, that judgment must be stated in a detailed way, and its rationale must be presented. That overall principle should include rules of decision for how the principle will be implemented in a consistent way with each question. I would argue that God's action in intimate human life, though not directly knowable, has effects that are knowable, and that some community of human knowers will be able to discern them. I would further argue that the theological community can articulate criteria, in principle measurable, that in most cases mark such action. Research could ascertain the presence or absence of such marks. Much of that research has been done, though it typically does not identify locating the action of God as its objective. Theologians can do that. Regarding each issue, the theologian would determine what empirical data would matter to the inquiry, along with the theological rationale by which a specific criterion has been deemed relevant.

A further necessary piece is to present the leading current theological positions regarding the issue in question: sexual pleasure, fidelity, contraception, and so forth, and to connect each of those positions to their historical sources from theology and sociology. The tradition is thus brought into dialogue with the present realities of data and theory. Principles salient to contemporary arguments are shown to emerge from positions implicit, if not explicit, in the history of the discussion. Hopefully, what will emerge is a description of a spectrum of beliefs from which a current position can be constructed.

Its construction would go through a two-step process. One would involve testing the various points on the spectrum in relation to the overarching theological position the writer is choosing, so that one could claim that a given position on the spectrum articulates the broader perspective most relevantly. Then that position needs to be tested against the empirical data that has been unearthed, which should result in either confirmation or the necessity of change. At that point a final statement of a position in regard to a specific issue should be possible.

When that is done, a list of discrete positions will have been generated. Its representatives must be tested against one another. A web of argument whereby each point supports the other must be presented.

My summation, which needs to be historically and theologically argued at length, is as follows. It is clear that God is re-creating human nature constantly. The things that are possible to us now are different from those in a setting before there was writing, or before there was philosophy, or before there was indoor plumbing. God assists into being, like a cosmic midwife, whole gestalts of cultural meaning, each successive one of which requires and creates a somewhat different human organism, living in somewhat different social structures, and subject to somewhat different expressions of the divine will.

Yet there do seem to be discernible directions and regularities. In every age in the history of the West, humans have been called to develop new capacities, and humans have dependably chosen to live in ways that call them to develop those capacities more fully. It has happened with tool making, with language, with marriage, and with the lengthening period of education and nurture for children.

There seem to be two developments over the Christian era that mark what we are being called to learn, to embody, and to perfect. The first is that when family groups of parents and children have the resources, they increasingly have chosen to live as separate units—not as isolated or disconnected, but to have clearer and clearer boundaries between them and their adult children, their parents, and the collateral lines of their community. This has certainly been the case for most of the last five hundred years, when resources have been available; and the striving to achieve that state has been important in the motivation to develop new resources.

Though this has brought about ecological problems we have not yet learned to solve and has carried with it the increased isolation that has enabled scattered pockets of increased abuse of women and children, it has also enabled and required the development of the second emergent: intensified communications between marital (and other) partners that deepen the spiritual potential in couple relationships and has made committed sexuality the most potent lure toward intensely humanizing love. The ultimate thesis of this book is that God is using passionate, committed sexual connection between faithful partners as an invitation to us to become the relational, mutually exploring, cosmically accountable, and lovingly celebrative beings that this age enables and requires if we are to deliver what God wills to be available for the generations who follow.

Bibliography

Anderson, Roy S., and Dennis B. Guernsey. *On Being Family.* Grand Rapids: Eerdmans, 1985.

Aquinas, Thomas. *On Kingship, To the King of Cyprus.* Toronto: Pontifical Institute of Medieval Studies, 1949.

———. *Summa Theologica.* London: Burns, Oates, and Washbourne, 1920.

Aries, Philippe. *Centuries of Childhood.* New York: Knopf, 1962.

Augustine. *City of God.* In *The Fathers of the Church.* Vols. 8, 14, 24. Ed. Roy Joseph. New York: Fathers of the Church, 1950–1954.

———. *On Marriage and Concupiscence.* Trans. Peter Holmes. In *The Nicene and Post-Nicene Fathers,* First Series, vol. 5, ed. Philip Schaff. Grand Rapids: Eerdmans, 1956.

Barthelemy, Dominique. "Civilizing the Fortress: Eleventh to Thirteenth Century." In Duby, *A History of Private Life*, vol. 2.

Beecher, Henry Ward. *Lectures to Young Men.* New York: Newman, 1851.

Beecher, Lyman. *Plea for the West.* Cincinnati: Truman and Smith, 1835.

Benton, John F. "Clio and Venus: An Historical View of Medieval Love." In F. X. Newman, *The Meaning of Courtly Love.* Albany: State University of New York Press, 1968.

Bernard of Clairvaux. *The Letters of Bernard of Clairvaux.* Trans. Bruno Scott James. London: Burns Oates, 1953.

———. *On the Song of Songs.* London: Mowbray, 1952.

———. *The Steps of Humility.* Cambridge: Harvard University Press, 1940.

Bernard, Jessie. *The Future of Marriage.* New Haven: Yale University Press, 1982.

Blenkinsopp, Joseph. "The Family in First Temple Israel." In Perdue, et al., *Families in Ancient Israel.*

Blidstein, Gerald. *Honor Thy Father and Thy Mother.* New York: Ktav Publishing, 1975.

Bonaventure. *The Works of Bonaventure.* Vol. 2. Trans. Jose de Vinck. Paterson, N.J.: St. Anthony Guild Press, 1963.

Braunstein, Philippe. "Toward Intimacy: The Fourteenth and Fifteenth Centuries." In Duby, *A History of Private Life*, vol. 2.

Brav, Stanley R. "Marriage with a History." In *Marriage and the Jewish Tradition.* New York: Philosophical Press, 1951.

Brown, Peter. *The Body and Society: Men, Women, and Sexual Renunciation in Early Christianity.* New York: Columbia University Press, 1988.

Browning, Don, Bonnie J. Miller-McLemore, Pamela D. Couture, K. Brynolf Lyon, and Robert M. Franklin. *From Culture Wars to Common Ground.* Louisville: Westminster John Knox Press, 1997.

Brundage, James A. *Law, Sex, and Christian Society in Medieval Europe.* Chicago: University of Chicago Press, 1987.

Bucer, Martin. *De Regno Christi.* Trans. John Milton and published in *The Judgement of Martin Bucer Concerning Divorce* in *The Complete Prose Works of John Milton.* New Haven: Yale Press, 1959.

Bushman, Richard L. *From Puritan to Yankee: Character and the Social Order in Connecticut, 1690–1765.* Cambridge: Harvard University Press, 1967.

Bushnell, Horace. *Christian Nurture.* Grand Rapids: Baker Book House, 1979. The complete 1861 edition.

Campbell, Alexander. "Address on the Amelioration of the Social State." *Millennial Harbinger,* July 1840.

Campbell, Thomas. "Brief Memoir of Mrs. Jane Campbell." In *The Memoirs of Thomas Campbell.* Cincinnati: H. S. Bosworth, 1861.

Carr, Louis Green, and Lorena S. Walsh. "The Planter's Wife. The Experience of White Women in Seventeenth-Century Maryland." In Gordon, *The American Family in Social-Historical Perspective.*

Carson, Gerald. *The Cornflake Crusade.* New York: Rinehard, 1957.

Chartier, Roger, ed. *A History of Private Life.* Vol. 3, *Passions of the Renaissance.* Cambridge: Belknap Press of Harvard University Press, 1989.

Clark, Clifford E. *Henry Ward Beecher: Spokesman for a Middle-Class America.* Urbana: University of Illinois Press, 1978.

Coleman, Emily. "Infanticide in the Early Middle Ages." In Stuard, *Women in Medieval Society.*

Collins, John J. "Marriage, Divorce and Family in Second Temple Judaism." In Perdue, et al., *Families in Ancient Israel.*

Contamine, Philipe. "Peasant Hearth to Papal Palace. The Fourteenth and Fifteenth Centuries." In Duby, *A History of Private Life,* vol. 2.

Coontz, Stephanie. *The Social Origins of Private Life: A History of American Families, 1600–1900.* London and New York: Verso, 1988.

————. *The Way We Never Were: American Families and the Nostalgia Trap.* New York: Basic Books, 1992.

————. *The Way We Really Are: Coming to Terms with America's Changing Families.* New York: Basic Books, 1997.

Cott, Nancy F. "Divorce and the Changing Status of Women in Eighteenth-Century Masssachusetts." In Gordon, *The American Family in Social-Historical Perspective.*

D'Emilio, John, and Estelle B. Freedman. *Intimate Matters: A History of Sexuality in America.* New York: Harper and Row, 1988.

Davis, Justine Randers-Pehrson. *Barbarians and Romans: The Birth Struggle of Europe, A.D. 400–700.* Norman: University of Oklahoma Press, 1983.

Deferrari, Roy J. *Fathers of the Church.* Trans. Gerald J. Walsh and Grace Monahan. New York: Fathers of the Church, 1955.

Degler, Carl N. "The Emergence of the Modern American Family." In Gordon, *The American Family in Socio-Historical Perspective.*

Demos, John. *A Little Commonwealth: Family Life in Plymouth Colony.* New York: Oxford University Press, 1970.

Duby, Georges. *The Knight, The Lady, and the Priest.* New York: Pantheon, 1983.

————. *Medieval Marriage.* Baltimore: Johns Hopkins University Press, 1978.

————, gen. ed. *A History of Private Life.* 5 vols. Cambridge: Belknap Press, 1987–1991.

————, ed. *A History of Private Life.* Vol. 2, *Revelations of the Medieval World.* Cambridge: Belknap Press, 1988.

————. "The Aristocratic Households of Feudal France." In *A History of Private Life,* vol. 2.

————. "Solitude: Eleventh to Thirteenth Centuries." In *A History of Private Life,* vol. 2.

Duckett, Eleanor. *Death and Life in the Middle Ages.* Ann Arbor: University of Michigan Press, 1967.

Edwards, Jonathan. *The Great Awakening.* Ed. G. C. Coen. New Haven and London: Yale University Press, 1972.

Epstein, Barbara Leslie. *The Politics of Domesticity: Women, Evangelism, and Temperance in Nineteenth-Century America.* Middletown: Wesleyan University Press, 1981.

Fichtner, Paula Sutter. *Protestantism and Primogeniture in Early Modern Germany.* New Haven: Yale, 1989.

Fiske, John. *The Dutch and Quaker Colonies in America.* Boston and New York: Houghton Mifflin, 1899.

Flandrin, Jean-Louis. *Families in Former Times: Kingship, Household and Sexuality.* Trans. Richard Southern. Cambridge: Cambridge University Press, 1976.

Fuchs, Eric. *Sexual Desire and Love: Origins and History of the Christian Ethic of Sexuality and Marriage.* New York: Seabury, 1983.

Fuchs, Victor R. *Women's Quest for Economic Equality.* Cambridge: Harvard University Press, 1988.

Gardella, Peter. *Innocent Ecstasy: How Christianity Gave America an Ethic of Sexual Pleasure.* New York: Oxford University Press, 1985.

Genicot, Leopold. "On the Evidence of Growth of Population in the West from the Eleventh to the Thirteenth Century." In Sylvia Thrupp, *Change in Medieval Society.* New York: Appleton-Century-Crofts, 1964.

Gladden, Washington. *Applied Christianity: Moral Aspects of Social Questions.* Boston: Houghton, Mifflin, 1894.

——. *Ruling Ideas of the Present Age.* Boston: Houghton, Mifflin, 1895.

Gordon, Michael. *The American Family in Socio-Historical Perspective.* 3d ed. New York: St. Martin's Press, 1983.

Graham, Sylvester. *A Lecture to Young Men.* 1834. Reprint, New York: Arno Press, 1974.

Gregory of Nyssa. *On Virginity.* In *St. Gregory of Nyssa. Ascetical Works.* Vol. 58 in *The Fathers of the Church.* Ed. Joseph Deferrari. Washington: Catholic University of America Press, 1966.

Greven, Philip. *Child-Rearing Concepts 1628–1861.* Itasca, Ill.: F. E. Peacock Publishers, 1973.

——. *Four Generations: Population, Land, and Family in Colonial Andover, Massachusetts.* Ithaca: Cornell University Press, 1970.

——. *The Protestant Temperament.* New York: Alfred A. Knopf, 1977.

Groover, Ralph Edwin. "Alexander Campbell and the Family: Precept and Example." Ph.D. diss. Emory University, 1982.

Haroutunian, Joseph. *Piety Versus Moralism: The Passing of the New England Theology.* New York: Henry Holt, 1932.

Hauerwas, Stanley. *A Community of Character.* South Bend: University of Notre Dame Press, 1981.

Hopf, Constantin. *Martin Bucer and the English Reformation.* Oxford: Blackwell, 1946.

Hunt, Mary Fierce. *Tenderness: A Feminist Theology of Friendship.* New York: Crossroad, 1991.

Hunt, Morton, and Bernice Hunt. *The Divorce Experience.* New York: McGraw-Hill, 1977.

Ihinger-Tallman, Marilyn, and Kay Pasley. "Divorce and Remarriage in the American Family: A Historical Review." In Pasley and Ihinger-Tallman, *Remarriage and Step-parenting: Current Research and Theory.* New York: Guilford Press, 1987.

Ingersoll, Andrew J. *In Health: Sex, Marriage, and Society.* 1877. Reprint. New York: Arno Press, 1974.

Jerome. *Against Jovinian.* Trans. W. H. Freemantle. In *The Nicene and Ante-Nicene Fathers.* Second Series, vol. 6. Ed. Philip Schaff and Henry Wace. Grand Rapids: Eerdmans, 1892.

John Paul II. *On the Family.* Washington, D.C.: United States Cathiolic Conference, 1981.

Kellogg, J. H. *Plain Facts for Young and Old.* Burlington: I. F. Segner, 1884.

Kerns, Joseph. *The Theology of Marriage.* New York: Sheed and Ward, 1964.

Kuhns, Oscar. *The German and Swiss Settlements of Colonial Pennsylvania.* New York: Eaton and Main, 1900.

Lazareth, William H. *Luther on the Christian Home.* Philadelphia: Muhlenberg Press, 1960.

Lea, Henry C. *History of Sacerdotal Celibacy in the Christian Church.* 4th ed. London: Watts, 1932.

Levy, Barry. *Quakers and the American Family: British Settlement in the Delaware Valley.* New York: Oxford, 1988.

Lindsey, Ben B., and Wainwright Evans. *The Companionate Marriage.* New York: Boni and Liveright, 1927.

Luther, Martin. *Luther's Works.* Ed. and trans. Walther I Brandt. Gen. ed. Helmut T. Lehman. Philadelphia: Fortress Press, 1962.

———. "The Estate of Marriage." In *Luther's Works.* Vol. 45.

———. "That Parents Should Neither Compel Nor Hinder the Marriage of Their Children, and that Children Should Not Become Engaged Without Their Parents' Consent." In *Luther's Works.* Vol. 45.

Lynd, Robert S., and Helen Merrell Lynd. *Middletown: A Study in Contemporary American Culture.* New York: Harcourt, Brace, and Company, 1929.

Mace, David R. *Hebrew Marriage.* London: Epworth, 1953.

Marty, Martin. *Righteous Empire: The Protestant Experience in America.* New York: Dial Press, 1970.

Martyr, Justin. *The First Apology.* Vol. 56 of *Ancient Christian Writers.* Ed. Walter J. Burghardt, John J. Dillon, and Dennis D. McManus. Trans. Leslie William Barnard. New York: Paulist Press, 1997.

Mather, Cotton. *Diary of Cotton Mather.* New York: Frederick Ungar Publishing, 1957.

May, Elaine Tyler. *Great Expectations: Marriage and Divorce in Post-Victorian America.* Chicago: University of Chicago Press, 1980.

McNamara, Jo Ann, and Suzanne F. Wemple. "Marriage and Divorce in the Frankish Kingdom." In Stuard, *Women in Medieval Society.*

Mead, Sidney Earl. *Nathaniel William Taylor, 1786–1858: A Connecticut Liberal.* Chicago: University of Chicago Press, 1942.

Meyers, Carol. "The Family in Early Israel." In Perdue, et al., *Families in Ancient Israel.*

Morgan, Edmund S. *The Puritan Family.* New York: Harper and Row, 1944.

Mulder, John M. "Introduction." In Bushnell, *Christian Nurture.*

Munger, Theodore. *The Appeal to Life.* Boston: Houghton-Mifflin, 1887.

———. *Freedom of Faith.* Boston: Houghton-Mifflin, 1883.

———. *On the Threshold.* Boston: Houghton-Mifflin, 1884.

Nelson, James B. *Embodiment: An Approach to Sexuality and Christian Theology.* Minneapolis: Augsburg, 1979.

Niebuhr, H. Richard. *Christ and Culture.* New York: Harper, 1951.

———. *The Social Sources of Denominationalism.* Cleveland and New York: World Publishing, 1929.

Nottingham, William J. "The Social Ethics of Martin Bucer." Ph.D. diss. Columbia University, 1962.

Ozment, Steven. *When Fathers Ruled: Family Life in Reformation Europe.* Cambridge: Harvard University Press, 1983.

Palmer, Phoebe. *The Promise of the Father.* Salem, Ohio: Schmul Publishers, 1981.

———. *The Way of Holiness, with Notes by the Way.* New York: Palmer, 1871.

Patai, Raphael. *Sex and Family in the Bible and the Ancient Middle East.* Garden City: Doubleday, 1959.

Pedersen, Johannes. *Israel, Its Life and Culture.* Vol. 1. London: Oxford University Press, 1926.

Perdue, Leo, et al. *Families in Ancient Israel.* Louisville: Westminster John Knox, 1997.

Pivar, David. *Purity Crusade: Sexual Morality and Social Control, 1868–1900.* Westport: Greenwood Press, 1973.

Post, Stephen G. *Christian Love and Self-Denial: An Historical and Normative Study of Jonathan Edwards, Samuel Hopkins, and American Theological Ethics.* New York: Lanham, 1987.

Rauschenbusch, Walter. *Christianity and the Social Crisis.* New York: Macmillan, 1910.

———. *Christianizing the Social Order.* New York: Macmillan, 1912.

Reed, James. *From Private Vice to Public Virtue: The Birth Control Movement and American Society.* Princeton: Princeton University Press, 1978.

Rothman, Ellen. "Sex and Self-Control in Middle-Class Courtship in America, 1770–1870." In Gordon, *The American Family in Socio-Historical Perspective.*

Rouche, Michel. "The Early Middle Ages in the West." In Veyne, *A History of Private Life,* vol. 1.

Rousselle, Aline. *Porneia. On Desire and the Body in Antiquity.* Trans. Felicia Pheasant. Oxford: Blackwell, 1988.

Sanger, Margaret. *Happiness in Marriage.* Garden City: Blue Ribbon Books, 1926.

———. *My Fight for Birth Control.* Fairview Park: Maxwell Reprint, 1969. Originally copyrighted, 1931. Cambridge: Harvard University Press, reprint of 1837 edition.

———. *What Every Boy and Girl Should Know.* New York: Maxwell Reprint, 1969 reissue of 1927 edition.

Scanzoni, Letha Dawson, and John Scauzoni. *Men, Women, and Change.* New York: McGraw Hill, 1981.

Shammas, Carole. "The Domestic Environment in Early Modern England and America." In Gordon, *The American Family in Socio-Historical Perspective.*

Sidel, Ruth. *Women and Children Last: The Plight of Poor Women in Affluent America.* New York: Penguin Press, 1986.

Sirluck, Ernest. "Introduction" in John Milton, *Complete Prose Works,* vol. 2. New Haven, Conn.: Yale University Press, 1953.

Stone, Lawrence. *The Family, Sex, and Marriage in England, 1500–1800.* Abr. ed. New York: Harper, 1977.

Stuard, Susan. *Women in Medieval Society.* Philadelphia: University of Pennsylvania Press, 1976.

Sweet, William Warren. *Religion in the Development of American Culture, 1765–1840.* New York: Charles Scribner's Sons, 1952.

Tertullian. *On Exhortation to Chastity.* In *The Writings of Tertullian,* vol. 3, *Ante-Nicene Christian Writings,* vol. 18. Ed. Alexander Roberts and James Donaldson. Edinburgh: T and T Clark, 1869.

Tuchman, Barbara W. *A Distant Mirror: The Calamitous 14th Century.* New York: Ballantine, 1978.

Van Horn, Susan Householder. *Women, Work, and Fertility, 1900–1986.* New York: New York University Press, 1988.

Vannoy-Hiller, Dana, and William W. Philliber. *Equal Partners: Successful Women in Marriage.* Newbury Park, Calif.: Sage, 1989.

Veyne, Paul, ed. *A History of Private Life.* Vol. 1, *From Pagan Rome to Byzantium.* Cambridge: Belknap Press, 1987.

Wallace-Hadrill, J. M. *The Barbarian West, 400–1000.* New York: Hutchinson's University Library, 1952.

Waller, Altina. *Reverend Beecher and Mrs. Tilton.* Amherst: University of Massachusetts Press, 1982.

Wallerstein, Judith, and Sandra Blakeslee. *Second Chances: Men, Women and Children a Decade after Divorce.* New York: Ticknor and Fields, 1989.

Weitzman, Lenore J. "The Economics of Divorce: Social and Economic Consequences of Property, Alimony and Child Support Awards." *UCLA Law Review,* no. 28, November 1981.

Welter, Barbara. "The Cult of True Womanhood." In Gordon, *The American Family in Socio-Historical Perspective.*

Wertenbaker, Thomas J. *The Planters of Colonial Virginia.* Princeton: Princeton University Press, 1922.

———. *Plebeian and Patrician in Virginia.* In *The Shaping of Colonial Virginia.* New York: Russell and Russell, 1958.

———. *Virginia Under the Stuarts.* Princeton: Princeton University Press, 1914.

Wesley, John. "The Doctrine of Original Sin, According to Scripture, Reason, and Experience." In *The Works of John Wesley.* 1872. Reprint, Nashville: Abingdon Press, 1986.

———. "On the Education of Children." In *The Works of John Wesley.* 1872. Reprint, Nashville: Abingdon Press, 1986.

———. "On Obedience to Parents." In *The Works of John Wesley.* 1872. Nashville: Abingdon Press, 1986.

Wesley, Susanna. "On the Education of Her Family." In Phillip Greven, *Child-Rearing Concepts 1628-1861.* Itasca, Ill., F. E. Peacock Publishers, 1973.

Whicker, Marcia Lynn, and Jennie Jacobs Kronenfeld. *Sex Role Changes: Technology, Politics, and Policy.* New York: Praeger, 1986.

Willard, Samuel. *The Compleat Body of Divinity.* New York: Johnson Reprints, 1969. Originally published 1726 from lectures and sermons delivered beginning 1688.

Witherspoon, John. "Letters on Education, No. 2." In *The Works of the Rev. John Witherspoon.* 3 vols. Philadelphia: William W. Woodward, 1800.

The World Almanac and Book of Facts, 1995. Mahwah, N. J., World Almanac, 1995.

Index